D0418508

Till the Cows Come Home

Till the Cows Come Home

Sara Cox

CORONET

First published in Great Britain in 2019 by Coronet
An Imprint of Hodder & Stoughton
An Hachette UK company

This paperback edition published in 2020

4

Copyright © Sara Cox 2019

The right of Sara Cox to be identified as the Author of the Work has
been asserted by her in accordance with the Copyright,
Designs and Patents Act 1988.

All rights reserved. No part of this publication may be reproduced,
stored in a retrieval system, or transmitted, in any form or by any means
without the prior written permission of the publisher, nor be otherwise
circulated in any form of binding or cover other than that in
which it is published and without a similar condition being
imposed on the subsequent purchaser.

A CIP catalogue record for this title is available from the British Library

Hardback ISBN 9781473672734
Paperback ISBN 9781473672703
eBook ISBN 9781473672710

Typeset in Electra LH by Palimpsest Book Production Ltd,
Falkirk, Stirlingshire

Printed and bound in Great Britain by Clays Ltd, Elcograf S.p.A.

Hodder & Stoughton policy is to use papers that are natural,
renewable and recyclable products and made from wood grown in sustainable
forests. The logging and manufacturing processes are expected to conform
to the environmental regulations of the country of origin.

Hodder & Stoughton Ltd
Carmelite House
50 Victoria Embankment
London EC4Y 0DZ

www.hodder.co.uk

In loving memory of our darling brother
David Cox
1963–2019
We love and miss you

Foreword

I really really enjoy talking. Anyone who's ever stumbled upon one of my radio shows will have no doubt about that.

I also love words and language. Maybe it's a hangover from my A level in English Literature – I do appreciate a clever turn of phrase. Or maybe this love precedes my years at sixth form – perhaps the seeds were sown in Dad's farm kitchen, my nana's front room or the pub where Mum ruled the roost as landlady: conversation, gossip, wry observations, banter – all swirling around me in a whirlwind of words as I sat quietly in the eye of the storm, soaking it all up.

Painting pictures with words is something I try to do on the wireless – conjuring up images that will hopefully transport the listeners to another place, whisking them away from their desks or the gridlocked traffic on the M6.

I love the buzz of making people laugh too. As the youngest of five I worked out pretty early on that the best way to get any attention from the grown-ups was to clown about. Not much has changed.

This book, then, is an extension of all the above. A big wordy pie packed with all the people, places and ponderings from my first twenty years on this glorious planet. I hope you enjoy tucking into it.

I wanted to tell the story of my upbringing on the farm because whenever I chatted to anyone about whether I could write AN ACTUAL BOOK I discovered my most vivid memories were always about the farm – wherever the sentence began it'd inevitably finish on a pony, by a tractor or in a field with some cows.

The farm is my dad's – he still lives there. I've always been a certified daddy's girl so it's been really rather lovely documenting our relationship, which, aside from my husband Ben and the kids, has been the biggest love story of my life.

Having said that, there's a little twist in the book. No, I'm not adopted (despite my four older siblings occasionally telling me I was found wrapped in chippy paper by the barn door), but writing this book has certainly helped me to unearth the person who I really have to thank/blame for making me who I am today. Typical – only I could write a book and surprise myself with its punchline.

The farm is the place where my story began and now it's part of my children's story too; Lola, Isaac and Renee love being at Grandad's to fuss over a newborn calf or clamber over the hay bales in the barn, just like I did.

They are another reason for writing this book. They just know me as Mummy – shouter of 'HURRY UP, we're now officially late!' in the morning and 'For the umpteenth time, BRUSH YOUR TEETH AND GET TO BED!' in the evening . . . and someone who talks on the radio and pops up on the telly.

I want them to know that as well as head chef and bottle washer I'm another person – a farmer's daughter, a former bullying victim, an ex-supermodel-cum-barmaid. I'm also hoping that if they know where I've literally come from then they'll understand better where I'm coming from when I nag them about wasting food, working hard, respecting their elders – all the stuff that punctuated my childhood (and therefore this book) and is a big part of who I am.

Now I'm older and approaching my thirties (OK, my mid-forties, whatever) I've become more fascinated by what – or rather who – came before me. I want to keep the memory alive of those people who shaped me but are no longer here. Through this book my own children can get to meet their maternal great-grandparents for the first time. I've tried to freeze-frame some moments from our family's history for my children (and perhaps theirs one day) to savour.

I think it's human nature that as we journey further away from our childhood, we yearn to return, to arc round, circle back towards the things that shaped us from the beginning – the people, the places, the food, the music. The land we lived on. For me it's my dad's farmyard, the streets where I played out, the lanes I drove down to my boyfriend's, the outdoor steps in faraway countries I sat on smoking with my best friend.

Like a thousand-piece jigsaw, all these places slot together to make me who I am. Each friend, each holiday, every family member has added a pencil stroke to the sketch of my life – the portrait of me as a person.

From idolising Lady Diana and several regrettable perms, to being spooked by Michael Jackson's 'Thriller' video, the polyester-clad eighties feature heavily in my story and it's a decade I remember with fondness and relish still today.

Looking back helps us to focus on who we are now. I don't feel I'm much different to the scrawny girl who was insecure and shy at school, but so secure at home nestled among my family that I was a confirmed show-off. Now I guess I'm just brave enough to do my showing off in the most public of ways, on the radio or telly.

Self-belief is a fragile, intricate structure, built up over years, getting stronger over time but still easily wobbled by a setback or criticism. How different am I now from the kid in the corridor praying the teacher arrives at the classroom before the bullies do?

Writing this book has also allowed me to accept my weaknesses and forgive myself for being bullied. I've felt frustrated at my seeming willingness to allow myself to be picked on, but as I've rifled through those memories I realise it wasn't my fault; I was powerless and scared – stuck between a rock and a hard-nosed thugette.

We should all look back and be proud of where we've come from and how we've grown. Occasional pluckiness should be applauded – from riding injuries to crossing continents pocketing adventures and a bit of cash along the way. And moments of fear should be met with compassion and kindness.

I hope you enjoy my jaunt back in time to Bolton, the glorious north – the place whose name runs through my very centre as if I were a stick of seaside rock.

Bolton is a town that's seen many changes through the years and has struggled to find a new identity since its traditional industries disappeared, but what makes the place is the people – stoic, friendly, practical, kind and hilarious.

Like any working-class town we know how to work hard and play hard. And I'm hoping this book will be a bit like a night in the pub, swapping stories about our upbringing – some funny, some poignant, some far-fetched. So pull up a stool, mine's a G&T, and let's begin . . .

1. One Girl and her Head

'Just jump!' So I did. It didn't go well. Let me explain. I was perched on the end of the loft platform in the barn on the farm where we lived. It was summertime, just before haymaking when all the lovely fresh hay would be brought in by an army of pals and helpers, fuelled by tea and ham butties.

Now, though, the barn was almost empty save for a few old bales knocking around on the dusty floor and a pile of half a dozen or so right next to the loft. These were to be my crash mat. All I had to do was launch myself from my position sitting up in the loft and push away from the wall, gliding majestically onto the scratchy landing below. Think 'falcon fledgling's maiden flight from its perch on a cliff'. It was a drop of perhaps eight feet, but to my seven-year-old mind the chasm below might as well have been the Grand Canyon. Or, seeing as this was Bolton, the 'Reet Grand Canyon'.

My older sister Yvonne was the one encouraging me to jump. I was grateful that she was playing with me so I was keen to impress. As the youngest of five I was used to being a walking,

talking booby prize to my older siblings. An unwelcome addi-
tion. A skin tag on the neck of fun. Like stabilisers on a bike I
slowed them down and made them look uncool.

The unruly gang of scuffed-kneed siblings was led by Robert,
the eldest, boasting a full twelve years on me. He was tall and
bonnie with a snub nose and dark hair. He had a deep author-
itative voice even as a teenager and was caring and sensible in
equal measure. Next came the twins, a mere twenty months his
junior. David – tall and slim, matching dark mop above a shower
of freckles, and a practical nature but more shy than Robert.
Dot – younger than David by two minutes and comfortable in
the protective shadow of her older brothers, sensitive, willowy,
with a sweet face and pale aqua eyes framed by fine mousey
locks. Next was Yvonne, much younger than them but a full
four years older than me – she wore her seniority with pride;
long dark-blonde hair, olive-green eyes and porcelain skin, lips
often chapped during winter so that in old faded photos she
looks like she's wearing a smudge of red lippy. They were bigger
than me – faster, stronger, busier. I seemed to stand rejected in
their slipstream whenever they went about their business.

If they tried to sneak off on some adventure they'd edge away
along the farm lane and just as they thought they'd escaped,
Mum's loud, bird-startling voice would boom out, 'Take Sarah
with you!' I'd emerge from behind her (while I still could before
I outgrew her – Mum is tiny, a 4'11" pocket-sized, bespectacled
badass, with an impressive bosom and cracking legs) and, with
her cropped permed hair – blonde, auburn, hazelnut-coloured
depending on the week – quivering, she'd holler instructions to
them. She's a force to be reckoned with even now – a sharp
tongue but a soft heart – you always know where you are with
Mum and even if you're in the doghouse she won't let you
languish there for long. Confident, funny. Really loves to natter

on. This apple hasn't fallen far from the tree.

Back then though I was half girl, half forehead – a trait that was a target for classmates, both figuratively with a plethora of nicknames (slaphead, fivehead, fodder) and literally as they'd heartily slap it while running past, high-fiving my fivehead.

So the fact my sister had agreed to hang out with me and my forehead was a big deal. Sure, the downside was she wanted me to jump off high stuff to certain death for her own amusement, but at least I'd die knowing I wasn't a chicken. Turns out I wasn't a falcon either.

I took a deep breath. I jumped. I didn't push away from the platform, though, I sort of nudged my bottom over the edge, so instead of springing away from the wall I slid down it like a blob of custard dripping down a kitchen tile.

In fact I stuck so closely to the wall, hurtling down on my shoulder blades like sledge runners, that I didn't even make it onto the bales below but tumbled between them and the wall, like a lost mitten down the back of a radiator.

I looked up to see my sister's horrified face frozen in a grimace – part sympathy, part worry in case I grassed her up to Mum, and part admiration at how I'd managed a vertical human bobsleigh down a barn wall.

The good news was I didn't die and I didn't break any bones. The only evidence of my misjudged jump was the two red raw tramlines down my back that made me look like I'd been mowed down by a joyrider in a Silver Cross pram.

2. Making an Entrance

Growing up on my parents' farm in the seventies and eighties was like having my very own slightly deadly adventure playground, and us kids were often getting into scrapes.

Grundy Fold Farm is still there and my dad still runs it. It isn't vast – discard the picture you may have in your mind's eye of rolling hills stretching as far as the eye can see, like a giant's patchwork quilt. In a soft furnishing analogy it's less quilt, more fabric swatch.

It's a small tenanted holding. It used to be around forty acres but now is more like fifteen thanks to the surrounding housing estates, the semi-detached red-brick homes seeming to shuffle silently ever closer to the farmhouse, tarmac inching over the outskirts of Dad's fields, steadily nibbling away at its edges.

From the farmyard you can look out over the front field and imagine you're in the countryside but a quick glance to the left and you see the homes that now hug the farm lane, back-garden trampolines peeping over the fences.

Still, it is a proper farm and my dad's a proper farmer, as

were his dad and his own father before him. In fact, farming goes way back in our bloodline. A TV show about family history asked me to feature, to look at my forebears' role in the world wars, but after further investigation it became apparent that on Dad's side no one fought in any conflicts because as far back as records went the menfolk were listed as 'farmer' or 'butcher' – occupations excused from call-up because they provided food for the nation. My Cox ancestors brandished not a bayonet during wartime but a joint of beef.

My dad, Len, is still working hard on the farm. He's over six feet tall and gifted all us offspring his long legs. A face that's as handsome as it is lived-in, with pale-blue eyes, kind and crinkled, sitting underneath a nearly bald head that's tanned from being outdoors all seasons. He has a slight limp thanks to a badly broken ankle years ago, so he walks like he's got a bit of gravel in his boot. Driving the tractor, handling the cattle, lugging bales around and 'shovelling cack' (his words, not mine) have kept him fit and strong. His hands are the size of dinner plates and he's tough.

I've seen him smash through ice with his bare hands when the cows' water troughs have frozen over. It may or may not have been a coincidence that he did that once in front of a new boyfriend I'd taken up to meet him; a kind of 'Watch it, son. If I can do this to three inches of solid ice imagine what I could do to your neck if you dick my daughter about.'

The few boyfriends who were deemed good enough to get to the farm always looked meek and slightly pathetic, stood in my dad's mighty shadow, quivering in their borrowed wellies that looked as alien on them as kitten heels on a cow.

Spoken like a true daddy's girl, I know.

Like any family ours has had its dramas, and when my mum met Dad she was a petite nineteen-year-old and he was a divorced older man with three young children to look after: a boy of six called Robert and four and a half year-old twins, Dorothy and David.

Mum fell in love with Dad and with his kids, raising them as her own. Having kids now myself, I find that pretty bloody mind-boggling – it was a testament to how much she must've loved Dad (and how gorgeous the kids were too) that Mum didn't saddle up the nearest heifer and gallop off into the sunset. I'm glad she stuck around because a few years later they had my sister Yvonne and then, in December 1974, I put in an appearance.

Mum's story of my birth was less *Call the Midwife* and more *Carry on Through the Cervix*.

Being an awkward madam, I decided I wanted to rock a breach vibe and come out feet first, which, you don't need to be a genius to work out, stings a bit for the poor labouring woman.

Mum recalls how, with it being mid-December (Friday the 13th no less), the doctor who had been summoned to help had arrived straight from the hospital's Christmas party.

I like to think he'd been pulled out of the midsection of a conga chain and diverted to the labour ward, possibly with a few pissed orderlies still attached.

I also imagine his tie was wonky and he was still wearing a cone party hat held on with an elastic chinstrap. This was 1974 so I'm certain he'd have been wearing a swirly pattered shirt, possibly in orange, with brown flares. According to Mum he'd been enthusiastically putting the 'merry' into Merry Christmas and was half-cut to the extent that, once I was safely out, when Mum needed a little patching up, he had to close one eye as he struggled to thread the needle, tongue poking out of the corner of his mouth in concentration.

Knowing my mother, this last detail could be an embellishment, but she swears it's true. In fact, when I recently put it to

Mum that these details seemed a little over the top she even added to them, saying the young doctor had a bottle of Cinzano tucked under his arm.

My entrance into the world wasn't straightforward. Not only was I greeted at the door by a pissed man wearing a party hat like some rubbish seventies housewarming, but I was born with a dislocated hip and an allergy to milk.

Mum had to sit my four siblings down and gently explain that I was a 'special baby'. It's probably best they had a heads-up; I wasn't wearing the usual newborn attire of a cute Babygro but instead a contraption that was half dungarees, half tree-surgeon harness, with straps over my shoulders and round my waist and connected to my ankles. This look was topped off, literally, with my magnificent forehead, a bonnet stretched over the tip, like a tea cosy on a missile.

Despite being fixed by the clever doctors my legs have let me down on occasion. During times of extreme pressure and phys-ical exertion I'd often come a cropper. I'm no natural athlete and I maintain to this day a spring onion shape. Some women lament being apple- or pear-shaped but with my aforementioned acre of forehead plastered across my huge head and my lack of hips that whittle away down to skinny long legs I'm a dead ringer for a scallion.

I was never therefore very aerodynamic and struggled with running fast, my long legs going like the clappers with my gargantuan noggin bobbin about on top. From a distance I probably looked like I was running holding a helium balloon.

I dreaded sports days and struggled to find an event I could master. I sacked off the sack race and wasn't particularly smashing at the egg and spoon.

On one sports day I decided to go for glory. I was to compete in the 100m sprint. In fact, that's probably overstating it. I was five years old and the track was about twenty yards of a dusty sports field. As I stepped up to the starting line I looked sideways at my competitors, ready to take them down. I managed to block out the roar of the crowd (a few teachers and a handful of mums) so I could focus.

We took our positions and as the firing pistol rang out (whistle was blown) we surged forward, necks straining, arms pumping, legs flying.

At least that's what the other kids did. Not me. The pressure to perform and the flood of adrenaline through my skinny limbs meant that when the whistle blew, my legs gave way and I crumpled to the floor like one of Fred Dibnah's chimney stacks.

As the other kids streamed through the finish ribbon, I was marooned at the start. Mum came and gathered me up from the floor and dusted me down. Usually after an unsuccessful race your mum can say 'It's not the winning that's important but the taking part' but I didn't even manage that.

My school had two fantastic assets. The first was chocolate custard – a now rarely seen substance served at the same temperature as the earth's core and the same consistency as emulsion. The Farrow & Ball colour equivalent would be 'wet spaniel' or 'conker vomit'. The other good thing was the school's proximity to our farm.

The sports field that witnessed my start-line humiliation ran parallel with my dad's fields, separated by a line of prickly yew trees and a wooden fence.

Beyond that lay Dad's fields, split into wonky slices by trees and barbed-wire fences, the broad iron gates allowing passage from field to field.

Each gate swung out over a worn-away area. In wet times it

was a welly-snatching trap to navigate – all ploughed up by the cattle, congregating in the hope of being let into the dry or at the very least getting a few slices of sweet hay. In summer it became bald and dusty from the tractor and trailer driving through, compacting the hard earth.

Beyond the front fields lay four more, each with a name: the pond (containing a pond), the open cast, the lane, and Stopes, named after the road that ran alongside it.

From the school playground I could see the front fields and the barn, a vast light-grey brick block, its upper section made up of slats of pale wood.

The proximity of the farm was a source of both joy and pain; although it was torturous in that I was so close and yet so far away from home (just taking off and popping home for a swift half of Vimto was firmly discouraged by the spoilsport teachers), I still loved to be able to gawp out of the windows daydreaming and see home.

Not only could I see home, unfortunately I (and everyone else) could often smell it too.

In early spring Dad would take a huge orange tank, like a massive can of pop on its side, fill it with liquid slurry, hook it up to his tractor and take off around the fields, liberally spraying ample amounts of nutrient-packed but extremely whiffy poo smoothie.

The aroma would travel quickly and at playtime us kids were hit with the dense stench; a bit like the famous gravy advert, but as the wisps of scent danced through air towards their eager nostrils, instead of 'Mmmm . . . Bisto' they said 'Urgh . . . poo', quickly followed by shouts of 'Oi Coxy, that's your dad making that smell.'

I began to dread this time of year as I knew the kids would give me as much shit as my dad was spreading.

3. Benji and the Missing Ball

Masefield Primary welcomed me back recently to film a documentary there on friendship. It was lovely to sit watching the kids run riot round the playground, some completely oblivious to the cameras, others lobbing a ball towards us so they could coyly retrieve it while smiling shyly at the camera.

It would've been a great shot, me stood in the playground staring into the middle distance and saying wistfully 'I remember when all this was fields,' but it IS all still fields. Happily, not much had changed in over three decades, apart from a new wire fence cordoning off the playground from the grass beyond, which back in the day would've scuppered mine and Benji's fun.

Benji was a Lakeland terrier, a real jaunty, self-assured little fella who'd occasionally trot across the field from Dad's and swagger around the playground causing near hysteria among the kids.

Shouts of 'Dog! Dog!' would go up and I'd be packed off to grab him and return him home. Obviously for 'safety' reasons

I'd need to take a friend, so my chosen pal and I would escort Benji across the playing field like security ejecting a troublesome festival-goer. Dad would welcome us with open arms and crack open the ice pops. I've lovely memories of hastily munching snacks at the breakfast bar in the farm kitchen, knowing we'd have to leg it back to school sharpish.

Benji was gorgeous – just below knee height and compact, with small dark intelligent eyes and wiry chestnut-coloured hair on his face, legs and chest. He sported a superhero cape of black glossy curls along his back.

If he had had a superpower it would've been 'Mega ratter!' – the scourge of all whisker-twitching vermin daft enough to set paw on his territory. He was a working dog and was never happier than when snout-deep in rodent scent, like a wine connoisseur with their nose in a spicy Shiraz. He was often found wriggling his bendy frame behind bales of musty hay, on a one-dog mission to catch whatever rat was lurking in the crevices of the barn.

The 'Norway' or 'brown' rat population (which, puzzlingly, isn't remotely Nordic and isn't uniformly brown, rat fact fans) has been on the rise over the last thirty years thanks to warmer winters, which means longer breeding periods. With their fondness for merrily defecating near enough constantly, spreading diseases, damaging buildings and machinery and causing fires by gnawing through electricity cables, it's fair to say that rats really aren't high on the list of farmers' most favourite things, which, judging by my dad, I think begins with a brew at No. 1, then biscuits, then talking with his farmer buddies about cows; 'rats' is at the end at about No. 41,349.

We did our best to keep the buggers down and Benji took real pride in helping. Just as a rat is hard-wired to breed, to gnaw, to poop, this tough little terrier was bred to take them down.

At the height of summer when the barn needed ridding of the dusty old hay before the new fresh stuff was brought in from the fields, we'd gather to shift the bales that had lined the barn walls since the year before like the pastry casing of a huge square pie. The workers and friends who'd arrived to help with haymaking knew that the first morning would be taken up with clearing out not only the hay but its inhabitants as well.

On a couple of occasions I would perch on the edge of the loft next to my siblings (I wasn't tempted to jump – lesson learned) and as my dad's pals dismantled the remaining walls of hay like huge Lego blocks, we'd poke a pitchfork down the back of the bales, creating a kind of Indiana Jones-style obstacle course for the rats, who had to run the gauntlet down the corridor of prongs jabbing them towards the concrete floor. At these moments I secretly hoped I wouldn't feel the soft thud of furry flesh underneath my fork; that'd be too much. This was Bolton, not *Game of Thrones*.

As their empire steadily disappeared the rats would have to make a run for it through the vast barn doors and out to the open fields with Benji in hot pursuit.

More often than not they'd escape to freedom, but occasionally a cheer would go up when a slightly slower one was unlucky and Benji could be seen shaking his prize like a rag.

Looking back it all seems a bit gruesome and it was. It's a million miles from my own kids' lives. The only rodent they'll encounter is our hamster Cheddar; and our dogs Beano and Dolly, fluffy white Maltese ruled by the cat (Watson), might like chasing squirrels but if they came face to face with a rat they wouldn't know what to do with it. Beano would be just as likely to bake it a quiche as he would to break its neck with a few deft shakes.

By the time Benji died he had a few bits missing – a goolie and a corner of an ear had been lost in battle, as had a few teeth. If I have one resounding memory of that dog it's that if he worked hard, he played even harder.

He had his hobbies – he loved brawling, fast women and fast cars. Benji picked fights with any big dog that crossed his path despite being snack-size to them. It was like he was channelling every badass character Vin Diesel had ever played. He also was quite the romancer – if any bitch was on heat within a two-mile radius Benji would be up her garden path in no time.

His liking for fast cars, or at least chasing them, caused us no end of worries. On one side of our house was the farm proper, the buildings and fields, but on the other side, through a heavy, squawky-hinged blue gate, lay a housing estate.

Like a Bolton version of *The Lion, the Witch and the Wardrobe*, that gate was the door through which you'd step into a new world: not a snow-covered Narnia full of curious characters, but a vast estate with a fair few colourful characters. Hundreds of neatly kept small semis spread across a myriad of avenues and crescents. Little has changed; maybe the family Cortina and the kids' Chopper bikes have been replaced by Ford Focuses and scooters, but it was and still is a nice enough area. It was never rough – not mattress-in-the-front-garden rough.

Beyond the gate always felt like a different land; on the farm we were in our own little kingdom, we were safe, knew the rules and could gallivant around the yard, fields and buildings with no worries. But beyond the gate was the real world and this is where Benji would get into scrapes.

On the farm he barely batted a darkly lashed eyelid at Dad trundling past on his tractor and neither did he pay any attention to visitors pulling up in their cars, but once through the gate and onto the estate, Benji had an inexplicable and pathological hatred of vehicles and would pursue them, barking furiously. If it had an engine and four wheels it was fair game. His absolutely favourite quarry to chase through those streets was the ice cream van.

You've gotta admire this plucky terrier; he certainly had balls (well, one at least). Choosing a pastel-coloured ton of van as his mortal enemy, he'd set off towards the estate as the unmistakable strains of 'Greensleeves' chimed into audio range, announcing Mr Whippy's arrival.

If I'd managed to find Mum or Dad in time to cadge 50p I'd join the queue of kids, salivating at the thought of a lemonade or banana lolly, high on a heady combination of anticipation and the diesel fumes pumping out of the van's exhaust.

Benji would satisfy himself with sniffing around on a nearby lawn, acting as if the ice cream van was of no consequence to him. But when the crowds of kids had dispersed and the monster's engine roared and pulled away from the kerb, that was his cue to attack.

I'm not saying Benji wasn't a smart dog but to try to bite a moving wheel isn't the brightest idea. It's not only highly dangerous but must've hurt too – as the van trundled off Benji would be running alongside the rear wheel trying his damnedest to get a gobful of rubber tyre. He must've had gums of steel.

Luckily he never fully got a purchase on it or he could've become attached and whizzed round and round, thwacking road and mudflap in quick succession like some macabre wheel decoration. It was only when the van groaned from first to second gear and picked up speed that Benji's little springy terrier legs could no longer keep up and his nemesis would make its getaway, disappearing into the sunset; well, into Chester Avenue at least.

I like to think there's a real possibility that one or two of Benji's peggies are still lodged in a tyre lying in a scrapyard somewhere.

4. Cold Jubblys

Grundy Fold Farm lies just on the outskirts of Little Lever and Bradley Fold. The latter is quite remote. Dad knows a few farmers over that way. Narrow roads wind round sloping fields dotted with sheep. Stone cottages, the occasional tractor slowing the traffic and blind corners hiding horse-riders mark it out as being rural. It has its picturesque moments even in winter, its bare hedgerows framing the bleak but beautiful land. The former, Little Lever, is a place I often refer to on the radio as a 'charming little hamlet' as an in-joke to anyone who knows it. If Little Lever is a hamlet then I'm Dame Shirley Bassey. I love it though and I know my way round it better than anywhere I've lived since. I think the place where you ride your bike as a kid is the place you truly know back to front. I might not know all the street names but I know the footpaths, the ginnels and the short-cuts.

Residents refer to it as 'the village' but that's not accurate either – a village conjures up images of vicars, hanging baskets, duck ponds and thatched roofs.

What it is is a collection of sprawling estates and residential areas surrounding a high street that boasts my most favourite chippy in the world, a couple of chemists, shops and these days a massive supermarket, replacing the long-dead local minimarts, one of which was Hanburys. God, I loved that place, whose shelves were so cluttered it looked like one of those Channel 5 documentaries on hoarding.

Despite the aisle space being narrowed down to the width of a Weetabix by all the produce bulging from the shelves they still had little wonky trolleys, used mainly as mini cages on wheels to stop lil' darlings like me running riot and sliding a multipack of Blue Riband in among Mum's everyday essentials.

Recently while filming *Back in Time for Tea*, a BBC2 show about food and social history in the north, I discovered Hanburys had thirty-one stores in the north-west, eight of them in Bolton. They were first opened in 1889 by Jeremiah Hanbury and were among a handful of thriving independent supermarkets that could be found before the Big Four came striding into every town and swept aside all competition.

I find as I get older I care more and more about history, about where we come from, what went before.

If I'd told my twenty- or even thirty-year-old self about the beginnings of Hanburys I would've been met with the same blank stare I get from my own kids now when I point out a statue or interesting bit of architecture.

I first had an inkling I was heading towards middle age way back in 2005 while on a train to, ironically enough, a massive Radio 1 festival called the Big Weekend. Each summer the station would take the music line-up to a less obvious area than the usual big destinations. This year it was Sunderland's turn to welcome the circus to town. Tens of thousands of locals were allocated free tickets as world-class headliners rolled in for the weekend, hosted by all the Radio 1 DJs. They were huge events but as we approached Durham train station I wasn't struck breathless by the thought of the Foo Fighters, Kasabian or No Doubt – no, I was bowled over by the beautiful railway bridges with their high, narrow arches in warm yellow stone that framed the green hills behind.

Since then of course the signs have come too thick and fast to list or even notice . . . I now take pride in my full-blown middle-age symptoms and even took a puzzle book to do by the pool on holiday this year.

Back to the overstuffed aisles of Hanburys. In summertime Mum would treat us to Jubblys (stop giggling at the back), which were ice-pops encased in curious pyramid packaging made of the toughest cardboard ever created. I'm sure NASA would have some use for it if they realised its durability. Looking back, maybe Jubblys weren't that delicious and it was just such a mission to rip, bite and gnaw the packaging open that when the sweet, partly melted lolly eventually flooded your mouth the flavour was accentuated by relief.

Apart from Jubblys, Mum didn't really embrace too many food fads despite the early eighties being a hotbed of new, exciting convenience food. I'd watch the adverts on the telly for Findus crispy pancakes with their tagline of 'Every day has a different taste' and I'd think 'Yes! That's me! I want every day to have a different taste!' – the close-up of a slightly bobbly looking half-moon of pancake the colour of Homer Simpson, being sliced open to reveal its lumpy brown innards oozing out like some gravy mudslide, looked unbelievably scrumptious to my young eyes.

Much to my dismay, Mum insisted we ate proper food made from scratch and no amount of pleading would budge her. I absolutely love Mum's cooking though; her melt-in-the-mouth beef in red wine sauce was a thing of true wonder. Her Christmas lunch had mash AND roasties – potatoes two ways? What a woman.

Her broth was my absolute favourite though and she's now given me her old broth pan. Forget inheriting Great-Aunt Fanny's pearls, I was over the moon with my broth pan, which is silver with a few scorch marks and is big enough to bath an Alsatian in. The recipe involves some embarrassment as the main ingredient sounds like a sleazy bit of cockney rhyming slang – you need a certain confidence to walk into a butchers and ask for a ham shank without breaking eye contact. It's worth it though. The ham shank is so salty that if you were to throw it into the Dead Sea it'd gag and spit it back out, so it needs soaking. Once soaked you lob it into the pan atop a mountain of diced veg and boil the bejesus out of it, adding soaked soup mix along the way. The result is a greyish (stick with me) liquid with a flavour as deep as a mother's love. Each spoonful brings with it tiny treasures of celery, turnip, onion or lentil with a chunk of soft, stringy, pink ham.

If there is a national broth society I'm hoping they'd approve of the PR job I'm doing here.

Sadly, however, no amount of spin can convince my own family to eat it. After hours of me slaving over the stove, my face shiny with hope and condensation, only my eldest will have some and even then I suspect it's a sympathy slurp. No matter, I make it anyway and freeze it. Like salmon are driven to swim upstream to spawn, I make broth because it's in my genetic make-up.

It doesn't sound like much but this and her chilli con carne are the two recipes my mum has handed down to me and they were the two pillars that held up my childhood teatimes.

When I say Mum handed down the recipe for her chilli it's a slight exaggeration. After decades of eating the rich, dark chilli with rice, washed down with cold milk, I thought it was maybe time for her to pass on the secrets of its deliciousness. I was also about to appear with potty-mouthed chef Gordon Ramsay on his show *The F-Word*. The challenge was for us to compete to make the same dish, which would be blind-tasted and judged by a panel. I thought that chilli con carne would be perfect – who could beat Mum's home-made delight? The conversation went thus: 'Mum, please can I have your chilli recipe?' Now at this point I hoped for a hushed whisper, revealing a complicated list of rare spices sourced possibly from a rainforest, but instead she just said 'Oh, I've always used a packet mix, Schwartz is quite good.' I was genuinely gobsmacked that one of my all-time favourite meals had come from a packet. Seems Mum was up for convenience foods after all. Her secret trick was to put half a tin of baked beans into the chilli to soften the kick of the spice for us kids. Suffice to say I lost the cooking challenge and Gordon was almost lost for words that I'd committed such culinary crimes.

Despite the trauma I still make chilli with baked beans for my kids and they like it, whatever Ramsay reckons.

Mum's cooking skills came in handy on the farm as there were often extra mouths to feed, especially during haymaking, one of the busiest times on the farm, when there'd be a small army of helpers turning up to get the hay in. Arable farmers have for centuries watched the skies, trying to predict the weather and fathom its patterns. During haymaking my dad was at the mercy of the rain, which we get a lot of up north.

The far two fields in winter were knobbled and gnarled, but they transformed in the summer and grew lush long grass that towered above me. Once dried out by the warmth of the sun, it turned a beautiful golden and green hue and could be cut and left in long rows, ready to be gathered up by the metal fingers of the baler, swiftly knitted into neat blocks of compacted hay and then dropped out of the back like a huge mechanical goose laying oblong eggs.

For it to be cut and baled it had to be dry, which meant relying on the Great British Summertime. Farmers now use minute-by-minute weather apps to help save time and avoid disaster but Dad just had Michael Fish and luck.

Once Dad had had a couple of days of dry weather and the go-ahead from the weathermen it was all hands on deck in a race against the rain. Make hay while the sun shines isn't just a cute quip. Dad would rally the troops: my big brothers Robert and David plus a couple of their mates, including Andy with the metal-rimmed specs who had a look of Freddie Mercury, and Diddy, a lad from the village who was a right rum 'un. He reminded me of a pirate with his shining eyes, pierced ear and inky black hair. His nickname became the only name anyone knew him by, earned by him being what is technically known as a shortarse. There was also Mel, who helped out on the farm – a lovely man, quiet and considered, who Dad relied on; he sported a five o'clock shadow at 10 a.m. and had a head of dark curls with a matching tache. Then there was John, a family friend – bleached blond hair, toothy grin, daft as a brush – who was as much of a joker as he was a hard grafter.

John would be joined by Kim, his future wife, though neither of them knew it yet – then he could only dream of such riches. Kim had kept her horse on Dad's farm and was a similar age to my eldest sister Dot. She became a good friend of Dad's (now ex) wife. Kim was striking – tall and slender with bright hair the colour of pumpkins that fell in thick waves to her shoulders, and a dusting of pale freckles scattered over her nose. She was a grafter too, strong and athletic. She would muck in with the best of them and could cope with both the bales and the banter. John's face always lit up whenever he clapped eyes on Kim but it'd be another decade or so before she finally gave in to his charms.

Once the welcome cups of tea had been drained and the barn had been cleared and swept, haymaking proper would begin. Dad would be pulling a trailer with a tractor, following along behind the baler, with a couple of people picking up the bales and chucking them up to the men waiting on top of the trailer, balancing with their feet wide as if snowboarding. Chucking a bale upwards is most efficiently done using one smooth motion – lifting the bale first by the two lengths of orange twine holding it together, then a knee to propel it upwards momentarily onto your forearms, the momentum then helping the last upward movement as you push it up and away and onto the trailer.

The key was to get into a rhythm, using each body part like a footballer doing keepy-uppies. It was a schoolboy error to be seduced by the sunshine and wear shorts and a vest top – knees and arms would bear angry red scratches from the prickly bales, battle scars from a day's haymaking.

I was too little to gather the hay but I had the important duty of providing lubrication in the form of tea. As the crew toiled away I would make my way over the fields with a tray bearing cups of hot tea and coffee. It was hot, dusty, thirsty work haymaking, so I would feel like an important cog without which the whole machine wouldn't work. Each mug would be filled and then cling film stretched over the top; a genius idea, otherwise by the time I'd made it over the bobbly field most of the tea would've sloshed out onto the tray, like a small-scale *It's A Knockout* game.

There was plenty of banter, practical jokes and mickey-taking to lighten the load of so much physical slog. As well as the shouted instructions from Dad and Mel, laughter rang out across the field from this merry band of men – they were here because they liked Dad and my brothers, enjoyed the craic and were paid well, in sandwiches and maybe a turkey at Christmas. Mum would construct vast piles of butties ready for when the towering hay trailer came trundling steadily towards the barn for unloading – soft white bread, butter, ham, sliced in half, arranged on big dinner plates and devoured in seconds by the workers, like a swarm of locust through a barley crop.

I loved haymaking; it was one of my favourite times of year. The farm would be bustling, cars and vans bumping up the lane and pulling into the yard as the helpers rocked up. There was a real energy to the place, the feeling of folk mucking in together. The buzz of bringing in all the hay, the camaraderie and little me in the middle, fetching tea and trying not to get under everyone's feet. Once the barn was packed and stacked, fit to busting with new fresh hay and the massive blue sliding doors closed and padlocked, there was a real feeling of achievement. Knowing the hay was safely in and livestock could be catered for for the next year was something to celebrate; back at the farmhouse cans of cold beer were cracked open, more butties made, and the banter continued long after the sun faded over the newly bare fields.

5. Twelve Pots of Pond's

Away from the farm, on the weekends my eldest siblings would let their hair down at the local nightspot. Its name was Touch of Class but it had a few nicknames including 'Touch of Ass' or, my personal favourite, 'Touch of Crotch'. I never got to feel my feet stick to the dance floor of that particular establishment, though; instead I was down the pub. A family favourite was the Queen Anne – a vast red-brick building, a myriad of different rooms accessed along cream-tiled floors through dark wood and opaque glass doors.

These were the glorious eighties – decades before smoking bans, when parents thought nothing of sparking up centimetres from their offspring's faces.

In fact, so smoky were some of these pubs that kids got skilled at recognising their folks by their footwear peeping out below the dense fog of fag smoke. Once through the door of the snug the men became grey clouds wearing brown leather slip-ons.

My mum's mum, Nana, was the only woman who made having a fag seem remotely glamorous. Her packet of Benson & Hedges would be decanted into a silk purple paisley-patterned case with a golden clasp and she would hold her glowing ciggie between long fingers adorned with sparkling rings and always immaculately manicured fingernails, painted fuchsia pink. I have Nana's long nail-beds so they look decent even when cut to the quick – it's kind of comforting to think that once you're gone there are still whispers of you that echo through those you left behind.

Nana always smelled gorgeous, of face powder and perfume. Her golden-blonde hair was set into smart, slightly bouffant curls, framing a kind face with smooth skin and a dab of frosty pink lippy. Nana never washed her face with water, preferring instead Pond's cold cream. Each year on her birthday my grandad bought her twelve pots of the stuff to last her the year. It's not as showy as a dozen red roses but I think it's a thousand times more romantic.

Nana was pretty chic, often dressed in a floral number made at her dressmaking classes. I'd go along with her when I was really little. I remember her and her pals in the community centre, cutting out dress patterns, bent over sewing machines and gossiping over tea and fags.

Nana was a member of a few groups, including the fabulously named Lady Glades. Sure, in retrospect it sounds more like a feminine hygiene product than a secret society but that's exactly what it was, like the Masons but for working-class women. The Lady Glades gathered every Monday night in a room above the Queen Anne pub.

My grandad was in the male version of which the Glades were an offshoot. They had come up with their own female version as they weren't allowed to join the male one: the Royal Antediluvian Order of Buffaloes, or 'The Buffs' for short. Funny to think now that a group of middle-aged men in Bolton called themselves buffaloes. I like to imagine how the name came about in the first place, when the group was founded in 1822:

'OK, so settle down please, gents. Jeff likes Stag but there's too many connotations with that – there'll be no being stripped naked and tied to a lamp-post in this society, unless specially requested ha-ha, no, seriously though . . . Alf said Rhino but they're expensive – they charge too much – little joke there. Reg likes Buffalo cos like him it's heavy, hairy and has a slightly hunched back.'

'Last orders, gents.'

'OK, Buffaloes it is. Let's pop a "royal" at the front to make it fancy. Mine's half a mild if you're buying, George.'

Both groups were philanthropic organisations, raising money for charity, and each had a hierarchy and used badges, medals and sashes. I found the sashes fascinating – I'd only ever seen them on beauty queens, so seeing my nana slip hers on was like watching a grown-up playing dress-up.

But I suspect this generation that came through a war also enjoyed a bit of pomp and ceremony and were comfortable with order and rank. And liked getting together with their pals and having a drink.

On Remembrance Sunday I'd march with my mum, nana, grandad and the Buffs and Lady Glades. It being nippy in November, my grandad Vince would wear a massive dark-chocolate-coloured coat that I thought made him look especially buffaloesque. Maybe it was the pelt from an alpha buffalo he had to wrestle and kill and skin to gain entry to the Buffs . . . unlikely, in retrospect – buffalo weren't common in Little Lever and my grandad was only five foot in his stocking feet.

The procession of dozens of people of all generations, cagoules and perms fluttering in the breeze, solemnly wound its way through the village from the community centre, past the news-agents, a couple of chippies and the minimarket to outside the library, where the names of the village's war dead were carved on a huge stone plaque.

Grandad and his pals all proudly wore their medals on bright ribbons on the left breast of their coats. Some frailer than others, some in wheelchairs. I loved the feeling of us all marching for one reason, moving en masse.

I really got a sense of how important that day was, as the wreaths were laid and speeches made and then someone from the local church band played 'The Last Post' – a few bars of music that still has the power to move me to tears. It's always stuck with me and always will.

Years later, including during the time the tabloids would probably call the 'Party Girl Years', I'd always observe a minute's silence on both the eleventh of November and Remembrance Sunday, finding a quiet corner at work or pulling over in my car to bow my head and remember those who died in the horror of war so I could be free, glaring at the people around me who clearly weren't noticing the hour, the day, the month.

During the war Nana and her girl pals all worked in an aircraft-building factory. She didn't tell me much about it apart from she fixed the wings to planes. She made it sound pretty casual and well within her capabilities – popping a wing on a Lancaster Bomber, no trickier than hemming a pencil skirt.

My grandad Vince fought in World War Two but like many who served he never really spoke about it. Maybe it was more that I never asked, something I thought about too late.

As a nipper it's hard to imagine your elders as young people, in colour rather than in faded black and white. In my mind he was always just Grandad, the slightly grumpy one with a pot belly poking over his belt who would open the door to us with one hand while simultaneously turning down his hearing aid with the other. We didn't mind; we would just run to mither Nana. Grandad had his own armchair that no one else was allowed to sit on, a maroon velvet affair that he guarded like a swan guards its nest. If you dared perch on it for a moment when he'd popped to the loo, you knew to scram sharpish on his return. To be fair, Grandad's health wasn't the best – he had a vivid purple scar that ran from his chest and down his belly from his heart bypass and was often breathless and tired. But he never seemed frail to me – little yes, curmudgeonly sure, but never frail, and to the day he died he had a full head of shiny black curls and a large black tache – he looked like one of the old dudes playing dominoes in the background of *The Sopranos*.

Down at the Conservative Club he held court like a Mafia boss with his crew. He was naturally funny and quite the raconteur – he loved to make people laugh with his stories. Mum reckons I've him to thank for passing down the entertainer genes that have stood me in good stead in this crazy business we call show.

Vince had been a master baker (careful how you say that) but he had dreams to hang up his apron and take to the stage; he wanted to be a stand-up and even went to a 'comedy school' – night classes teaching the necessary skills to be a stand-up – but in the end he didn't get much further than writing down some of his favourite funny stories and jokes.

After he died Mum came across a small tan leather pocket-book full of his jokes. Because I love an emotional moment I savoured opening it, slowly leafing through the pages, hoping to maybe be brought to tears of both mirth and wonder at these incredible lost works.

The contents did actually take my breath away, not so much with their majesty but because . . . how do I put this? They were very much 'of their time' – written in the 1970s when nobody batted an eyelid about jokes about minorities cos it was just a bit of fun. I reckon if I'd told a couple of these gags to Bernard Manning even he might've thought I was out of order. Put it this way, at the time I was going out with a black guy and now I'm married to a Jew and I couldn't have shown the book to either of them.

When a few years ago a TV company asked me to take part in a history show called *War Hero In My Family* for Channel 5, I jumped at the chance. I was hoping to find out who he was before old age, deafness and a triple heart bypass moulded him into the Grandad I knew.

Old photos of Grandad as a young man showed him in his army uniform. He had more than a touch of David Niven, with a glint in his eye and a slight smile tipping up the corner of his moustache.

His army records revealed a mischievous lad who'd once, as a dare, nicked an officer's Land Rover and done a few laps of honour of the exercise yard with pals clinging onto the back, a joy ride during a joyless time. He was hauled out of the driver's seat and thrown before his superior, who handed out a fine and made a note of the disciplinary action on his record. It was amazing to be there seventy-odd years later looking out over the same exercise yard in which Private Vincent Fulford permanently blotted his copybook.

Our search led us to Italy, where, although obviously it was no longer wartime, I feared for my life a couple of times. My poor producer wasn't overly familiar with driving abroad, and inched along the dual carriageway, winding through the mountains in the style of a one-car funeral cortège with a slow puncture. We nearly needed a funeral as the Italian wagon drivers became incensed by her leisurely pace in our tiny hire car and roared up behind us in their trucks overloaded with fruit and veg, so close that we could almost smell the sweat forming on their furious brows.

We arrived in one piece at our location in the rolling hills near Naples. Once the scene of a desperate battle, now it was lush, green and peaceful, the only noise being birdsong. The idyllic surroundings made it even more difficult to imagine the horror that happened here in 1942.

It was my job to explain to viewers exactly what had happened – the Italians advancing on the British army in the valley below. How my grandad drove a makeshift ambulance – a Land Rover Defender – down into the battlefield and loaded up and ferried the injured back to safety.

I can't imagine how scary that would've been – bullets whistling past him as he drove back up the rough track with his fellow soldiers, his pals piled in the back as he bounced over the rough terrain, screaming in agony from their injuries, some already dead and others dying en route.

I really wanted to do the story justice and get across the nightmare that had unfolded in the beautiful valley below. I was to stand on the edge of a sheer drop and deliver my lines.

The only problem was that at that moment Grandad and I had more in common than any of the crew knew – as well as a penchant for performance my grandad also bequeathed to me a crippling fear of heights. I vaguely remember him lying on his back on the floor in their cluttered front room with his maroon-slippered feet up, when he had a vertigo attack, his little legs barely reaching the seat. I too have had to excuse myself from various social gatherings on charming roof terraces to avoid completely ruining the barbecue by flinging myself over the edge and onto, in my mind, the 'safety' of the pavement below, even if it's four storeys down. The fact that I would've, to keep with the Italian cuisine theme, splatted into a margarita pizza seems irrelevant to the vertiginous mind: the floor is where it's at. Only a surprisingly small voice in your subconscious whispers not to jump. Freaky.

So there I was, standing in the spot where Grandad bravely shuttled his friends to safety, and I could feel the drop behind me luring me backwards into its delicious void. To be fair, I was a good couple of metres away from the edge, but I still felt panicky, the palms of my hands seemed to have developed their own sprinkler system and my legs felt as sturdy as spaghetti. The cameraman looked puzzled as I kept taking fairy steps towards him and away from the abyss. If the director hadn't stepped in I probably would've kept going till my breath fogged up the lens.

I explained in a small voice how frightened I was and of course they let me move further away, though the view in the distance was even more distant than they'd intended, and I'm not sure the piece to camera had the same impact. It wasn't my most intrepid reporter moment. You've never heard Kate Adie say 'Ooh, can I just go and broadcast from behind that van – the gunfire really makes me jump?' or Sir David Attenborough refusing to film next to a giant African ants' nest cos they give him the heebie-jeebies.

At the end of the shoot the producer gave me a large brown envelope that I was to open on camera. As you'll know, with these sorts of shows emotional moments are encouraged, compulsory even. A sob, a sniffle, even a subtle lip-wobble would suffice. They set up the shot. I was to sit at the foot of a large tree and read the contents of the envelope.

The crew were speaking in hushed tones, clearly trying to create the right atmosphere so that when the director murmured 'Action' I'd feel able to openly weep at what I found, creating light entertainment magic as ex-party girl and 'Former Hellraiser' (copyright *Daily Mail* and Jeremy Vine's nickname for me) broke down in racking sobs.

The pressure was on.

I opened the envelope and peered inside. I was relieved – the sombre mood had for a second made me wonder just how bad things were. Was it a photo of Grandad wearing a French maid's outfit while cavorting with German officers? Did it, in a strange and unexpected twist, contain my surprise adoption papers?

No. It was in fact a letter from my grandad's group captain. I learned that after the war, when soldiers were discharged from service they were given a document that was somewhere between a school report and a CV to help them blend back into their former life on Civvy Street and rejoin the workforce. As I held the photocopied papers in my hand and read how Grandad had shown great bravery under pressure and had proved to be an honourable, hard-working soldier, I felt beyond proud.

Like farmers in a drought scanning the skies for rain clouds, the film crew watched my face, poised to zoom in as my emotional heavens opened and the first sweet drops fell. But my cheeks remained bone-dry. Usually I'll skrike at anything – news reports, songs, butter adverts – but like a kettle being watched that doesn't boil I couldn't just cry on demand.

I felt their eager faces watching me closely, so as I turned and delivered my final piece to camera I paused and stared thoughtfully into the distance and into a handy breeze, which at least made my eyes moisten a touch.

I came back from that trip with a fear of Italian HGV drivers and, more importantly, a fresh new respect for Grandad. I felt like I'd seen past the belly and hearing aid and met the brave, bright young soldier, popular with his fellow soldiers and respected by his superiors.

6. Bee's Knees, Ankles and Toes

Despite nearly dying at the hands of wagon drivers in Naples I have a huge respect for the much-maligned haulage community, thanks to me and my dad often hitting the road in his DAF lorry.

When you're one of five children and you're vying for attention not only with them but with a whole herd of cattle, time alone with your pa is so precious. As well as being a farmer my dad also drove a wagon. He was basically a man with a van but on a slightly bigger scale. He was freelance and had a rotation of regular clients who'd need their goods – from paint to tiles to garden furniture – transporting all over the UK.

Dad drove a modest flatbed DAF with a bright-blue cab. The back, as the name suggests, is flat, so the goods are loaded onto it on pallets and then covered with vast sheets, which are secured with long ropes thrown over and tied to hooks running along the underside.

I absolutely loved going with my dad in the lorry. I did it from the age of about seven, when I guess I was big enough to obey instructions but small enough to fit on the little bunk with him, up until the age of twelve-ish, by which time I was quite skilled at 'roping up'.

We'd rise ridiculously early. Or so it seemed. On winter mornings he'd wake me at 5 a.m. while it was still pitch black outside. Dad is a gentle soul and always woke me up really nicely, stroking my hair till I came to.

Mum on the other hand was much more vocal in her style, enthusiastically encouraging us to wake up by loudly shouting our names and telling us the time while whipping open the curtains and switching on lights.

Looking back of course I know it wasn't because Mum was a tyrant and Dad was an angel – it was because Mum was in charge of getting everyone up and off to school, and despite my efforts to be more gentle with my own kids, again this apple hasn't fallen far from the tree when it comes to mornings.

I try to coax my own offspring awake with kisses and whispered welcomes to a brand new day but with the clock ticking, dogs needing feeding and three of them to get up and out for 7.40 a.m. I usually resort to the curtain method. Recently I've had to try my very best to be more soothing, as my son banned me from waking him on account of my harshness and requested for his dad to be on wake-up duties instead.

On those dark mornings I really appreciated Dad's bedside manner. It didn't take much to get me up – not only was I excited to be going out in the wagon with him but I also saw myself as some kind of colleague or assistant on these trips and I didn't want to risk holding him up in case it jeopardised future invites.

Sure, being seven and feeling like a co-driver on a haulage job was totally normal. It felt like me and Dad against the world.

Traffic jams, middle-lane hoggers and tachograph frustrations held no fear for us if we had each other on these road trips. Like Thelma and Louise, if Thelma was a wagon driver with a bald spot and Louise was a scrawny nine-year-old in a hand-me-down polo neck.

I would get dressed quickly, partly due to keenness and partly cos it was always bloody freezing at the farm. Downstairs to the breakfast bar in the kitchen, feet swinging off the high stool as Dad dished up Shredded Wheat with hot milk.

And we were off. Well, once the wagon had rumbled into life, the heaters had kicked in and the windscreen mist had cleared. We'd bump down over the ruts and through the puddles on the farm lane and make our way through the sleeping village to the glorious M61.

All my school holidays would be spent out in the wagon with Dad. It felt like anything was possible on these trips – they were a real adventure to me and the world was our oyster. I imagine Dad saw them less romantically – loading up pallets of undercoat in Yorkshire and delivering them around Cumbria.

Dad is a quiet guy and so the deafening roar of the engine on these trips meant quality time together without the pressure to talk. I'd watch Dad and think he was not only the bee's knees but the bee's ankles and toes too. I loved stealing glances from the passenger seat as he drove this massive wagon. I thought he was the most handsome and brilliant man in the world.

We were higher up than most of the other vehicles on the road and I loved looking down from our lofty position. On long journeys with my own kids now the back seat looks like we've done a ram-raid on WHSmith – so many books, colouring pens, magazines and snacks to distract them from the hours on the motorway, as well as iPads and phones.

I didn't take anything to entertain myself in the wagon, though – I was quite happy to watch the world whizz by through a windscreen that seemed as big as a billboard.

I thought it was so cool how wagon drivers would flash their lights at overtaking lorries to signal that it was safe for them to tuck in in front of them, and in a thank-you for the courtesy the overtaking lorry would indicate left-right-left as they manoeuvred into position. It felt like a community – lorry drivers looking out for each other.

People sitting in the middle lane are the scourge of wagon drivers as the middle lane is their fast lane and if it's necessary to take evasive action and overtake a very slow wagon then it can be pretty dangerous if Clive and Claire in their Vauxhall Zafira are pootling along at sixty-eight in the middle lane, so engrossed with PopMaster that they're oblivious to the twenty tons of truck on their left needing to swing out to avoid a pile-up and potentially recycling the Zafira and its contents into a Turner prize entry.

I've not seen Dad angry much but middle-lane hoggers proper wound him up and I'm the same now – I never plonk myself in the middle lane and when pulling in front of a wagon I use my indicators in the left-right-left sequence favoured by HGV drivers as if deploying a secret handshake to identify myself as a member of their secret society.

I like to imagine they think 'The blood of a rich haulage heritage flows strong through yonder lass, she's one of us' and not 'Why's that daft cow in her Volvo indicating all over the shop?'

These trips with Dad were in the days before satnav, so Dad would smooth a bedsheet-sized map out over the steering wheel as we searched for an anonymous industrial estate tucked away somewhere in the drizzle of Yorkshire.

On the road with Dad we never really stopped at services except to use the loos. I was desperate to go to these brightly lit meccas of Big Macs and pick 'n' mix but they were seen as extortionate so instead we'd go to truck-stop cafés where ladies with upper arms the size and shade of partly defrosted legs of lamb, blue gingham tabards straining over their matronly bosoms, dished up sausage and chips and sloshed out our brews into white mugs.

I always felt quite like Sophie in *The BFG* in these places – everything seemed super-sized, from the truckers' bellies to the fry-ups they were wolfing as they leafed through the *Sun*. I was often the only kid in there, so I enjoyed feeling like a stowaway among the giants.

Sometimes we wouldn't have the fine dining experience of a truck-stop; instead Dad would pop into a shop and emerge with a pack of bread rolls and a packet of ham and, without cutlery (we were hardcore truckers, not picnicking at Downton!), he'd use his thumbs to create a crevice in which to poke a couple of slices of the ham. He was ahead of his time really. 'Len's Ham Pockets' could've been a thing if 'ham pocket' didn't sound like some horrible Shakespearean description of a bar wench's genitalia.

Whenever we were at a depot, collecting or picking up, I usually had to stay in the cab to dodge the wheels of the fork-lift trucks buzzing around. But if being confined to quarters in the cab was the dullest bit, one of the best bits was the occasional visit to a pub. ''Ey up,' Dad would say, 'do you fancy some pop? Let's go have a quick leg-stretch.' Zipping up his body warmer and smoothing down his hair we'd set off, me trotting alongside trying to keep up with his long stride.

The bracing walk took us from Dad's parking spot outside the depot we were delivering to first thing, through Whitehaven town centre, past the fishing boats bobbing about in the harbour, huddled together as if for warmth, and through the doors into the bright lights and cosy welcome of the local pub. After weekly trips delivering on this route for a few years Dad had become pally with the landlord, who bent the rules to allow me in. 'Alreet, Jeff,' Dad would say, 'pint of Guinness for me please and a lemonade for the ankle-biter.' There'd also be Smith's crisps, cheese and onion flavour, the green bag ripped right open by Dad and laid out like a sharing platter.

After a couple of drinks we'd head back to the wagon. I loved the sleeping arrangements. It felt a bit like camping. Behind the seats in the cab was a bunk that was about the width and length of a stick of chewing gum. Somehow all six foot two of Dad and me with my large head both squeezed onto it in sleeping bags, assuming the classic 'top to tail' position. It's a mystery how we got any sleep at all, but I imagine we were both knackered – Dad from map-reading and being angry at bad drivers and me from gawping out of the window – because after a quick 'Night night, sweetheart, love you' from Dad, we would both immediately zonk out.

The next thing I'd know it would be morning and Dad would have already wriggled noiselessly off the bunk and be busily going through his morning routine, accompanied by the strains of Derek Jameson braying and shouting his head off on Radio 2's breakfast show.

The cab of the wagon consisted of a driver's seat, a passenger seat and a big, hard plastic dome bit between the two that hid all the technical gubbins necessary for a truck to work, possibly involving spark plugs or something.

There was the thin bunk that ran behind both seats and, of course, a glovebox, full of tachograph cards.

That was it. But in my dad's hands this small space became like Mary Poppins's bag. From every nook, cranny and crevice Dad would produce stuff, like a plastic washing-up bowl for us to wash in – 'But hang on, Dad, we have no water!' – eau yes we do; he'd produce a big container of H_2O to soak the flannel and soap he'd just whipped out of a toiletry bag that he'd magicked from Lord-knows-where. Toothbrushes and toothpaste would be produced with a flourish, along with a fluffy towel. Finally Dad would dig out his electric razor and shave his greying bristles, gurning as he did so.

In my mind's eye it's like a movie montage flashback, Dad whipping out all this stuff, me watching all shiny-faced and goggle-eyed to the strains of Wham!'s 'Wake Me Up Before You Go-Go'.

The most regular run Dad and I would do would be the Cumbria one: Carlisle, Workington, Whitehaven, then round the coast to Barrow-in-Furness.

The last leg to Barrow involved Dad negotiating his wagon round roads that seemed to wind endlessly up and up with a stomach-bothering sheer drop at one side. I hated that road; with my fear of heights I always felt like we were inches from certain death – just one wrong twitch of the steering wheel, a violent sneeze perhaps, and us two plus wagon would hurtle over the edge to oblivion. Dad would never have admitted he was nervous driving this route but his face, set in grim concentration, spoke volumes. I always felt safe though.

Whitehaven was where a couple of tins of paint would always seem to fall off the back of the wagon and we'd then mysteriously acquire a massive haul of prawns, fresh from the sea and triple-bagged in plastic packed with ice to keep them cool all the way home.

When we arrived back it was my job to shell them in the

outhouse sink, snapping back their grey heads and gently tugging out the long black thread that was their intestinal tract. Like I say, these trips had ups and downs both literally and figuratively. The main up was the special time alone with my dad and the downs definitely included getting prawn poo down my nails when we returned home.

7. Seventies Tangerine

To get into the farmhouse you first went through the porch, which was added on in the nineties. This was painted white and housed a small loo cubicle so you could pop for a pickle without all the fuss of wrestling your wellies off. The porch was also a handy place to store mucky wellies and wet dogs.

From there and into the kitchenette through an ancient wooden door, made from wide planks joined vertically together and painted black with a cast-iron gate latch that had a knack to opening it to get in and on the other side a huge, cast-iron bolt as big as one you'd see on a castle door, to keep people out.

On the back of the door hung so many waxed jackets it was as though the door had grown its own shell from multiple layers of thick, dark-green skin. Behind the door was a dog bed, cosy next to the airing cupboard, a cork noticeboard beside the land-line that was hung on the wall, and in later years in a never-seen-before (or since) embracement of technology, a cordless handset with a metre-long aerial, like a radio control for a toy boat.

There was a small padded bench underneath the phone, a

perfect perch for yakking on the blower or taking off your wellies. The metal sink that Dad alleges I used to be bathed in was under the big square window looking out over the yard. The cupboard underneath the sink held all the medication for the animals, like something from the pages of Harry Potter – old-fashioned medicine bottles, huge syringes and brown glass ampoules jumbled up with plastic plungers, bandages and aerosols of purple antiseptic spray.

Next to the sink stood a tall freezer, often containing half of one of Dad's cows, and the top of which was the domain of Cindy, the dark-brown Burmese cat, who I loved. Like a feline version of Angie Watts, she was clingy and fiery. Depending on her mood she'd either be mewing loudly for your attention from her furry nest in the sky or would silently swat at the top of your head with a paw as you passed, just so you didn't forget who was boss.

When she wanted love she'd meow until whoever was nearby would eventually give in and stand still next to the freezer so she could climb slowly down onto their shoulders, using her front paws to inch down the vertical drop of the freezer's plastic door until both gravity and common sense suggested she was close enough to make the leap onto their upper back.

You'd have to brace yourself, for two reasons – not only was she pretty sturdy and heavy for a cat but for the first couple of seconds after landing she'd use her powerful claws to gain her balance; then you could set off to the sofa or wherever with Cindy hitching a lift too, her long brown tail helping her to balance, wrapping round your neck and across your face like a rogue handlebar moustache.

Cindy and our Jack Russell Sally were sworn enemies, so she'd always time her hitchhiking with Sally's absence and skedaddle the moment the dog bustled into the room.

*　　*　　*

46

Like most houses the kitchen of the farm was, and is, where all the action is, the heart of the home. Although the cupboard doors have moved with the times – from seventies tangerine to eighties pine to a more understated cream in recent years – the shape has remained the same, a square of units with windows looking out towards the coal shed and the small garden, the public footpath and gate beyond. As you enter from the kitchenette you get to the breakfast bar and wooden stools.

It's in this room that Dad knocks up a cracking roast beef and one of his 'home-grown' turkeys at Christmas. It's here that everyone gathered after haymaking or during calving season. It was in this room that Robert frantically shook the ketchup bottle without checking the lid was on properly, liberally spraying the walls behind him with the red stuff, much to our delight as we all watched agog from the safety of the breakfast bar. It's in the kitchen that a teenage David helped himself to a jar of yoghurt only to find out it was actually worming liquid for the calves that Dad had put in the fridge to keep cool, and it's into here that Robert came home drunk after a big night out and liberally spread pâté on some hot buttered toast before falling into bed. He was told the next morning that he'd actually snacked on the dogs' brawn.

Rivers of hot tea flowed as births, marriages and deaths were discussed here; all life was in that room and it was all debated over a couple of fig rolls at the breakfast bar.

Sitting in the kitchen never felt particularly private – in summer the door that led out across the concrete pad and to the coal shed was always open and people would often be popping their heads round, from the girls who stabled their ponies in the yard asking for the barn key, to the local policeman saying how-do to Mick the Tip – no, not a gangster from the Mafia who got his name because he liked to lure his victims to the local tip but a wagon driver who kept his tipper truck on Dad's land, bouncing up the lane every night, the chains on his truck clanging like a haulage ghost of Christmas past.

If the kitchen was a hub of activity then the lounge was a sacred place of relaxation, as this was where the carpet began and may the good Lord have mercy on the souls of those foolish enough to venture from the kitchenette to the lounge without first taking their wellies off. The lounge was where Dad could finally relax after a long day. In winter evenings a coal fire would be built and lights dimmed, and humans and animals alike would snooze in the soporific glow of the flames. The fireplace was surrounded by brick that travelled about two-thirds up the wall, upon which Dad's ornaments of porcelain Herefords grazed, a bull, cow and calf. I loved the porcelain calf and would always secretly play with it.

The lounge was a long rectangular room with an oxblood leather chesterfield sofa and matching armchair in front of the fire, with a telly the size of a skip at one end and a polished mahogany dining table at the other. It was at this table that I broke the news to Dad that I was a vegetarian and it was at this same table that I tucked into a leg of lamb a week later when the whiff of a cunning plan cooked up by Dad worked a treat and the smell of the roasting joint wafting in from the kitchen overwhelmed me and banished any notion of not eating meat.

New Year's Day buffets were spread on this table and home-work pored over, all watched by a fox's head that's still there today and is the focus of much macabre curiosity from my kids. It is a fox that met its demise on Dad's farm and is mounted on a wooden plaque with its tail hanging on a hook next to it, which to me seems in poor taste – bad enough you get shot and stuffed but then to have what was previously dangling off your rear end placed next to your face for eternity seems a little unfair, like having your own arse stuffed and popped up next to your head.

The fox obviously has some fake bits – glass eyes and plastic gums and teeth set in a snarl – though its expression is one of slight surprise, which I guess yours would be too if you were met with the wrong end of a farmer's gun.

Dad actually wouldn't bump off foxes if the red-coated buggers would just pop in to steal one hen for tea and leave the rest alone but, in a henhouse, foxes will decimate the entire coop and barely eat anything.

The upstairs was made up of three bedrooms and a bathroom where the shower used to go cold whenever one of the cows would take a sup from the automatically refilling drinkers; the house shared the same water supply as the cattle sheds and it was all connected – at least that's what Dad used to tell me. 'DAAAAAD! The water's gone freezing!' I'd holler and he'd shout his reply 'The cows must be thirsty, it'll warm up again in a minute.'

Us three girls used to share the biggest room and there were bunkbeds on one side and a single bed on the other. It's the room my husband and I sleep in now when we visit and it's tiny, although it seemed massive to my six-year-old self. It's in this room that I'd sashay up and down singing Gloria Gaynor's 'I Will Survive', coached by my sister Dot. Across the landing from where Dot would swing me over the stairs on the draft excluder was the boys' room.

The farmhouse always has a slightly wonky feel to it; the carpeted floors always seem slightly sloped and creaky, like the whole building has been pushed to one side by a giant hand and then hastily straightened. To be fair, one side wall of the house had to be knocked down and rebuilt at one point, the bricks removed to reveal the boys' bedroom, like an opened-up doll's house.

From the outside during my childhood the farmhouse looked like a child's simple pencil drawing – painted white, two windows upstairs, two down, a door and smoke coming out of the chimney. Only in winter obviously, and only at night-time. The only time I remember a daytime fire in the hearth was on Christmas Day and New Year's Day, and the rest of the time the house was – and still is – a bit parky. One winter there was a heavy snowfall and the house was absolutely freezing, so Rob begged Dad to let him light a fire, to which Dad responded by pointing at the three inches of snow on the roof and saying, 'See that snow, it's insulating the house so it can't be cold.'

These days my husband reckons it's colder inside the farm-house than out but he's wrong – there's no such thing as a cold house, just the wrong jumper thickness. Dad used to be a firm believer that central heating made you ill by making you warm and cosy and – I imagine – a bit soft and therefore a more attractive target for germs. Not sure how the science of this plays out but let's just say Dad is still going strong and is to hardy what James Bond is to suave. My brother Robert has a fondness for made-up medical facts – for example, that long toes are a sign of intelligence (he himself has very long toes). I can see where he gets it from.

The house had a long double garage behind it that could've been a prop from a horror movie – made from wood and painted treacle-brown, it was always dark inside and was cluttered with junk and tools on the floor and old thick cobwebs hanging like grey garlands from the rafters. Its pitch-black interior meant that the bare bulb dangling from the ceiling couldn't throw enough light to illuminate the very rear, so it was as if the garage just dropped off into a black hole. The boys tinkered with their motorbikes in there but it was a self-imposed out-of-bounds area to me.

Beyond the garage was a small grassed enclosure that ran from the rear of the garden and along the tarmac path that led down to the estate. In recent years a small allotment area was created by my brother-in-law Gary, where sprouts sprouted and cabbages cabbaged with huge success – Dad reckoned the soil was so rich thanks to it being a former burial site for many of the farm's pets.

Before the deathly vegetable patch, my pony Gus would some-times be put in for a pick of grass, as would Leeroy the goat or the occasional orphan; not the curly red-headed all-singing all-dancing variety – no, Dad's mate farmed sheep and during spring we often adopted a little lamb after it was orphaned at birth or if it was one of twins and its mum didn't have enough milk for two. This was the stuff of dreams for a young girl – these little spares came to us to be hand-reared. At first it was pretty full-on – like any newborn they'd need feeding every few hours, including through the night. The lambs would be white, fluffy and the size of a big cat, eighty per cent skinny legs like pipe cleaners, with big doleful brown eyes, long pale eyelashes.

Their feed bottles would be the size of big glass pop bottles, with a long black rubber teat on the end. They'd suckle furi-ously and as they got bigger feeding them became like pulling a cracker that wouldn't crack, the lamb pulling one way while you'd try to cling onto the bottle.

The lambs would snooze in a big cardboard box filled with a couple of old jumpers before graduating to a spare dog bed, until eventually they were strong enough to be turfed outside. I'd read enough children's fiction to know exactly what was supposed to happen with these lambs – a strong bond would form, the lamb would follow me everywhere like a dog and people would comment in wonder at our special relationship, the likes of which they'd never witnessed in all their years dealing with sheep/children. The lamb would blossom into a sheep and we'd go through a rocky patch after a misunderstanding but then one day the sheep would rescue me by raising the alarm after I got wedged somewhere remote. Sheepy would then escape the chop and not become chops – and we'd head off into the sunset, hand in hoof.

What actually happened was I'd get terribly attached to these furry friends and one day they'd disappear. Just like that. Gone. Laters. TTFN. The clue could've been in the names my dad bestowed upon twin lambs who ended up in our care - 'Freezer 1' and 'Freezer 2'.

Still, I didn't ask too many questions of Dad as he's known for his no-nonsense answers, plus I'd grown up with the legend of Larry (there's more on this later) as one of our family folk tales, so instead I chose to believe they'd gone to live somewhere charming, possibly with a name like Honeysuckle Farm, where they had all the sweet grass they could ever need.

8. Nuzzle that Muzzle

Returning to the farm after a trip away with Dad always gave me a sinking feeling.

As we slowly bounced up the farm lane I knew that coming home meant I had to share my dad again – with my siblings, the farm helps, the cattle and also Dad's then wife.

By this time my parents had divorced – a drawn-out, traumatic time for everyone except me; the heartbreak was over my head as I was only six at the time. Even though the consequences rippled through our family for years – the hurt, the divided loyalties, the politics – I was cushioned from it by my siblings, especially my eldest sister Dot, who was always there with a hug and a gentle explanation of any drama.

By now I was living half a mile away from Dad in a little council house with my mum, stepdad Ken and sister Yvonne. The three eldest had remained on the farm with Dad and his new wife.

I still had my old bedroom at the farm and spent loads of time up there as it was only a ten-minute walk away and there was a pony who needed mucking out. Still, coming home in the wagon meant back to reality and the end of mine and Dad's adventure.

The pony that needed mucking out was the result of our fat little Thelwell-esque Exmoor pony Muffin having a dalliance with a local part-Arab stallion. This in itself was a marvellous yet puzzling thing, as Arabs are the equine equivalent of annoying people you see dancing in bars in Bacardi adverts – sexy, vibrant, beautiful things, big eyes flashing and slender hips swinging.

Muffin, however, was less white rum and more half a stout – she was no looker, bless her; I can only presume she had a great personality or the stallion had his sugar-beet goggles on.

Quite the opposite of a leggy filly, she had short, sturdy legs placed at all four corners of her like a small coffee table. Now imagine the tabletop had begun to give and sag under the weight of a large barrel that had been perched atop it and you've kinda got her silhouette, her low-slung belly almost grazing the long grass of her field. She was a bright bay colour and so unbelievably stubborn that any mule who encountered her would've concluded that sometimes compromise can be a good thing.

She provided hours of fun though for Dot, who rode her endlessly round Dad's fields. Muffin was like a little tank – you could trundle around on her and no one got in her way, calves and ground-nesting birds scattering as she approached at a thunderous trot. As long as you didn't expect to be able to steer her or adjust her speed she was a cracker.

The result of Muffin's dalliance with the stallion was a little bay colt with a white star on his face and one white sock on his back left ankle.

He was born in the early hours of 1 August 1979 and was named by Mum, who chose a moniker subtly inspired by his birthday – Augustus the first, Gus to his friends.

And he had many friends – Gus grew up to be a beautiful boy. He grew bigger than his mum and ended up 13.3hh. He was definitely sturdy, but slinkier than her thanks to his dad's genes, with a pretty face and huge dark eyes with full lashes.

He was super-affectionate with a personality as big as his arse, which was sizeable thanks to Muffin.

I truly believe that the relationship between a young girl and her pony is pretty unique. I think Gus was probably my first love – I spent so many hours whispering sweet nothings into his ear and nuzzling his muzzle, breathing up his nostrils, fancying myself as a bit of a horse whisperer. I'd clasp Polo mints in my lips and Gus would gently nibble them from me. Who needed real boys when I had this dark, handsome chap to cuddle, waffle on to, kiss and love? And Gus didn't want me to drink cider with him or try to put his hoof up my top.

When teenagerdom struck, I'm sure my dad felt this last point keenly. As members of the opposite sex began to catch my eye and I started to swerve slightly from Gus, my dad knew that keeping me interested in ponies would at least delay the inevitable.

I'd been riding ponies since the age of six. Dad used to take me to a local riding school. I loved it – each week you'd ride a different little pony for an hour, all of our charges following nose to tail round the edge of a large indoor school. We'd be put through our paces from walk to trot to canter, go over trotting poles and at the end of each lesson practise our balance exercises – the excitingly named half scissors and more advanced full scissors, where you'd have to swing your legs around like a shonky circus act without sliding off the pony and onto the dusty floor, and 'Round the world' – basically this involved taking your feet out of your stirrups and awkwardly shuffling round in the saddle till you had rotated 360 degrees, while hoping your mount didn't suddenly set off for a jog. Luckily the experienced little ponies saw it as a perfect opportunity for a quick standing-up nap.

On the way home we'd stop off for chips and I'll always remember the guy behind the counter giving me a single chip wrapped in paper. Either I had extraordinarily tiny hands or spuds back in those days were the size of rugby balls, because I remember holding this one chip, gripped in my fist, and it was the size of a Crunchie.

As well as the mammoth chips, my other main memory of that time is of my massive head almost thwarting my equestrian ambitions. My dad took me to a tiny saddlery to fit me with my own riding hat. Before then I'd popped on any old adult hat that was rattling round the farm – dusty affairs with no chin straps, the torn velvet faded by the sun. Now, though, with the introduction of Kitemarks and safety standards, Dad thought I'd better get a proper hat.

I loved and still love a saddlery – these days if I treat myself or my eldest daughter to some horsey gear the smell of leather from the tack takes me straight back.

There's something so special about a shop dedicated to one hobby or pastime, because not only will you find everything you could ever need for your passion all under one roof but you're only ever in there with other people who also love what you love. It's the same with all specialist shops – no one ever really goes browsing through the bait bins in a fishing shop – 'Ohh, I might treat myself to a pint of red maggots!' – or idly peruses the trombones in a brass instrument emporium. These are more than shops, they're hives for kindred spirits to gather and nod admiringly at a split cane bamboo fly rod, curved soprano sax or, in my case, new riding boots.

The shop I went to with Dad was tiny with high shelves, reachable only by one of those ladders that wheel along rails, heaving with everything from lead ropes to boots and brushes.

Despite having a nogginous maximus I manage to go about my daily business and, apart from occasionally knocking it on low-hanging shelves, I cope. The only time a big head becomes a real problem is when one needs to borrow or buy headgear.

The trouble is that my head is deceptively large and, as I've painfully learned, people aren't always willing to accept its true size.

So there's me, six-year-old Sarah, standing in the saddlery with my dad. The shopkeeper eyes me for a few seconds and then reaches under the counter, producing a box containing a beautiful velvet navy hat. She whips off the white tissue paper with a confident flourish and pops the hat on my head. It's too small and perches like a thimble on a beachball. She seems puzzled but nevertheless produces a hat one size bigger; again it's too small. She repeats this about four times and each time becomes more puzzled and more determined to make the hat fit, trying to wrestle it further down each time, forcing it over my increasingly tender scalp, my face reddening as it becomes perfectly clear I have an abnormally huge head. What next? Maybe Dad will sell me to a travelling freak show or the circus. I'd spend my days combing the bearded lady's face and my nights displaying my planet head to the crowds.

Luckily, out of nowhere (well, I imagine out of the back room) the lady's husband appears with a hat that he's clearly dug out from some specialist area as the box is so dusty. The huge hat slides on like it was meant to be. Relief floods the room – Dad hasn't had a wasted journey and I've got my Kitemarked, navy-blue-velvet-covered hat.

A repeat performance of this scenario occurred again about

twenty years later, this time with a motorcycle helmet in a biker shop in Essex with my then-boyfriend, who rode a very fast bike around very winding country lanes and wanted me to join him on the pillion. The scalp and my ego were just as bruised as the first time.

Riding was something I just loved. I always felt, and still do, that when I'm not riding regularly there's a piece of the jigsaw missing – I have that feeling that there's something not quite right, like Kevin's mum in *Home Alone* just before she realises she's left her youngest child behind.

Where there is light there must be darkness, and what goes up must come down. The darkness and the down came in the formidable shape of my riding instructor.

The shadow she cast was a big one in all senses. She was my stepmum's mate and they'd have a catch-up over a Mellow Bird's and a couple of fags before we went up to the field where she taught me. To be fair, maybe I was an easily intimidated child, but to me she was truly terrifying. I got the distinct feeling that, like the lost sibling of Miss Trunchbull, she loathed children. No smiles or chit-chat from me could melt the frozen Arctic tundra that was her heart. What she lacked in empathy she made up for in disdain. In jodhpurs and boots, her cropped bleached hair standing stiff in the breeze and holding a whip in one hand like a Disney villain, she'd stand in the field as Gus and I trotted in a circle round her.

When I struggled to get Gus to do as I asked, she'd holler instructions dripping with sarcasm, shredding any wisps of confidence I may have had in my possession.

I hated those lessons; they were my most miserable hour of the week. Seeing her thundering across the yard made my heart thump with dread.

One of the consequences of being born with a dislocated hip is that my legs are kinda wonky and no matter how many times she shouted at me I just couldn't keep my knees in the correct position – so one day she tied my stirrups to the saddle's girth with some baling twine, then tied my feet to the stirrups. Now, I'm no health and safety nut but even I knew that to be tethered to half a ton of animal with its own mind was pretty dangerous. Gus was a sweet pony but like all ponies had irrational fears and would occasionally take off if something spooked him (mostly carrier bags and buses). He was also a bit clumsy, and if he'd tripped with my feet tied into the stirrups I could've been crushed and killed.

Luckily none of that happened. But when I was untethered my knee was so sore from being held in an unnatural position that I came up with some cruel fantasies about my instructor from hell being sucked into a slurry pit or trampled by a thousand cows.

As I limped away from the lesson that day I think we all knew a line had been crossed. I must've said something to Dad because lessons with her soon stopped.

Riding should be fun, and I had to make up for lost time. I did just that on what were known as the sandy paths. Just a fifteen-minute hack down a disused railway line, these paths wound around a huge country park away from roads and civilisation. Clip-clopping past the stables and a couple of rows of cottages trussed up in flower-covered trellises and into the paths felt like entering a whole new world – the Kingdom of the Ponies! Like gangs of outlaws romping round the Wild West, herds of teen girls trotted their fat ponies round the paths, pausing only to catch their breath or smoke a mint Consulate. I knew a few of the girls but I was a bit of a loner – I've always been perfectly happy with my own company.

Plus, as a teen I loved it being just Gus and me – off on our escapades. I just loved the silence; the space to breathe, the only sound Gus's hooves clip-clopping along.

When I did hook up with a couple of the girls who I knew from the paths, bonds would quickly be made by shooting the breeze about each other's ponies and we'd light up ciggies and chat. Smoking in the saddle was the thing to do. It always felt like a ridiculously rebellious act.

Now of course I see it for what it was – just a ridiculous act. Trying to give off an air of nonchalance while wrestling a Clipper lighter out of your tight jodhpurs pocket and sparking up a fag wasn't easy. If there was a breeze you'd need to cup your cig as you lit it, meaning not only were you setting fire to something while sitting on top of an animal, you now weren't holding on to the animal either. Smoking is already bad for you without adding an extra edge.

Luckily Gus never took off with me during a ciggie break, not that he was averse to the odd gallop. Near the sandy paths was a huge hill, and we'd all hurtle up it. That was the plan anyway – what usually happened was we'd get to the foot of the hill and the other girls would set off at a canter up through the grass towards the brow of the hill, but Gus would get so excited at the prospect of going fast with his mates that he'd express that excitement the only way he knew how to – by bucking. Gus was a master bucker (on these occasions I used to call him a little bucker, or something similar at least).

He'd dip his head down low and put it between his front knees, instantly pitching me forward slightly, then he'd throw both his back legs up together and with some force. I did my best to lean back and stay on. I got quite good. If a vacancy had come up for a part-time cowgirl in a rodeo I reckon I would've been in with a chance.

It was like a real-life game of Buckaroo except I didn't have a plastic lasso, spade, sombrero or guitar. Once the bucking bronco sideshow had ended, if I was still in the saddle, Gus would gallop up the hill at a decent clip to join his mates. We'd arrive at the top pink-cheeked (me) and breathless (both of us).

Trying to avoid serious injury/death by either being thrown or setting fire to myself really worked up an appetite, so most hacks around the sandy paths ended with a trip to the fish and chip shop.

As the old saying nearly goes: 'You can take a horse to a chippy but you can't make it fit through the doors,' so Gus would wait on the pavement while I popped my head in and ordered a chip barm, a soft white circle the size of a CD crammed with hot, fat chips. With one hand holding Gus's rein I'd stretch with the other to pop my 50p on the counter. My usual fare from a chippy is chips and gravy but I wouldn't attempt that on horse-back – I may have been daft enough to smoke on board but I wasn't a lunatic.

I had some brilliant times with Gus – he was my best friend and annoying sibling rolled into one slightly roly-poly pony. When I got started in TV on Channel 4's *The Girlie Show* (if you didn't see it, it was a rather stuffy late-night political discussion show, no need to google it, just take my word for it, OK?) and had done a few interviews with the press, one paper, let's call it the *Maily Dail*, ran an exposé on me poo-pooing my working-class roots and insinuating I was actually a poor little rich girl whose daddy was landed gentry and I had had my pick of world-class ponies, golden unicorns and a candyfloss castle, or something like that.

The image of me as some Veruca Salt character trotting around Daddy's vast estate couldn't have been further from the truth. I was definitely lucky – I knew most girls my age would've killed for a pony – but I wasn't spoilt and this was never more apparent than when Bolton Horse Show was on.

It was held a few miles away on some land behind a mill. I think it's fair to say that most if not all the competitors arrived with their horses in a trailer being pulled by Mum or Dad in the family car. The few more serious contenders rocked up in a horsebox. I hacked there on Gus with my pal Vicky on her dapple-grey pony. Show days meant that everyone had to be smartly turned out – I'd be up at the crack of dawn, stomach churning with excitement, tiptoeing out to Gus's stable to give him the works. It was like a spa day for him; he was buffed, brushed, plaited and combed to within an inch of his life. I would just stop short of a vajazzle.

Poor Gus often didn't have much mane to plait as he suffered with sweet itch – I know it sounds like a seventies R 'n' B song but it was actually a skin irritation caused by allergies and midges that made him rub the skin around his mane raw, removing much of it in the process. We tried all sorts of lotions and potions and even put garlic powder in his feed, hoping the pungent garlicky scent of his sweat would deter insects from nibbling him, but it didn't work and he merely always smelled like he'd been out for an Italian the night before. In the end it was easier to hog him – closely shave all his mane off so he'd rock a look that was half yard brush, half Annie Lennox eighties buzz cut.

Still, with his hoofs slathered in hoof oil, leather tack all cleaned and coat shinier than a conker, he looked the part, which was just as well as he wasn't attending the show for his skills.

Despite there being loads of showjumping classes and cross-country, Gus and I chose to shun them in favour of the more beauty-based events – 'Prettiest Pony' and the classic 'Pony the Judge Would Most Like to Take Home'. This class was a thinly veiled attempt to make sure there was at least one class everyone could win. For 'Prettiest Pony' the pony had to on some level be cute, but 'Pony the Judge Would Most Like to Take Home' was open to interpretation – any ol' mule could mooch round the ring as long as they paid the couple of quid entry fee.

The reason we didn't attempt any proper jumping classes was more to do with my lack of skills than Gus's. I'd popped over many a little jump in Dad's field, made from fencing poles painted in pastel paint and propped up on empty oil drums, and Gus was pretty good. The only problem came when I had to remember my way round a jumping course. With my heart thumping in my ears and adrenaline gushing through every fibre of my body, I'd forget the order of the jumps. Like one of those news stories about a pensioner driving four junctions the wrong way along the M62, I'd get completely confused and overwhelmed. Each jump was numbered and the first two would be pretty straightforward but then it'd be a left or right turn to number three and this is where I'd fall apart, nerves shredding my memory of the course.

It was so humiliating when a crackly voice announced over the tannoy that you'd messed up – they might as well have said 'SARAH COX RIDING AUGUSTUS FIRST IS DISQUALIFIED FOR BEING A COMPLETE IMBECILE – PEOPLE PLEASE GATHER ROUND TO POINT AND LAUGH.'

They could've just flagged me down and discreetly informed me; that way I could've casually trotted out of the ring as if it was my choice because I'd just remembered there was a sale on at Tammy Girl. The humiliation stung enough to put me off for life.

Part of the excitement with riding is the unpredictability of it – but for all the thrills, what goes up must occasionally come down.

I've managed, in the main, to bounce on landing from errant equines with no real damage. However, as a twelve-year-old I found myself in the A&E department of Bolton Royal Infirmary. Eventually.

I was out riding with Vicky, a very gung-ho pal of mine who was also a kind of no-nonsense, jolly hockey sticks type, like a 1950s Guide leader crossed with Angela Merkel.

She kept her dappled grey pony on the farm, so we'd often go on a hack together, Gus skipping about excitedly at having a friend, trying but failing to play it cool, swinging his rear end around and generally acting like the Rizzo to the other pony's Kenickie.

We decided to head to the sandy paths. We could get there by one of two ways. The first was mainly roads and would mean negotiating the 'Seven Stars dip' – which sounds like an impressive astronomical event but was just the pub that stood at the lip of a huge steep drop in the road, a kind of narrow tarmac-covered valley. Mooching past the pub meant leaning back in the saddle to help your pony's balance as they negotiated the steep decline.

I was familiar with the sharp angle of this rollercoaster-esque drop as I'd ridden down it all my life on my sister Yvonne's Chopper bike.

From the age of around six, with scant regard for my personal safety, Mum used to let me get a 'backie' from Yvonne, and it was literally a backie – we'd travel back to back.

Yvonne would be facing forward, face set against the wind in a determined grimace, mousey long hair streaming behind her, flared denim dungarees flapping as we hurtled down into the abyss of the dip, sun glinting off her white knuckles as she gripped the big Harley-Davidson 'ape-hanger' handlebars and steered the Chopper round the gravel-filled potholes. There was me facing backwards – head jiggling with the vibration, knees tucked up to avoid the wheels – luckily the L-shaped saddle of the Chopper meant I was able to cling on to the vertical bit of the seat like a koala on a tree trunk.

At the bottom of this plummeting drop was the entrance to a builders' merchants, which meant that as I hurtled backwards down the hill there was often a lorry or tipper truck following closely behind, bearing down on us as my sister negotiated the grids and ruts at full pelt.

It was these lorries that played on my mind whenever I considered which route to take on horseback. Gus wasn't bad with trucks usually, having got used to Dad's being parked outside his stable most nights. His greatest nemesis were double-decker buses; the quiet swooshing noises they made freaked out his little pony brain.

However, the trucks from this builders' yard were operated by young drivers who I presume thought it'd be character-building for young riders to have a few tons of metal roar up behind them as they trotted along the road.

I decided on that fateful day with Vicky that the disused railway tracks would be a better and safer bet. This route ran for a couple of miles from near enough the bottom of my dad's farm lane all the way to the entrance to the sandy paths.

The railway lines were really overgrown and actually quite picturesque – lots of bushes and greenery with the odd glimpse of wooden sleeper or track peeking through the weeds and the nettles.

There was only the occasional hazard. One of the best things about riding is you don't have time to think about any of your own worries because you spend the entire time thinking like a horse.

To the untrained human eye it may just be a carrier bag

caught on a bit of barbed wire fencing, but when you see it with your pony eyes you know full well it's actually a small monster, fluttering in the breeze and ready to fly at you and eat your face.

Hear a scrambler motorbike in the distance? Sure, it's a slight annoyance to our human ears but to our pony ears it heralds the arrival of a terrifying roaring dragon, again who could try to eat your face and possibly bite your bottom. Thinking like a pony is rather lovely because it helps you to subtly brace for any potential upcoming drama. I never went too method, though; me wearing a bridle and pooing on the road would've been a step too far.

This day on the disused railway seemed to be particularly hazard-free. It was bright and warm and only the sound of birdsong filled the air. It was the sort of sunshiney, woodland-creatures-smiling-at-you, dickybirds on your shoulder morning mainly found in fairy tales.

Once away from the road we pushed into a trot, which became a canter, which became, out of the blue, and entirely decided by Gus, an emergency stop.

My pony brain was too busy looking ahead for hazards to be able to see this one coming. If I had been approaching a jump I wanted him to clear, a stream I expected him to cross or even a path with unfamiliar zigzag road marking I could've braced for a stop. But this? This seemed to be an emergency stop made entirely from mischief. I truly believe he did it just to see what would happen.

What happened was this. Gus stopped but I didn't. The speed we were travelling and the surprisingly sudden nature of him slamming on the brakes meant the momentum kept me travelling forward for what felt like a long time. Going by the double-decker bus, the measurement tool popular for record-breaking skyscrapers, blue whales etc., I reckon I kept floating through the air for at least the length of one bus.

When I eventually landed, I managed to take the full impact of the fall on my left elbow. Yup, when hurtling through the air, always best to choose the pointiest boniest bone to land on.

I remember sitting on my arse in the shrubbery, looking up at Vicky, who'd turned back and was now looking down at me from her pony a few feet away. Both rider and mount were wearing confused expressions, their eyes wide, heads cocked quizzically to one side.

Gus meanwhile took the opportunity to grab a few mouthfuls of grass. Behaving like a complete dickhead had clearly given him an appetite.

The art of falling from a horse can be mastered – the tuck and roll is the method professional jockeys use when they come off their charges among the clatter and chaos of dozens of horses' hooves hammering past you on the racetrack. I'm certain 'Try to land on your elbow' is not part of the tuck and roll because it bloody hurts. I struggled to my feet and grabbed Gus's reins with my right hand and somehow managed to swing my sorry ass back into the saddle. We were only a few minutes from the farm, so I pulled Gus round ready to head back to the safety of the yard. Vicky had other ideas; it was a lovely day after all.

Combining all her medical training with her impatience at the hack being hampered by my dramatics, she said 'You OK to carry on, yeah? Reckon you're just a bit bruised and it'll feel better in a bit, let's just do a quick hour and we can cut back if it's still sore,' at which point I should've replied 'No thanks, because I may well vomit with pain down my horse's neck any minute,' but being a young teen and not yet equipped with the confidence to vocalise what was best for me, even when in agony, I replied meekly, 'OK, well, can we go slow please?'

I was within sniffing distance of Dad's farmyard and there I was, willingly trotting away from help. I didn't want to be a wimp, but it can't have been much fun, a tentative shuffle around the railway lines with a girl quietly whimpering over every lump and bump.

At last we made it back to the farm and I slid out of the saddle gratefully. I found my dad, as usual tinkering with something, trying to fix a bit of tractor. I didn't want to panic him so I calmly told him what had happened.

Dad looked at me, ruffled my hair with one of his huge hands and reassured me that I'd 'Be alreet', and to get Gus 'fed and mucked out'.

Not the usual medical advice admittedly. In agony? Faint with pain? Go lug around a couple of feed buckets and pick up some pony poo – it works a treat for all injuries! Available from NO major pharmacies because IT'S MADNESS!

It wasn't what I was hoping for, to be honest. But I didn't protest; I think I just trusted Dad's judgement implicitly, plus with him I was always conscious of not wanting to seem soft or make a fuss.

By the early evening, having mucked out and fed Gus literally single-handedly, I was feeling terrible and my left elbow was throbbing sickeningly; a dull thud that reverberated up my arm towards my throat, making me bilious. I remember sitting on the big oxblood chesterfield couch in the lounge feeling woozy and hoping someone would notice this pale, unusually quiet child and take pity on me. Luckily they did – Dad suddenly realised that even for me, pretending to be in pain for six hours just to get attention was a bit much, and decided I needed to be taken to hospital.

Dad didn't take me himself – it was calving time and he

didn't dare leave one of his prize cows that was showing signs of going into labour. Given the choice between his youngest offspring and a bouncing baby Hereford there was no competition – I wouldn't fetch as much at market.

I eventually made it to A&E thanks to my stepmother's dad giving me a lift. I arrived home from Bolton Royal Infirmary with my arm in a foam sling and a confirmed fractured humerus – I'd broken my funny bone. It was, ironically, no laughing matter.

9. Spiral Permed Butterfly

It was around this time that I started a new school. I was twelve years old and had had to leave Bedford High, the school I liked and the friends I loved to become the new girl at a secondary school back in Bolton. For a couple of years we'd moved a few miles away but we'd now returned to our home town. My very first day was after the Easter holidays in the second year of 'big school'. Although the pupils had only been there eighteen months it was, in their short lives, plenty of time to make friends, form bonds and subconsciously create tribes – the swotty, the sporty, the rebellious. It wasn't easy to infiltrate an already established school hierarchy. It didn't help that my arm was still in its foam sling after my riding accident. It wasn't a great look, to be honest – a plaster cast earns gasps of excitement as people excitedly crowd around you, pens at the ready to joyfully graffiti it, but a flesh-coloured foam strap that had become a bit manky and bobbly on the edges wasn't really the focus of any envy.

Unfortunately, my ear-length, permed bob (yes, there's such a thing), lanky legs with three pairs of long socks scrunched down round the bottoms so I looked like a foal with heavily bandaged ankles and my general lack of confidence didn't make up for the un-coolness of the sling.

No worries, I thought on my first day, I'll just keep my head down and once my arm is fully recovered I will fling off my sling and emerge like a spiral-permed butterfly from a chrysalis.

This plan was slightly derailed when the headmaster spotted me at lunchtime struggling to carry my tray of food one-handed and, before I could protest, insisted he carried it for me and found me a seat.

It's easy to forget what an important figure the head is. A bit like when a police car pulls up behind you on the road and you automatically start driving like you're on your driving test, hands at ten-to-two, sitting up straight, hiding your shooter and cocaine in the glovebox – OK, not really, but you know what I mean, you don't fully relax until they've driven off.

With the head teacher everyone eyes them and tenses until they've glided past. So it was on this day; as the headmaster strode through the canteen holding my tray of chips and beans aloft, everyone was watching him and the girl with the knobbly knees following behind, her cheeks burning bright red at the unwanted attention.

I may as well have been wearing an A-board saying 'Wanted – full-time bully. Must be able to work individually or as a team'. The post was soon taken up by two girls who were to make my school life miserable for the next couple of years. Like cartoon baddies, one was a big oaf who towered over the other – a short, scrawny, mean-faced girl with long thin hair and a pinched expression. Let's call them Big and Little.

The bullying, as is often the case, ranged from so subtle it was barely noticeable to others – snide whispering, passing notes, elbowing me as I made my way past – to more physical, humiliating stuff like shoving me or tripping me up so I'd land with a bang on my knees. I went to speak to the teachers about what was happening but Big, although not the brightest, was popular with the teachers because she could be quite a fun, nice character when she wanted to, so I was dismissed as the new girl not settling in and being a little oversensitive.

I had friends but they were too afraid to stick up for me in case the bullies turned on them. What was worse was that the bullies would often be charm personified to my friends so I felt truly alienated. It's a tried and tested formula: be so nice to your target's friends that it's difficult for the friends to defend the target fully. Secondary school politics were fragile and it was a minefield to negotiate. As much as I'm sure my friends sympathised, they didn't want to put themselves in the line of fire by defending me too stridently.

My two best friends at the time were Sakira and Firoza. I'd latched on to these two pretty soon after starting at Smithills School, no doubt drawn by Sakira's mischievous dancing eyes and bright toothy grin and the shy smile of Firoza with her big brown eyes, soft, round shape and a contagious giggle (hiding a wicked sense of humour) never far from her lips.

Sakira was actually quite sassy, so the bullies would try to befriend her, and Firoza had such a placid and serene nature that to be horrible to her would surely incur the wrath of the gods.

Rather than defend me, they just listened to my woes. 'God I hate Big, such a stupid cow,' I'd whine and they'd agree. 'She's a silly bitch,' Sakira would hiss angrily, nodding in agreement as I recounted the injustice of being heckled and shoved in the queue outside the science lab.

Sakira would sometimes make a joke to distract Big from picking on her prey and that would work, temporarily earning me a reprieve from the bullies' attentions as they switched their focus to whatever teacher Sakira had made a wisecrack about, but at other times she'd be a bystander to the abuse, unable to intervene. It was a calculated stance – she had to choose her moment to defend me carefully without winding Big up or humiliating her in front of her rapt audience (usually of one – Little) and becoming her new victim. Big liked Sakira but, make no mistake, if Sakira pushed her luck too much Big would flex her bully biceps in her direction.

Sakira was from a big, loving family. Her mum was a quiet, calm lady who I'd see after school preparing the evening meal, cross-legged on their living room carpet peeling a mountain of vegetables onto a layer of newspaper. Her dad, though they were really close, was pretty strict about who she hung around with and I didn't quite meet the criteria for the sort of girls he wanted his daughter to be pals with – this girl with the big perm and big voice. Sakira was very funny and we'd often be giggling and roaring with laughter. It was usually about completely daft, childish stuff but I suspect her dad thought we were plotting about boys and bad behaviour. She asked a few times for sleepovers at mine but permission was always denied; she'd call him at work, slipping into Urdu as she tried to convince him she'd be on her best behaviour, but it was no use.

So although I was close to Sakira we never got to hang out much after school. We still managed to have fun at school though; at least, we did when the bullies weren't around.

Anyone who's been bullied knows it can become debilitating and all-consuming. It was one of the first things I'd think about every morning before school. There would be those lovely nano-seconds before I was fully awake, barely conscious and still blissfully ignorant, but then with a thud I'd be down to earth, remembering the horrible treatment that awaited me. I'd feel instantly deflated before the day had even begun.

Mum tried her best. 'You OK, sweetheart?' she'd ask as I ate my Weetabix at the little round white wooden table in our tiny dining room in the terraced house where we lived. I'd sullenly watch the portable telly on the sideboard, Anne and Nick warbling away happily as I forlornly spooned up my soggy cereal. 'I'm fine, I just hate Big, she's such a cow to me.' I could never really say the 'b-word' – bullied. It would seem like an admission of weakness and I felt such a failure being a victim. Pathetic. Mum was really busy and worked so hard – I felt she had enough on her plate without my woes adding to her load. Occasionally she'd notice me looking tearful in the morning, but I imagine she presumed I was just tired and in the case of Big she just thought it was the usual teen squabbles, as I didn't point out exactly how bad things were. To quote one of Mum's favourite lines, 'I'd be in a tent on Blackpool prom if I could read minds' – she had no idea how much I was suffering because I suffered in silence at home. I'm a little like that still; for someone who talks for a living I'm very good at keeping schtum and internalising my worries.

Very occasionally there'd be proper tears in the morning and Mum would let me stay off school; at those moments it'd be like the valve had been loosened on Mum's pressure cooker and all the negative energy would fizz out and evaporate.

Mum would leave me at home with reminders of the chores I had to do, which I'd immediately put off to settle down for a day on the squashy foam sofa bed we had in the lounge. These would be 'double *Neighbours* days' – the ultimate in sloth-like behaviour, watching both the lunchtime and teatime showings of the same episode from my horizontal position inches from the screen.

I couldn't be off every day though, so the next morning I'd get the bus with the same feeling of dread rumbling in my stomach – it was pretty exhausting worrying about walking down a corridor in case a foot or elbow came flying out at me, because the school day in general is walking down lots of corridors (walking, mind – NOT running, something the teachers were obsessed with preventing).

If I could travel back and have a word with myself I would probably tell the twelve-year-old me to retaliate. To push back. I was a strong girl from lugging buckets of water and bales of hay and probably could've battered them. But I didn't because ultimately I was a bit of a chicken and not naturally violent and they took full advantage. While I was at it I would probably also tell myself to maybe rethink the spiral perms.

Both the perms and the bullying pockmarked my early teens. I didn't confide in Yvonne as she was away at uni and my older siblings weren't around as much – they were all married off. When I did see them the last thing I'd want to do was prattle on about my woes. Eventually Mum talked to the school but I hadn't fully accused anyone of anything, so it was difficult for her to go in there and read the riot act. It meant that they didn't take her concerns seriously and just fobbed her off, promising to keep an eye on me and reassuring her I just needed to settle down.

I never would've guessed that I would be eventually rescued, in a roundabout way, by Mr Whippy.

One day at breaktime the head of my year looked out of his office window and witnessed a kerfuffle in the playground – Big was holding my arms behind my back as I struggled while Little shoved a cone of ice cream into my face. I remember I tried to struggle free but couldn't, so I gave in, staying still just to get it over with. Having seen Little mush the ice cream into my face, it coating my chin, my nose, getting into my eyes, as other pupils shrieked with thrilled shock at what they were seeing, he finally believed that I was indeed being bullied. He apologised to me and Big and Little were hauled into his office, warned off me and put on detention. Other teachers were tipped off. It did the trick and the bullying ceased, but I've never eaten ice cream since. Ha, not really. I joke but it had been a truly horrible time and, with the bullying finally over, at last I felt like I could breathe, like a breeze block had been lifted from its resting place on my chest.

I'll never know if Big realised how hellish she made those couple of years. But I do know that Little seemingly had no clue that she was my bully, because years later she texted Radio 1 when I was hosting the breakfast show, wanting a 'shoutout'. I was flabbergasted.

The text she sent was a fond one, as if we were long-lost school pals. Didn't she realise the tears I'd shed thanks to her? The anxiety she caused, the humiliation, the dread, the sadness? She got her shoutout all right. Though not the one she was expecting. I relished dedicating an entire link to reminding her of her horrible treatment of me. Was revenge sweet all those years later? I'm not sure. I'd waited fifteen years to get a voice loud enough to answer my tormentors. Was outing her on the radio to millions of people tantamount to bullying . . . ? Probably. Did I care? Not really. I wouldn't do it now but back then, in my late twenties, I was much more hot-headed and I suppose still hurting.

Perhaps as a response to the bullying, I began to assert my authority in other ways and embarked on a short rebellious stint at school. But my one attempt at wagging a class ended in disaster when I decided to skip a lesson and spend my illicit freedom hanging out in the school toilets with Sakira and Firoza. After about ten minutes we were busted by a teacher. How on earth did she know we were there? Why was our cunning plot halted in its infancy? We didn't have long to wait to find out because the teacher told us: she'd spotted our silhouettes leaning up against the big frosted window in the girls' loos. Our hearts clearly weren't in this wild behaviour. She didn't even punish us, just sent us on our way to class.

Life at secondary school had some welcome distractions, mainly playing in all the sports teams despite me being the least talented member of each squad. In netball I was GD – Goal Defence. Anyone who knows the game knows the court is divided into three sections, with restrictions on which thirds you can enter. Most players can enter two zones, but Goal Defence is allowed in only ONE. Which spoilsport (literally) thought of a game that restricts its participants from using most of the court? It's like being given a delicious trifle but only being allowed to eat the jelly. There's only one position that can run free and gazelle-like around all three zones – Centre. It seemed to me that there was always a particular type of girl who got to be Centre. Glossy-haired, bouncy, not knock-kneed and goofy. I think I can spot a Centre girl even now. Gabby Logan, Myleene Klass, Susanna Reid, Alexandra Burke; they are the Centres, determined, gritty, dedicated – they get the jelly, the cream AND the custard.

Still, I made the team. I enjoyed standing stock-still, marking my opponent, arm in the air and fingers outstretched like I was feeling along a tall shelf for some door keys.

I also didn't excel at hockey. I can remember standing on an all-weather hockey pitch in deepest winter and glancing down to see my legs had been replaced by two sticks of corned beef, pink-and-purple-mottled. My hands were frozen to the hockey stick, it was dark and I could see my breath as I panted, chasing the ball in the white glow of the floodlights.

I loved it though. I rarely scored, whether it was netball, hockey or running a rounder in rounders. Maybe I just enjoyed the smell of sweaty changing rooms, the rumble of the school's clapped-out minibus or wearing an elasticated bib.

Maybe it was that I felt like I belonged. I'd always felt loved at home but being younger than my siblings I never quite made full membership of their club. Humans are naturally pack animals, even if we occasionally enjoy our independence; the feeling of being in a clan at school was one I treasured – perhaps the spectre of bullying, which potentially could've raised its head again, made me feel that safety in numbers was the wisest choice. Even if I was a bit of a butterfingers during netball, misfired at goal during hockey or rarely scored a rounder, the teams still accepted me.

If my team track record was mediocre, my actual track record was abysmal. To look at me back then, with my long coltish legs making up three-fifths of my body, you'd think I was built to run. Nature had other ideas and had also gifted me slightly knock knees, and the ensuing nicknames knocked my confidence so much that I hated even walking in front of people, let alone running. Of course, when you're fourteen you may not have the emotional intelligence to explain this to a tough Glaswegian PE teacher with a tight black perm and a mouth set like a pale pink hyphen. So what I did was a sulky half-run, half-galumph round the athletic track, like a wildebeest whose tranquilliser dart was just starting to take effect. It wasn't appreciated by the teacher and I was a constant source of frustration for her. Sorry miss.

10. Nailed It

I was a toddler with no toddle, thanks to being hypermobile – a fancy-sounding way of saying a bit wobbly. My joints – from elbows to knees to ankles – can bend in all kinds of unnatural and uncomfortable-looking ways and, when I was little, even getting upright was a struggle.

The only way I'd sit to watch telly was on my bottom with my knees and thighs together flat on the floor and each shin folded out at my side. I had to sit like this in school assembly too as forcing my gangly legs into a crossed position used to really hurt – after a couple of Bible stories, some announcements and a rousing rendition of 'All Things Bright and Beautiful' unlocking my kneecaps from that unnatural shape was agony.

It wasn't all negative – my party trick as a child was to grab my left foot with my left hand and pull it sideways and then backwards towards my spine, arching my torso left till I could look over my left shoulder and touch my nose with my big toe, to howls of delight and disgust from my friends.

Being hypermobile may have been handy for those moments

when it was absolutely crucial to touch my face with my foot but it wasn't very helpful when it came to walking.

At around twenty months, a time when most kids are walking, I was struggling. I would pull myself up to a standing position but my knees – unsupported by my plasticine ankles – would give way and I'd crumple to the floor, my nappy-clad bottom hitting the deck hard.

Watching my frustration gave Mum a brilliant idea. She knew I was ready to walk; I just needed a little support – literally. The helping hand arrived in the form of some little red wellies, my new best friends.

They came up to just below my knees and were of sturdy enough rubber that when my skinny legs weakened and wobbled, they'd provide just enough scaffolding to help me remain upright and grow stronger and more confident. In no time I was toddling about the farmyard, thrilled. I wore them all the time, often pottering around in just my nappy and my red wellies – I imagine I looked rather swish.

My own three children were late walkers too, having inherited my ankles. I knew from my own experience why they were struggling to walk and so at around twenty months I popped a pair of wellies on them and, hey presto, they too were walking within a day.

Once I was fully upright, my troubles really began. My legs picked up a fair few knocks from various exploits on the farm – one scar on my knee remains to this day. I was thirteen and Dad asked me to carry a crate of chickens from the shed to a new coop. The crates were about the size of a bale of hay and awkward to carry, made of heavy-duty brown plastic with slots for holding on to them. There's no way I could've managed by myself, so one of the farm helps took one end and I the other.

It was dusk and disgusting weather – blowing a gale with a helping of sideways rain – so over my jodhpurs I was wearing my waterproof trousers, which were as glamorous as they sound, but these huge navy rubber affairs did the job and kept me nice and dry.

As we slowly made our way through the gate into a little enclosure I slipped on the sopping wet grass and pitched forward, letting out a yelp. Not wanting to drop the hens, I clung on and landed on my right knee with a thump. My kneecap connected with a semicircle of smooth rock that was poking out of the grass like a discus that'd been thrown with such force that most of it had embedded itself in the earth.

My knee was sore but I staggered to my feet like a spurned lover after an unsuccessful proposal and eventually, in the howling wind, we decanted the clucking hens into the warmth of their new coop.

Job done, I went about my other chores with my knee slightly throbbing. I fed and watered Gus and as I pushed a wheelbarrow of muck up to the midden through the rain I realised that my faithful waterproof trousers had obviously suffered a tear when I'd fallen and the rain had got into them – my right leg felt very wet.

I leaned the barrow up and made my way towards the house. In the dim light of the kitchenette I wearily pulled off my wellies and peeled down my rubber trousers to reveal my jodhpurs, now looking rather snazzy as they weren't just cream but patterned red too . . . The wet I'd been feeling wasn't rainwater but my own blood, gushing from a pumpkin-seed-shaped gash on my kneecap. The blood had soaked through my jodhpurs and it looked like I had a bright scarlet bandana tied round my leg.

To this day, every time I shave my shins I spot that little

battle scar on my knee and feel strangely proud that despite everything that happened, I didn't drop those bloody hens.

Minor injuries were common on the farm. One day I was playing, as you do, on a huge pile of planks that had been stacked up against the side of the cattle pens and which Dad obviously had plans for. They were 'pre-loved' and thus had lots of nails poking out of them; huge, gnarly nails. The kind of nails you'd imagine Hagrid would have rattling round his pockets.

See if you can work out what happens next, like on a TV bloopers show where the host pauses the footage and you have to guess the outcome after the adverts. A five-year-old girl is playing on a nail-strewn plank pile while her dad shouts at her from his perch on the tractor, 'Get down or you're going to get hurt!' I, being five, obviously ignored my dad because a) these planks were tremendous fun, and b) Dad's control over me was limited as he was in the process of steering a tractor and moving silage bales.

I carried on merrily skipping up and down the planks until the inevitable happened. I went flying. As I landed I did what comes naturally – I put my hands out to stop myself. The nail that punctured the fleshy part of my right hand, the meaty bit below the thumb, pushed through with such ease and poked out the other side so cleanly, like a skewer through a chicken drumstick, that it almost looked like something from a joke shop. No one was laughing though. I instinctively pulled my hand up and off the nail and stared at the hole it had left in shocked silence. Then I snapped out of it – as the blood began to pour from the wound – and my screams echoed around the yard. Dad leapt off the tractor and came running over, his face growing paler with each stride. He reached me and immediately gave me . . . a massive bollocking.

That's what happens. When you ignore your parents' frequent warnings, then get injured, their frustration morphs into a brief, hot, fury.

Dad rarely got angry, so I must've really shaken him up. I was whizzed to Bolton Royal Infirmary and was patched up. I remember having to have a tetanus jab in my bum cheek and trying my best to punch the doctor away as he approached with the needle. I'd like to apologise, thirty-eight years later, to that no-doubt overworked, under-appreciated young NHS medic for being, in all respects, a pain in the arse.

11. Geese and Guns

Growing up the youngest of five meant there was always someone around to mither. Someone who'd hopefully let me tag along. I love being part of a big family – we're a clan, identified by our long lanky legs, toothsome grins and blue eyes. The kitchen, with its classic 1970s bright orange units, was always a whirl of activity when I was little – I'd stand in the eye of the storm as the rest of the family swirled around me, shoving past to put the kettle on, Mum rattling pans on the stove, Dad having a hasty brew, flicking through the *Farmers Guardian* or opening post. ('You can have the bills if you like, Sarah.')

There'd be various siblings entering and exiting with buttered toast or a cadged biscuit hanging from their lips. Robert and David didn't hang around – they always had something to tinker with or jobs to do around the farm. Dot was a calmer spirit, often quietly going about her business, helping with housework, tickling up. You'd find Yvonne in a quiet corner of the lounge curled up with a book.

I miss them now. I live 200 miles away in that there fancy

London where the streets are paved with sashimi and I miss being able to call on my older siblings for a quick brew and – let's be honest – free last-minute childcare and some DIY. Whenever my eldest brother Robert comes to visit with his wife Sarah-Jane he's barely through the door before he starts oiling a hinge here, bleeding a radiator there, and she's reading a largely ignored child a story while popping the kettle on.

Robert and I are really close. Because he's thirteen years my senior I've always been slightly in awe of him because he's eternally had an answer for everything – he managed to seem wise even as a teen. He's a fixer – he can turn his hand to anything – and has always been driven, from his first business selling mice and bunnies to owning various companies and now selling his art, thanks to a previously untapped reserve of artistic talent that means he can paint. So he's a do-er.

He's also a looker – in the eighties he became a bit of a gym bunny and loved a sunbed – back then lightly grilling oneself to a crisp on a sunbed tucked away in a spare room was all the rage, blinding white tubes mere millimetres from your face pumping out UVBs and Cs while you prayed your mate's mum didn't barge in and find you horizontal, sweaty and naked apart from a pair of tiny foil goggles.

Robert had it all – he was tall, tanned and muscly with a mop of jet-black hair and a bright white smile. He looked just like Dad if Dad had been put through some sort of heart-throb machine. My friends all fancied him like mad and would swoon whenever he popped round to Mum's and I'd kiss him hello. 'You're so lucky you get to kiss him!' they'd squeal – which was kinda weird; he was my big bro and, as much as I loved him, to me he was no Morten Harket.

Robert always had a knack of talking like he was incredibly knowledgeable about his subject, even if occasionally he'd have little evidence to back up his wise musings. Whenever he was in charge he'd not allow us to have the radio on because he claimed we'd get indigestion cos we'd 'eat to the beat' – something that still makes me chuckle to this day. I'm sure he just didn't fancy having the radio on, so he came up with this fantastical logic to be able to persuade us. He was good at making up facts to suit him, like his medical fact about long toes like his being a sign of intelligence.

It wasn't just my friends who thought he was gorgeous. Robert also attracted the attention of a goose. Geese are brilliant at seeing off intruders or potential threats because they're so ballsy – I was always wary of them, but when I was about seven this one gander called Max, behaving not at all like a typical fierce goose, developed a deep and all-consuming obsession with Robert.

It would follow him round the yard like a feathery shadow. At first it was funny but the novelty quickly started to wear thin and Robert attempted to avoid it. Whenever the coast was clear he would venture out and suddenly the goose would appear from nowhere as if it'd been hiding somewhere on surveillance. It'd waddle after him until it fell into step alongside him, all casual like. One boy and his goose. Robert eventually succumbed and just let the goose hang out with him. At the height of the affair, Robert would be on his back on an empty feed bag under his car, and while he tinkered with the engine the goose would settle on his lap.

Robert has the best stories about growing up on the farm – stuff that happened when I was still knee-high to a heifer.

Like the one about Dad's mate Brian, who was a 'real seventies copper' with a fascination for high-powered weapons, which he'd bring up to the farm to show to Dad.

One day he brought a machine gun with him, an actual machine gun. Rob was duly dispatched to go and 'borrow' one of our sister Dot's dolls, which was then tethered to a fence post in the field before Brian fired off dozens of rounds at it, machine-gunning the doll to smithereens.

Rob himself had guns and pistols from a young age because, as he explains now, 'There's always something to shoot on a farm.'

One time a bloke called Billy who lived down the footpath from the farm agreed with Dad to swap his .410 shotgun for six large trays of eggs. Rob was sent off to do the transaction, carrying the eggs down the overgrown path and walking back with the shotgun, an old thing that had been painted grey. Robert stripped it back, varnishing it till it was like new. Around the same time, Grandad Cox passed away and Dad ended up with an old box of bullets, likely from the war years, all different sizes. Realising none of these fit his new gun, Rob decided to have a bit of fun with them; he waited till everyone was out and built a small campfire next to the garage and put a handful of bullets on the fire to 'see what would happen'. Well, what happened was of course that the bullets, containing gunpowder, exploded.

Robert legged it into the garage and hid. It was only once everything had fallen silent, apart from his heartbeat thudding in his ears, that he saw the new small hole a few inches away from his head in the garage wall and realised how close he'd come to killing himself that day.

Always the entrepreneur of the family, when he was a teenager Rob bred mice in the coal shed. The bottom half was piled with coal and the top half was his home-made mousearium. It was a pretty snazzy pad for the mice – multi-level, linked by wooden ramps and tubes and enclosed by chicken wire. I remember standing on my tiptoes and peeping into the labyrinth of this rodent penthouse and thinking it looked quite magical. Ironic that his pets were kept in the mouse equivalent of P. Diddy's Miami mansion while their cousins the rats were being hunted and hated up at the barn. Rob sold these mice to pals and to Mittens, the pet shop, and before long he progressed to breeding rabbits for the same shop, making a few bob.

As well as being an astute businessman Robert was also quite the inventor. One day he made stilts by getting thin oblong lengths of wood and nailing tyre stops onto them. Similar to doorstops, they were wooden wedges shaped like cartoon cheese. He fastened the underside to the wood with the thin end of the wedge pointing down so his feet could stand on the square surface at the top. Ingenious. They weren't very high – when he eventually managed to get up he was perhaps two feet off the ground. We all trooped out into the garden for the demo. He could get up OK, but staying up and moving proved difficult. He'd underestimated the weight of the wood, and lifting these chunks of timber to take a step while remaining balanced was too tricky.

After numerous failed attempts, Robert's audience, by now bored, melted away. I popped back into the kitchen to carry on looking at the back pages of my dad's *Farmers Guardian*; I loved drawing biro rings round my dream horses in the classifieds, getting lost in a world of if-money-was-no-object fantasy ponies.

Something caught my eye. Robert seemed to have mastered the stilts – once, then twice past the kitchen window; he'd cracked it! What I didn't know at that point was that, in order to solve the falling off the stilts issue, he'd tethered his wellies to the actual stilts and, using the side of the house, had managed to get his feet back into the wellies, pull himself vertical and was now proudly strutting his stilty stuff around the lawn.

On his third walk-by there was a stumble that uprooted him. He started to fall and I remember watching and wondering why he wasn't jumping off like he'd done before. Instead he just fell, almost in slow motion, past the window. No arms flailing, no drama, just a silent fall, like a tall skinny tree being felled right outside the window. I imagine that was the exact moment he realised the main disadvantage to tying wellies to stilts. He landed with a crash, gashing his forehead on the corner of the garden wall.

When he wasn't being seduced by geese or crashing his stilts, Robert was very popular. His birthday parties were always wild affairs and I thought he was very cool – his mates were shaggy-haired lads in skintight double denim and girls with blonde perms and short skirts, all of them tumbling out of the tent put up in the farm garden, mysterious potent-smelling smoke billowing out after them.

From about the age of fourteen Robert loved motorbikes and would often bounce across the fields on them. My other brother David followed in his tyre marks and soon the two of them were obsessed with this new hobby. Robert started with a little Puch moped, which he soon tired of and sold to David. Makes me laugh that he didn't give it to him but sold it to him – both lads obviously knew the value of a quid! Plus Rob needed the cash for his next bike. This one is the one I remember the most vividly, probably because of the colour. Rob bought an old Lambretta scooter from his mate Warren for £15. He had great plans for it – he chopped off all the metal panels and painted the thing lime green and used it as a scrambler.

By sixteen he had a Yamaha FS1-E 'fizzer' – a bike that was small and spindly with big wheels but thin tyres that looked and sounded like a mosquito – that he'd razz off to school on.

Both lads would let me ride on their latest bikes, between their legs on the narrow seat, and I'd just perch there like a wild-haired mascot between their outstretched arms as they steered the bike up the farm's gravelly lane, avoiding the potholes.

David was tall and gangly with legs up to his armpits – a trait that connects all the Cox siblings. As a teen he had a mop of hair as dark and shiny as liquorice, a bright toothy smile and playful eyes sheltering under more serious brows.

We had a slurry pit, two cavernous underground tanks about ten feet deep that held thousands of gallons of liquid muck from the farm, ultimately intended for spreading on the fields. The pit had an old wooden cover and when David was twelve he fell through it. Robert saw the cover give way and David disappear into the darkness beneath. David would've drowned if it wasn't for Robert – he ran and screamed for Dad, who also came running, grabbed a long wooden ladder and lowered it into the slurry, scrabbled down it and managed to somehow grab his son from the pitch-black stench. Beyond terrifying. I was a baby at the time, so I don't remember this, but I'm crying as I tell the story. Thank God I didn't lose my lovely brother that day. Dad replaced the broken cover with a new steel manhole cover and no doubt relived the horror of what could've been again and again.

David doesn't like a fuss and when I asked him to describe the whole experience, he simply replied 'Smelly.' He said it wasn't the slurry pit that was his worst experience; his most frightening moment growing up on the farm happened when he was fourteen and I was two. David was in the garden, cutting the grass with old shears. I toddled up to him and grabbed at the shears and my tiny fingers got caught in the closing blades. I screamed. David froze. Luckily they were rusty and blunt so no real harm was done. It's touching that from all the dramas on the farm, including his own near-death experience, it's that one, when he momentarily thought he'd hurt his baby sister, that springs to his mind as the worst.

Both Robert and David always looked out for me when I was little and I remember them being gentle and kind to their kid sis. Thanks to the large age gap I was no competition and didn't have the wit or inclination to wind them up. I think I was seen as a harmless enough little thing who just occasionally got under the feet, like a cat.

There was only one time when they really upset me.

Pippi Longstocking was my beautiful rag doll. I was only six when I got her and she was similar in height to me. She had yellow wool hair tied in two neat thick plaits and huge round bright-blue stitched-on eyes with long black stitched-on lashes, and wore a matching pink floral cloth hat and sundress. Physically she was similarly built to the Cox clan – her legs took up four-fifths of her and it was these limbs that my teen brothers were attracted to. Not in a weird way – she was a rag doll. No, Robert and David would occasionally each grab one of my darling Pippi's feet and use her for a brief tug-o-war. This horrific practice would usually stop as soon as I clocked what was happening and would have the screaming abdabs until they stopped and I could snatch poor Pippi from their grip.

One fateful day things went too far – I screamed, I shouted, but my brothers continued with their tug-o-war, deaf to my pleas of 'GET OFF HER!' Both boys' faces were strained and pink with exertion and I realised this was no longer about Pippi or me – this was about them and no one was stopping till the tug-o-war was won.

Pippi's face flew back and forth, her plaits whizzing around, her blue stitched-on eyes looking wider with shock as the boys kept pulling and I screamed and shrieked, trying to rescue her. Something had to give, and what gave was Pippi. Or more specifically Pippi's lady area. She split right up the middle. White cotton woolly stuffing immediately started to peep out of the split seam. When I was little and attempting some unlikely gymnastic manoeuvre or eccentric dance move Mum would warn me that I'd 'split my difference', and that's exactly what happened to Pippi. Both boys snapped out of their hypnotic tussling, immediately dropped her and legged it out of the bedroom I shared with my sisters, hoping to make themselves scarce before I could holler the standard distress call; a double-syllable 'MU-UUUUM!'

Mum tried some emergency surgery and stitched up poor Pippi but she was never the same again.

I myself was treated more like a souped-up doll, rather than a little sister, by my sister Dorothy. David's twin, so eleven when I was born, she was all light-brown permed curls, large green eyes, a shy unsure smile and a quiet voice that faded before the end of every sentence as if she had little faith in the words that were coming out. She was tall with a willowy frame and, back then anyway, flared jeans. She cuddled me and fussed over me like you do with a favourite doll, but also did a lot of throwing me around.

One of our favourite games involved a draught-excluder snake. Back in the seventies and eighties, it seems now, instead of making doors that actually fitted into the frame someone decided it'd be easier just to ensure that every house had a few (usually home-made) draught excluders. These were long, thick, stuffed fabric cushions (usually, due to the shape, either styled as a snake or a sausage dog) that lay dolefully on the floor at the bottoms of doors to block the gaps left by shoddy workmanship, watching you with their button eyes.

Of course to kids these were just extra toys – at my nana's I'd always be faffing about cuddling the draft excluder, much to the annoyance of Grandad, who'd strongly insinuate that the entire room of adults were experiencing the first symptoms of hypothermia because I was preventing the excluding of the draught by messing with Sid the snake, who was made from conker-brown velvet so was very huggable thankyouverymuch.

We had a blue Aztec-patterned snake at the farm (Ooh, is that the sound of pencils being sharpened down at *Elle Decor* I hear?) and it was with this that Dot and I came up with a fantastic game. She'd loop the draught excluder round my chest and under my armpits, then, standing behind me, hold the snake's head and tail tightly in her hands. Looking back I'm pleased she held it tightly because once the snake was in place we'd manoeuvre to the top of the staircase and she would swing me out over the stairs. For a brief moment I'd be airborne, squealing with delight as I flew through the air, the steep wooden stairway my only cushion if Dot lost her grip. Luckily she never did.

The only time she mildly injured me was when she dropped me on my head. She used to like holding me upside down by my ankles so my head was just a few inches from the cold tiles of the farm's kitchen floor. She'd then sort of dunk me up and down like a digestive biscuit in a cuppa, as if trying to shake change out of my pockets.

I know as you're reading this you might be thinking 'Jeez Sara, if this is how the sibling who loved you the most treated you, what happened to you at the hands of the others?' but I loved it. I'd giggle as my face flushed and the blood ran to my head.

On this particular occasion there was only one voice that

could be heard above our whooping and laughing and that was
Robert's: 'Dot – you're going to drop her on her head, put her
down.'

Sure enough, at the climax of what was to be our last game,
Dot's grip loosened and she dropped me on my bonce. I
remember it really hurt. She didn't let go of me completely –
she just misjudged the distance between my head and the floor
and therefore the depth of her dunk.

Even as I screamed I became aware that to make a fuss would
get Dot in trouble and result in a severe case of told-you-so's
from Robert. I may only have been six but already I knew about
loyalty and so stopped screaming and instead laughed hysteri-
cally despite the pain. I don't know if they realised I was trying
to protect Dot, or if they just presumed my cackling was due
to serious concussion. Either way it did the trick and Dot escaped
a serious scolding from our big bro.

Even though he would get frustrated with Dot, Robert loved
her to bits. When they were a little older Dot used to do the
vast majority of the cleaning in the house – even in family
photographs she's scrubbing, wiping and polishing like some
kind of Boltonian Cinderella. But one day she got herself into
a bit of a pickle. She'd been cleaning the brand-new avocado-
coloured bathroom and matching carpet – it really was a sea of
milky green in there when it was new, although the carpet faded
over time until eventually it looked like a thin coating of lichen
had grown over the floor. Dot accidentally dripped some bleach
on the carpet round the bottom of the loo. I can imagine her
poor face as before her very eyes big spots of the carpet's rich
avocado shade started to disappear and in their place blossomed
splodges of pale sickly yellow as the bleach ate its way through
the pigment. Dot panicked, knowing she'd be in so much trouble

for wrecking this new and luscious mushy-pea-shaded carpet, and did what we all did (and still do) if there's an emergency – she went to find Robert.

Robert is, and already was back then at nineteen years old, what is called in Yiddish a 'mensch'. One of life's good guys, solid, kind, reliable, the kind of 'drop everything' bloke who is really good to have on your side. So in this emergency, Dot found Robert and he got his thinking cap on.

On surveying the damage, he asked Dot if she had any green eyeshadow. Luckily, this being the early eighties OF COURSE she had green eyeshadow. In fact, she had many shades of green to complement the various shades of frosted pink lipstick she sported back then. Some might say that pale pink and green isn't a good combination and you know what? They'd be right. But that's the eighties for you: bold fashion statements and avocado bath suites.

Robert sprang into action and used the palette of green eyeshadow to cover the bleach marks, perfectly blending Fir Forest with Parsley Punch until eventually the marks were no longer visible. It was a triumph and Dot was thrilled. She kept an eye on those spots and touched up the area whenever the eyeshadow faded and the pale bits started to peep through.

Fast-forward a fistful of decades and after various successful career moves, Rob is now an artist whose work sells well to his numerous fans. He creates mainly palette-knife oils on huge canvases, but I like to think that it was crouching by the loo back then, mixing Dot's eyeshadow palette and dabbing it on the bleach spots, that ignited the art impulse in him.

If Robert was the MD of us kids, Dot was head of the care department. She always looked after me and was my constant defender if I was under people's feet, being noisy or annoying.

During times of family strife she'd shield me from the fallout until the storm blew over. She always had time for me.

Dot was the one who taught me how to ride a two-wheel bike. Let's just say I wasn't a natural Bradley Wiggins – up until the age of nine I couldn't ride a bike sans stabilisers. The final reckoning came for me on a camping holiday – all the kids on the site were whizzing around in a gang on their hired bikes giving it the full *Goonies*, but there was me at the back of the pack on a tiny bike with stabilisers, my knees up to my ears as I pedalled clumsily after the others. I had to learn to ride a proper bike, but I was terrified of falling and didn't trust anyone to help me learn apart from Dot. Eventually she stepped in to make sure that I would be on two wheels by the time I was into double figures. It only took an afternoon at the local park, wobbling along the paths with me screaming 'Don't let go,' until eventually of course she did let go long enough for me to wobble off on my own.

It was for Dot's wedding that I got my first perm. I was twelve and on bridesmaid duties, and what better way to celebrate a wedding and top off a pale blue pouffy satin dress than with a perm? No ordinary perm, mind – I wanted to channel my favourite pop superstar and hairspiration Whitney Houston. I dreamed of having a spiral perm so I could recreate her head of bouncy sun-kissed caramel curls with my own fine, mousey brown hair.

After months of intense campaigning, Mum finally folded and agreed I could perm my hair and debut it at Dot's nuptials. She took me to her hairdressers in the village and I was encased in a plastic cape, my head slathered in perming solution so potent that I took shallow breaths to avoid inhaling too many fumes, and deposited among the old ladies under the huge dryers to wait patiently for the magic to happen.

Eventually I was rinsed off and waited with anticipation to

see a north-west Whitney emerge. But no curls tumbled down from the soggy towel, just a damp mass sat on my head – no matter! Surely once dry its full majesty would be revealed.

The hairdresser set to work with her hairdryer. Unfortunately, someone had missed the memo about which strong female eighties icon I wanted to resemble; with my jawline-length hair blow-dried not into springy corkscrews but big, blowsy curls, rather than Whitney from New Jersey it was Deirdre Barlow from *Coronation Street* staring wide-eyed back at me from the mirror.

My poor sister now had for a bridesmaid an awkward pre-teen with a terrible perm. On the big day I felt so mortified at being the centre of attention with my terrible middle-aged barnet that I was too nervous to actually smile; to stop my teeth chattering with nerves I clamped my jaws together in a determined grimace, creating the kind of underbite favoured by Les Dawson's Ada.

Still, it was a special day and I was thrilled to be part of it. Dot was marrying Gary, a nice lad from the village with dark curly hair, a snub nose and a brilliant sense of humour, would play-fight with me and let me duff him up, so he was a-okay in my book. And he and Dot had kept me tucked firmly under their wings since the beginning of their relationship – from letting me sleep on a blow-up mattress next to their bed on their first night in their first home, thus extinguishing any frisson of first-night passion, to my stint clutching a bouquet and trundling up the aisle behind my sister.

In fact, I like to think their marriage has stood the test of time for thirty years precisely because it had to strive to get over its slightly shaky start with a clingy little sis who was also the world's most awkward bridesmaid.

The sister closest to me in age – and closest in proximity, as we were occasionally forced to share a room – is Yvonne. The friendship closeness took time to nurture and grow thanks to the age and proximity closeness. We'd fight like cat and dog. I was, I think, an irritant to Yvonne with my annoying habit of trying and often succeeding to be, the centre of attention by making people laugh. Being the youngest is easy – it's the plum position in any family, I think – and it was a role I fully embraced. By the last child the parents have grown tired of discipline and control and the care given to the little one is similar to how you'd treat a cactus: feed and water it occasionally but mostly leave it to its own devices.

Being the youngest gives you licence to really rock the ol' cute card. Habits that in older siblings are seen as petulant and annoying, like sulking, are, when looked at through the kaleidoscope of kids who are the baby of the family, cute and endearing. I was famous for sticking out my bottom lip, a super-sulker – the Incredible Sulk, Grumplestiltskin – but instead of being told off for being a mardy arse it was 'Ooh be careful, you could trip over that bottom lip!' – all fond chiding. At family meals I'd perform rubbish impressions of the then prime minister Maggie Thatcher: 'Mum, please pass the sprouts,' I'd say in my best Iron Lady drawl and my mum and nana were enraptured, applauding wildly as if on the front row of a sell-out Broadway show.

No wonder Yvonne found me annoying.

Before I go any further I should make it crystal clear that Yvonne and I are now very close. She does still have the ability to make me grit my teeth in fury with a single seemingly innocuous comment – I call it top-bunk mentality. In my mind she was always top dog, the boss, the one to be feared/avoided, so I'm particularly sensitive to any criticism from her. Whenever we argued she'd win, because I'd get too emotionally involved and would muddle up my words. It was usually words I'd heard her say that I would then put through my brain-mangle until they were misshapen and spit them back at her, much to her amusement – 'You're so IGRANONT,' I'd shout triumphantly.

In adulthood, we became pregnant at the same time (not literally to the second, that'd be weird), and from then on our relationship defrosted and re-formed as a strong sisterly bond born out of our sudden similarity – becoming mums for the first time was a major shared experience for us. And I love her very much.

As a child I always demanded a lot of fuss and love, not just with epic sulking or Maggie Thatcher impressions, but from the moment I arrived with my wonky legs. No doubt Yvonne, then four, thought I was a right pain with my dislocated hip, stealing her thunder.

Loads of family photographs show Yvonne and me on Christmas mornings, looking tired and dishevelled having leapt out of bed before dawn. We're posing proudly with our favourite new toys, our matching light blue nighties clashing with the swirling orange seventies wallpaper behind us. We have the same mousey hair – 'fine but lots of it' is how hairdressers have often described it, which seems like a backhanded compliment – and in those photos we both look so pale, almost translucent – like ghost girls clutching their Tiny Tears dolls. We have always looked very similar – spooky twins in our long-sleeved polyester numbers – but we were always very different in personality. Yvonne has always been slightly quieter, more reserved. The Cannon to my Ball-ache.

We were thrown together when our family lived for a while in a two-up two-down in Boothstown, a little place that squats by the East Lancs Road just outside of Manchester. Our house was tiny, a little terrace attached to the Conservative Club that Mum and Ken ran, so Yvonne and I shared a room, her luxuriating on the top bunk and me roughing it in the lower. We considered trying to split the room in two so we each owned a side, strictly out of bounds to the other, but once the bunkbeds and chest of drawers were in, the floor space that remained was roughly the size of a baking tray, barely worth sharing. It was more of a cell really, and if either Yvonne or I had fallen in with the wrong people and became hardened criminals it would've been good practice for a ten stretch.

Trying to squeeze past each other to get in or out of the room was like something from *The Crystal Maze* – 'Left a bit, no, you go back and I'll step here, go right, right! Yes, we've got the crystal!' – not helped by that fact we were both blessed with long limbs and a lack of coordination. No wonder our tempers frayed – we were literally living on top of each other in our bunks and we used to have some horrible fights. Poor Mum would often threaten to 'Bang our bloody heads together' but luckily Mum is the size of a Borrower, so she was never physically able to carry out that threat.

Yvonne's frustration with me was compounded by my irritating habit of using her stuff without asking and then promptly breaking it. She always looked after her stuff – she was always more responsible and conscientious than me. She'd cherish her things and treasure them, so no wonder there'd be hell to pay when ol' sticky mitts Saz would come along and help herself, like a magpie in corduroy trousers.

The event that best sums up the difference in personalities between Yvonne and me happened every year at Easter. We'd get about seven Easter eggs each from various family members and by 11 a.m. on Easter Sunday all seven of my eggs would be open, some partly devoured, others polished off. It was carnage. Shards of chocolate poking out of the packaging, shreds of foil littering the immediate area. Like a fox in a henhouse, I couldn't just eat one egg at a time; I'd tear into every box in an orgy of consumption. We kept them displayed (do come in, admire our display of Cadbury's finest) on top of the upright piano, and mine looked like a crime scene.

Yvonne, however, would carefully open one egg, eat some of it, then neatly replace the foil so the egg still looked untouched. Like Ferris Bueller arranging his duvet so it looked like he was still in bed, Yvonne would cleverly reshape the foil so it looked like there was still intact choccie underneath.

She approached the eggs in the same cool, considered way she approached life and it drove me mad. It always seemed like Yvonne's eggs lasted for weeks whereas mine were gone in a few hours.

This analogy isn't really to suggest I'm wild and unbridled and she's stiff and controlled, but for sure she's much more considered and I'm more slapdash, so growing up there were bound to be clashes.

Despite our arguments we did love each other; we just couldn't live together, like Syrian hamsters.

When Yvonne was around fifteen she took herself off to stay with a cousin in London and do some work experience as a hospital cleaner. This now feels very 'of its time' – the eighties were clearly pre-health and safety and insurance concerns – 'You're fifteen? OK, grand. Here's a mop, go sort out that large pool of bodily fluids over there near that naked old man!' – but thanks to a mixture of adventurous spirit and, no doubt, annoying sister, Yvonne booked her train ticket to head down south and get stuck in.

I was eleven and to me London might as well have been Mogadishu – my only knowledge of it came from *The Bill*,

Minder and new soap opera *EastEnders* and it seemed to me that London was mainly made up of criminals, con men and large-haired, loud pub landladies. I was genuinely worried for Yvonne's safety.

In the days before she left we started to read Shakespeare together – I don't know why. I think we rather fancied ourselves as modern-day Little Women like in the books, huddled together reading by the light of a crackling hearth. Although in reality we were both squished into Yvonne's top bunk reading aloud by the glow of a 40-watt bulb. Yvonne would hold the *Complete Works* in her hands and we'd read all the different roles. I absolutely loved it.

Maybe she did the Shakespeare thing because before she left for the big wide world she wanted to do a bit to educate this knotty-haired gobshite who'd blighted her life so far. All I know is that when she did leave I was in a real state. Even the thrill of acquiring her top bunk for the summer did nothing to quell my fears. I imagined all sorts of murderers and ne'er-do-wells lurking in the shadows of London, waiting to harm my sister. I convinced myself she'd be hurt in some way and I cried myself to sleep for the first few nights she was away.

I think Mum was as touched as she was incredulous.

Of course Yvonne returned in one piece but I could tell shaking off the shackles of small-town life had had a profound effect on her. It was the beginning of a decade-long case of intermittent itchy feet – not a fungal infection but the desire to travel. Not long after London she acquired a short bob hairstyle, cut sharply like the girl from Swing Out Sister, and, in the spirit of their hit single, she was ready to 'Break Out' and discover the world. Me, on the other hand . . . never mind spreading my wings; I curled them round me, perfectly happy to keep things as they were, always happier as a big fish in a small pond.

Yvonne was really close to Mum and I in turn could wrap my dad round my little finger with a killer combo of cuteness and comedy. Whenever Dad, Yvonne and I were together I'd be jazz-handing all over the shop in a bid to hog the spotlight. My sister is a talented pianist and had lessons every week. Dad used to take us and while she was learning her arpeggios with a local lady, called Mrs McCartney, who had a dark-brown bob and an extensive range of flowing shin-length skirts, we'd scarper to a nearby park and I'd get Dad to myself.

I had lessons too, but for a very short time because I lacked Yvonne's dedication and patience. I also wanted time with Dad more than I wanted to squeeze up on a piano stool next to Mrs M in her stuffy front room. Swings and slides or scales? No-brainer.

Yvonne has always worked hard for things, from Grade 8 piano to A levels to a law degree, whereas things have often fallen in my lap. And if it wasn't for Yvonne and her fabulous brain, I wouldn't be where I am now. It was while I was visiting her in Paris, where she was studying, that I first got scouted for modelling.

12. Red, for the Winner

Before the heady days of modelling and the glamour of the French capital, though, I was often busy helping to beautify bevies of a different kind of supermodel, of the bovine persuasion.

Agricultural shows are amazing events showcasing the many different sides of farming, rearing animals and general country pursuits, and they were the highlight of our summers.

In vast white marquees folk hoping for a rosette would display everything from award-winning Cheddar to prize pumpkins, bantams, bunnies, pigs and pigeons – all churned, grown and reared with love and dedication. Spectators sitting in the temporary stands would watch showjumping, sheep-shearing and motorbike displays. Throw in stalls selling everything from wellies to woodcraft to waffles and it was heaven. To me these were the best places on earth. They were the Glastonbury of the farming world, where instead of Ed Sheeran on the Pyramid Stage you'd watch a Gloucester Old Spot boar taking home a trophy in the pig ring.

In the build-up to show days Dad would spend a lot of time

bathing the cows. Well, I say bathing, but although I love the idea of a cow leafing through a *Take a Break* in a bubble bath surrounded by tea lights, the reality was far less luxurious and I guess technically more of a shower, as he would use a hosepipe and maybe a bucket.

The shows all happened in summer, so luckily for the cows the weather would be warmish. 'Up north warm' though, which really just means no sleet.

Dad would pop a rope halter on the cow or bull and tie it to a metal ring attached to a wall, then the fun would begin, hosing down the beast with lashings of Fairy Liquid and lots of rubbing and scrubbing until the white bits were sparkling and the brown bits glossy and squeaky clean. The cows on the whole didn't really seem to mind – there might've been a bit of skipping about from the younger animals but I reckon most kinda enjoyed having their crusty mucky bits scrubbed and soaped up. The prep continued with tools from the show box, a big wooden chest filled with hairspray, brushes and combs, much like a Kardashian's weekend bag.

Added to that were the blocks of chalk to rub on their ankles, the bright white lead ropes with gold clips and the leather headcollars all polished up. The humans needed to be well turned out too; anyone entering the show ring with an animal had to wear a white buttoned-up coat, like a junior doctor on *Holby City*.

Everything would be loaded up and off we'd rumble down the farm lane, the cattle wagon packed fit to bursting with cows, calves, the big bull, show box, bags of grub (for humans and cattle), hay, camping stove, sleeping bags and a couple of Z beds – because when night fell the straw would be swept to one side and the main part of the wagon magically transformed into our cosy accommodation.

Then would follow three days of the show – hours and hours of hanging around interspersed with short bursts of manic preparation and intense, nerve-wracking turns in the ring.

I'd watch Dad on his stints in the ring and my stomach would churn with nerves for him. This wasn't just about a bull catching the judge's eye – this was business, and reputations were at stake. The more prizes Dad's bull won the more its offspring could be sold for and the more Dad could charge for the bull to impregnate their cows. Each breed had a small and close-knit community of farmers supporting it, so word would travel fast about what had happened at the show, good or bad.

Dad never looked nervous in the ring but I know the adrenaline would've been flowing. In the last half-hour before the class, he would become quieter, more serious. He'd check the cattle over and over again to make sure they were pristine. He'd nip to the loo and comb his hair, straightening his dark-green Hereford-patterned tie, smoothing his white coat. His slender face would be still, just his light-blue eyes darting around as he performed last-minute checks on the animals. Then it'd be time to head to the ring, spectators scattering as Dad steadily made his way through the crowds. 'Mind your backs, please,' he'd shout, and families would glance round to see half a ton of beast steadily bearing down on them. One of us would be bringing up the rear, literally, holding a handful of straw in case the cow or bull decided to poo en route. If it did their tail would be held out of the way to avoid getting muck in it and we would wipe the cow's arse with the straw.

In the ring, everyone looked so serious, faces set in concentration as they stood their animals well and made sure they held their heads right. Dad would manoeuvre his massive bull round the ring so the judge could watch how he walked. Dad's eyes would rarely leave the judge's face as he watched for signs of approval in their expression. The crowds of families watching would be near enough silent, kids in buggies munching ice-cream cones and old folk leaning on their sticks, all rapt, seeming to hold their collective breath as the air crackled with tension. Then, when the judge pointed at the winning beast, the crowd would erupt into cheers and applause.

I remember feeling so proud watching Dad in the ring – I've welled up just writing about it.

Now I have my own family I know the importance of having different hats. I'm always me but I have my mum hat, work hat, friend hat – different parts of my personality given expression in different roles. I think I loved seeing Dad in the ring because he wasn't wearing his hassled-dad hat or knackered-wagon-driver hat; here he was in his prize-cattle-breeder hat, skilfully showing off his animals and taking pride in all the hard work it had taken to get them up to that calibre.

Dad loved these moments in the ring. Relief and pride would wash over his features as he stepped forward to collect his rosette. He would be particularly proud when it was the best colour rosette of all – red, for the winner.

During downtimes at the shows, Dad would mainly banter with his farmer mates. I loved watching him chatting so animatedly with them all; he seemed so far removed from the busy Dad juggling everything on the farm. I'd watch as his face would darken when discussing serious stuff and then suddenly light up, his blue eyes crinkling at the edges as he cracked up laughing with his buddies. The one usually holding court was another Hereford man called Jack Henry, a small wiry fella who had a precise, pointed black beard and moustache like Guy Fawkes and merry dark eyes that would twinkle as he talked. He always took the mickey out of me and I loved him. His wife was called

Win and she was a petite bird-like lady with neat pale-blonde curls, as glamorous as a lady could be in a white pharmacist coat holding onto a massive cow. She was quick to roll her eyes at Jack's chat but you could tell they were very much in love.

At the end of each long day Dad and his pals would pull up a few bales of straw and someone would produce a bottle of whisky. I'd hang out a bit, ear-wagging their chit-chat before cosying up in my sleeping bag on the camp bed in the cattle wagon.

Thousands of people would visit the shows, crowds filing through the huge marquees that were the animals' home for the duration, pausing to admire the sheer awesome size of a bull or pointing out a calf to the kids. I loved nothing more than busying myself around the cows, wearing the world-weary expression of a kid whose life's work was to make sure the white end of a cow's tail was backcombed to within an inch of its life and brightened with chalk. In clouds of Elnett hairspray and chalk dust I'd toil away, loving having a few passers-by stop to watch me skilfully coif the tail into a replica of Bet Lynch's bouffant hair circa 1986.

We kids not only helped with keeping the cows pristine; we were also allowed into the ring to show the cattle. Usually Yvonne and I would be given a calf each to hold, although the sensible-seeming logic that the smaller the animal the easier it is to handle was kinda flipped on its head with Dad's cows.

The massive stock bull, all three-quarters of a ton of prime beef, was surprisingly easy to deal with, probably because he was so massive he couldn't be arsed to summon up the energy to try to run about. Apart from the odd sidestep and guttural roar at a rival beast (the bull equivalent of saying 'C'mon then, you want some, do ya?') the big fella was pretty quiet and docile.

But a calf weighs the same as your average twelve-year-old human when it's only a couple of months old.

When it's so young, a calf is always shown alongside its mum, so you'd think – or hope – it'd just want to stick close to her. However, like a toddler being dragged round the shops, a calf in a show ring would often get bored and want to wander off and have fun, and those Bambi-esque limbs were deceptively strong.

That's exactly what happened to Yvonne at Bury Show one year. She was leading a young bull calf when suddenly it decided to make a bid for freedom. We were all holding an animal of our own, so we couldn't really give chase to help pull up this high-speed Usain Bull. We just watched helplessly. Yvonne momentarily tried to dig her heels in and stop the calf from gaining enough momentum but it was too late; the bull calf took off, pulling her along with it. She should've let go but some weird instinct must have kicked in – she clung grimly on to the lead rope as spectators, families and stallholders all leapt out of the way of the runaway calf with the girl attached to it like a rag doll tethered to the tail of a kite.

When she was unable to keep up any longer she fell and was pulled along instead, bouncing over the grass on her front like the speedboat she was waterskiing behind had run out of lake. Eventually the bull calf ran too close to a marquee and Yvonne got caught on one of the guy ropes, forcing her to let go of it and come tumbling to a halt as the calf simultaneously got bored of its adventure, slowed to a trot and stopped a few feet away.

Yvonne was fine – just a bit bumped and bruised. She went up in my estimation that day, with her display that would've impressed the most hardened Hollywood stuntwoman.

* * *

Runaway calves weren't the only excitement to be had at the shows. Dad and his mates would get involved in a little competition to guess the age, sex and breed of cattle. Easy, I hear you say – look at the size, the colour and the dangly bits. The twist, though, is that these weren't live animals – they were butchered, cooked and served in little chunks on numbered platters, like the samples they put out on supermarket deli counters.

Dad and his chums would chew the beef and then chew the fat over which animal they thought it had come from. 'Hmm . . . what do ya reckon, Jack?' Dad would say. Between these two great friends there was always a healthy dollop of rivalry, whether it was serious, like in the ring, or a bit of fun as in the meat tasting. Jack would eye Dad: 'Eeh, I'm not reet sure, Len . . . tricky one this,' he'd reply, squinting thoughtfully for effect, and then suddenly, eyes widening in a Eureka! moment, he'd scribble down his answer on the printed-out sheet.

I was always flabbergasted that they could get even one right but more often than not they got most of them; apparently from the taste, firmness and texture they could tell a lot about the beast the meat had come from, stopping just short of eye colour, star sign and hobbies.

Every show ends with the Grand Parade, which is basically aversion therapy for anyone with a health and safety addiction. On paper it sounds dangerous and in reality it was always insanity. As a celebration of the day's success each animal that'd won its class was taken into the main ring to do a lap of honour for the watching crowds. Considering there are dozens of classes, that meant dozens of animals all jostling to get into the ring; all creatures great and small: prize rams, ponies with their rosette ribbons fluttering, loads of cattle – it was a bit like Noah had parked his ark nearby but the memo about only two of each species hadn't got through.

I'd inevitably be holding on to a calf and you'd end up getting carried along on the swell of people and cattle. Not only animals but horse-drawn carriages and tractors would do a circuit too, like the Wacky Races. All of this made more hazardous by the fact that nearly all the farmers would be slightly delicate after the revelry on the bales the previous night.

During the laps of honour someone would announce over the squawky tannoy each animal's fancy long show name and its accolade. Much to Dad's annoyance, they'd often mispronounce his bull's name. He was called Lowesmoor One Fatham but they'd drop the 'th' sound of Fatham and call him 'Fat ham' – a name suitable for a prize boar maybe, but not a bull. I would see Dad shake his head in annoyance.

Grand Parade completed with, miraculously, no serious injuries, we'd finally load up the animals and get on our way, joining a long line of cattle trucks, trailers and horseboxes trundling off home.

13 Turkey Spaceship

If summers on the farm were all about the shows then winter was all about the turkeys. Across the yard from the farmhouse were two large, long wooden sheds. To get to them you'd have to run the gauntlet past Radge, a rescue Alsatian that Dad had as a guard dog tethered on a long chain near the sheds. I don't know where he sprang from, but he was one of many strays that found a home and a role at the farm.

Radge was not blessed with good looks – he was scrawny with a slightly hunched back and had a touch of the hyena about him with his wild eyes and slathering mouth. He was also always filthy and wet, even on warm dry days.

What he lacked in looks he made up for in enthusiasm, and whenever you'd walk within range of him he'd bound up and fling himself at you, risking a garrotting if he misjudged the length of his chain. (Radge had an insatiable appetite for affection and also for neighbourhood cats, hence the chain.) It was like being scrubbed on the legs by a stinky yard brush, but still I loved him.

Once past Radge you'd reach the oblong sheds that had housed chickens when I was very young but which, in later years, were turned over to the turkeys Dad raised in the winter months. The huge wooden doors would slide open to reveal dozens and dozens of young turkeys that were spending the last weeks of their short lives on the farm so my dad could fatten them up in time for Christmas.

The turkey shed was warmer than a hospital ward and really stuffy, lit by glowing yellow heat lamps that cast massive monster-turkey shadows on the walls. The shed was lined with sheets of silver insulating foam, which made the whole place feel like you were in a spaceship made on *Blue Peter*.

The turkeys would mill about chunnering among themselves, making a low warbling noise. They had plenty of room and were pretty content but very nervous, sensitive to sound and sudden movement, so you'd have to walk among them like Tom from *Tom and Jerry* on tiptoes past Spike the bulldog.

They were hefty birds and if anything startled them they'd keel over, their little hearts already under strain from being overweight. The heart-attack victims would be boiled up for the dogs, semi-plucked and bouncing around in a massive boiling bubbling vat of greying water, scum gathering on top, smelling like death.

Dad would mostly take orders for them, but the odd housewife would come up to the farm and Dad would offer to take her to the shed and wind the woman up, saying 'Come and point out the one you want so I can put a ribbon round its neck.' Women have always loved Dad; the ol' strong silent vibe he gives off makes women keen to get his approval, to make him laugh, to get him to drop his quiet, serious demeanour. I'd watch ladies go all gooey around him, laughing at his teasing, secretly thrilled that he was winding them up, his bright-blue eyes shining mischievously.

Slaughter time and the laughter ended, though I imagine it was marginally worse for the turkeys than for Dad.

Living on a farm, you have to be pragmatic about the use of animals for food. I never really had any moral wrangling over it. I remember asking where various meats came from and the answer was always a straightforward 'That's pig/cow' or whatever. I'm the same with my own kids; I answer honestly and it's up to them to decide how they feel about it. My eldest daughter Lola is now a vegetarian, so maybe I've been a bit too honest.

When I was tiny, my older siblings had a much harsher introduction to the food cycle, when (so family legend goes) they asked at the dinner table where their pet lamb Larry had got to and Dad replied, 'You're eating him.' Dad farmed in a fair way, though – he always made sure the animals had good living conditions and were treated with respect before they met their end.

A stable was used as the killing room, turkeys held firmly by the legs upside down, their heads sliding between two flat metal rails, which had an electric current running through them – this would stun the birds unconscious. Dad would then neck them, twisting their heads between his fingers in a quick, deft movement, before placing them head first into metal cones. The body would be encased tightly in the cone to avoid bruising to the flesh, because the bird would continue to twitch and writhe even after death, as all the nerves would still be firing – it also avoided broken wings. Their purple heads would dangle out of the opening at the narrow end of the cone. Plucking the birds was my job, and it was almost comical. After being dipped in boiling hot water, a machine that was basically a cylinder of rubber fingers would spin at high speed, as I held on to the chicken's feet like they were the reins of a runaway horse and carriage, and the birds' carcasses bounced over the whirling fingers.

Writing this shines a light on the darker side of eating meat but it's what has to happen if on Christmas Day you want slices of succulent turkey alongside your sprouts and roasties. As much as I like the idea of animals living to a ripe old age and dying of natural causes while surrounded by loved ones in a sun-kissed meadow, and only then being used for meat, that just ain't the truth.

At Dad's it was a small-scale operation but an efficient one, and done as humanely as possible. There was a shed opposite the house where he 'cleaned' the turkeys, as he called it. Hour after hour Dad would stand in that freezing shed sporting a big cream rubber apron, smeared with blood like macabre toddler finger-painting. He'd use huge knives to slice off heads and feet before pulling the entrails and innards out of the turkeys like a magician conjuring endless ribbons from his sleeve, and neatly parcelling up the giblets in a little plastic bag. Next to him on the floor was a silvery metal bucket of doom containing all the cut-offs – a grim pile of pastel-shaded organs, pale lilac intestines, rose-pink stomachs, papery faces gawping blankly up at you.

I always felt sorry for Dad, whose back must have ached from standing so many hours in his wellies on the cold concrete floor. It was a smelly, monotonous task and the one part of farming he didn't relish at all, which is saying something cos – much like parenting small children – a lot of farming is monotonous and smelly.

Turkeys bagged, collected and paid for and Christmas could commence. It was always special, but it was super-special if we got a bit of snow because then Dad would hook up a plastic sledge to a rope connected to the back of the tractor, and with a shout of 'Right! Hold on, kids!' he'd tow us around the undulating front field at a breakneck top speed of 3mph (obviously it felt much faster).

Looking back I don't think about the safety of sliding along behind a huge beast of a vehicle or the diesel fumes we probably inhaled; I think of Dad's face as he laughed, steering the tractor, half turned round in his seat to watch us as we screamed and squealed all round the field.

Health and safety, or lack of, is a recurring theme in this book. It's a miracle we survived the seventies – if we weren't second-hand smoking we were sliding around in the back seats of cars without seatbelts driven by adults with relaxed views on drink-driving. Add to that the extra excitement that comes with being on a farm surrounded by unpredictable animals and reversing tractors, and the Cox clan were lucky to escape unscathed.

There were a few near misses.

We had a lovely old dog called Spud, a lurcher crossed with a collie. He was huge and black with a dickie bow of white fur round his neck and a white tip to his tail like a paintbrush that'd been freshly dipped. He had the long gangly legs of a lurcher and a taste for smaller family pets – so he was also kept on a chain. He guarded the front of the house and would always demand a cuddle when you went in and out, sort of like an affection tollbooth.

He'd lean up against me and nearly knock me over, the top of his bony head reaching to my chin. He was getting on a bit and by the time I was eight he looked like one of the Rolling Stones, his hip bones jutting out and his fur greying. In his day he had been a fierce guard dog but now his eyesight was failing and he was half deaf.

It was this that created a problem one day when Dad was at

the top of a very tall ladder at the front of the house fixing a bit of guttering. Dad's friend Mel, who often helps out on the farm, was supposed to be holding the bottom of the ladder but had been distracted and left his post. Spud was on his chain as usual and mooched his way over to investigate what Dad was up to. Dad clocked this right away and started to shout at Spud to deter him from coming closer.

Unable to see Dad and only able to hear him faintly, poor confused Spud, like the world's oldest morris dancer circling a maypole, walked slowly round and round the base of the ladder looking for Dad, dragging his chain behind him.

Dad started to shout louder, realising that if Spud gave up his search and started to make his way back to his bed in the shed he'd pull the ladder with him.

Spud's chain was getting shorter and shorter as he wound his way round. Luckily, hearing Dad's shouting get louder and more panicked, Mel legged it back across the yard and grabbed the dog, turning him steadily round and walking him back the other way, eventually untangling the bottom of the ladder – but not before a small crowd of us kids had gathered to supportively laugh and point.

Dad did eventually see the funny side, once he was safely back down the ladder feet first rather than face first.

14. Bovine Sally Gunnells

One of the commandments of living on a farm is 'Thou shalt grab yonder wellies, come rain or shine, when commanded to round up escaped cattle.' Usually after I'd fed, watered, mucked out and tucked up my pony Gus for the night, swept the yard, peeled off my soggy joddies and was lounging in my jammies in a prime spot on the couch in front of a roaring fire with a couple of biscuits and something good about to start on the telly . . . THE CALL WOULD COME.

The phone would ring. If it was after 8 p.m. it'd never be good news – no one rang for idle chit-chat at that time – so as soon as the first ring trilled out from the big cream phone hung up in the hall we'd all look at each other with dread.

Dad would haul himself out of his chair grumbling and head towards the phone in the kitchenette. We'd be straining to listen to his replies – 'Where about? How many do you reckon? Are they near the road? OK, love, thanks for letting me know,' then once he'd put the phone down, the cry would go up 'Cows are out!' and it'd be a mad scramble to get wellies on and head out.

Like the bell ringing at a fire station or the Bat Signal being shined into the air, we'd all spring into action. Maybe Dad should've used a more exciting alert, some sort of klaxon or a cowbell.

Either way, we'd trudge through the fields to find the cows, who would be having a whale of a time, having pushed and leaned on a fence post until it gave way or found a weakness in the barbed wire thanks to the handiwork of some of the charming local teen vandals who often amused themselves by dicking about with Dad's fences.

The cows usually didn't actually go too far, none of them having the energy or inclination. Let's just say they lacked an adventurous spirit. They'd only roam onto the park that ran parallel with the bottom boundary of Dad's land or onto my school's fields, where they'd be spotted by a local, who'd ring the farm.

Depending on the weather the ground could range from squishy to knobbly to slippy, making it tricky to run after cows in the dark wearing wellies and your nightie.

The usually docile cattle could suddenly turn into bovine Sally Gunnells, skipping away at high speed and dodging past us in a zig-zag like they were scoring a try on the rugby pitch.

Us kids and Dad would be spread out in a circle like some weird dance performance, arms outstretched like scarecrows, slowly closing in on the cattle, hoping to shoo them back towards the field they'd come from. After a bit of pratting about the cows would eventually get bored of their new game and make their way back home whilst Dad patched up the fence.

We'd all pull our wellies off and flop back onto the couch, knackered, rosy-cheeked and strangely exhilarated by the adrenaline rush of an impromptu cattle drive.

*　　*　　*

Occasionally a call would come to say that something altogether more sinister was happening – there was a dog in the field with the cows, calves and expectant mums.

This was a less jolly affair – even the sweetest family pet who may by day like nothing more than a belly tickle and snooze on an armchair can undergo a transformation when in a field with a bunch of frightened cows and many hark back to their wolf ancestors, becoming slavering predators, like when the Hulk gets cross then can't remember anything after.

A dog suddenly appearing in the field barking and nipping at the ankles of the animals causes a mass panic among the herd, which is particularly bad for the cows that are with calf. Any woman with kids knows the last thing you want to do when you're heavily pregnant is run around a knobbly field in the dark being chased by dogs. You'd much rather lie on a squishy sofa eating custard creams. Although that obviously wasn't an option for the pregnant cows, having a relaxing time in the fields, chewing the cud and snoozing, was important. There'd also be new calves in the field that were at risk of injury from the dog or being trampled by the running cattle.

When Dad got a call about a dog that'd be the cue for him to go and unlock his rifle cabinet. Dad, like lots of farmers, used to have a gun for clay pigeon and rough shooting and had a licence to use it to protect his livestock.

That'd be my cue for hysteria. Weeping and begging Dad not to shoot the dog, I'd try to block his way and make him promise not to kill the family pet currently stalking the poor cows out in the field.

Once, I remember it was my job to run up the lane to the top field and swing open the big iron gate so Dad could drive through in his jeep and head up towards the cows and the dog. Instead of wrestling the old frayed blue rope off the tombstone-esque gatepost I stood there in the glare of the head-lights, refusing to open the gate, arms folded and face set in a determined grimace. It was vital to get to the dog before it did any damage, so this protest was probably pretty annoying. Dad jumped out the jeep, gently but firmly moved me out of its path, swung open the gate and roared off in the jeep, shouting 'I'll only pepper its bum.'

This charming phrase meant that he would only fire once the dog had scarpered, so it'd get nothing worse than a few tiny bits of shot in its rear end, hurting it just enough to deter it from returning.

What usually happened was Dad would get to the cows and find that the dog had gone. Or sometimes he would indeed just pepper its bum – I don't know if he meant to miss but let's just say that Dad wasn't always the best shot.

15. Death Row Gameshow

On a few occasions Dad would take me to the cattle market when he had a couple of bulls to sell. I loved it. Bustling, huge sheds with corrugated metal roofs containing rows and rows of pens holding all manner of livestock from sheep, pigs and cattle to geese, goats and hens.

Animals being loaded and unloaded from wagons; market workers and farmers shouting, watching the auctions, queueing for a polystyrene cup of tea. Men with red, weather-beaten faces as creased and crinkled as old leather satchels would gather round the indoor rings. These were metal enclosures with a gate on either side that could operate like a one-way system – livestock in one gate to be seen and bid on and out the other side once sold, hopefully off to a new farm and not the abattoir.

Dad always hoped for the former – a farm only needs one big stock bull, so he'd need to offload any spares. They were still good-quality young bulls with a great pedigree for showing and breeding, so ideally Dad would want them to go off to a new farm to service their own bevy of bovines, like a hoofed Hugh Hefner.

To help raise the stakes and stop his bulls becoming steaks, Dad would get me to walk them round the ring. This was a very different experience to showing cattle. It felt like some death row game show – 'Ladeeeez and gennelmen, will this young girl impress the crowd and save this beast from certain doom or will the farmers make mincemeat out of her . . . AND the bull?'

Either way, our plan often worked. I'd walk the bull on a rope headcollar round the ring and the auctioneer, before launching into his special hyper-speed babble as the bids began, would do a little spiel on the microphone about how easy the bull was to handle as 'a nice young lady is leading it round'. I would try to make light work of encouraging this slightly freaked-out animal to walk smoothly round the ring, smiling beatifically if it skipped about or misbehaved. ('C'mon, you schmuck! I'm trying to save your life here!')

Let's be clear here, by the way, this was when I was fourteen, with a terrible wavy bob just below my ears, boobs still a distant dream and registering about 250 on the awkward scale. I wasn't like one of the girls they used to have at the boxing, sashaying round the ring in between rounds using my cute looks to sell a bull.

The audience of mainly men would cross their arms on the gates and lean their chins on their forearms, burying their mouths in their jacket sleeves, possibly to hide their expressions so they could play their cards close to their chest about what beasts they were interested in. This left a narrow strip of face available between their nose and the pulled-down peak of their flat cap. Nevertheless, they still managed to bid, communicating with the auctioneer with the most minuscule of movements – a wink here, an eyebrow-raise there or the most minute twitch of an index finger were enough to place a bid. People joke that at an auction you could sneeze and end up accidentally purchasing a painting or expensive vase. At the cattle auctions your pupils contracting could buy you a cow.

16. Pine – the Wood that Powered the Eighties

When we left the farm we moved about half a mile away and lived in a red-brick three-bedroom council house on School Street. I was about six and a half when we left – the kind of age where you don't really question the whys and whats, you're just taken along for the ride. I can't remember feeling sad about leaving the farm – I had the priorities of a six-year-old and I'm sure the promise of my own bedroom was enough to quell any lingering unease about why we were moving home. Over the following weeks, months and years I'd gather enough information to piece together what had happened: ear-wagging on whispered conversations between Mum and Nana amid clouds of cigarette smoke; hearing curt greetings between my parents when Dad dropped my sister and me off at Mum's that occasionally escalated into shouty arguments – the frosting of civility still too fragile and cracking under the weight of Mum's heartbreak. It was a sad time, especially for Mum, but I was sheltered from a lot of it. Before I knew it, Mum was in love with a man called Ken and we were suddenly a shiny new little family and

Mum was much happier. Dad was with his new wife and we all had to readjust, now the dust had settled slightly. It wouldn't fully settle until twenty years later when I saw my mum and dad chatting warmly at my sister Yvonne's wedding. It took both the other partners to be gone – Ken through death and Dad's wife through divorce – before Dad and Mum could allow the old wounds to finally heal enough for them to become friends again. It was a surreal thrill, seeing the two people responsible for my existence talking together after all that time.

Life on School Street turned out to be a golden time. It was a quick walk from the farm – you could nip out of the farm gate and, depending on the season and therefore how overgrown it was, usually go down the little footpath that hugged Dad's paddock and continue along the side of Masefield School and out onto Masefield Road, which had neat little semi-detached houses on the left and the Lorival factory on the right, although you couldn't see it thanks to the high ivy-covered railings. First right and onto School Street and our house was the second on the right.

We lived at number 69 and I loved this house for many reasons: it had steep steps at the front that led up to the garden path, so to me the house seemed like a mansion on a hill; my nana and grandad lived just over the road at number 32; the back garden seemed huge – it was long and narrow with big leafy trees lining each side and, at the bottom, a rockery, something that was very popular in the eighties (I mean, rocks half-embedded in the earth and clumsily painted white; not surprising they were so popular); and my bedroom had the most amazing wallpaper – of sweet rosy-cheeked cartoon cowgirls riding their plump, peachy ponies, all in faded golden hues.

The house was always warm and cosy – in the lounge thanks to the gas fire and in the kitchen thanks to Mum's cooking. The window overlooked the back garden, not that you could look at it through the steamed-up windows created by a lack of ventilation and Mum's enthusiastic use of a pressure cooker.

I always found Mum's pressure cooker faintly terrifying, a huge silver vessel with a thick, screwed-on lid that was more 'engine part that's fallen off a spacecraft' than a pan. It squatted on the kitchen counter, hissing and spitting like a cornered cat and generally giving off the impression it was going to explode at any minute, blowing the entire kitchen and me all the way to the rockery.

From the pressure cooker and the slow cooker came a constant flow of delicious meals, from her melt-in-the-mouth beef in red wine sauce to chicken stew.

Our kitchen was dominated by the table, which was like a bench from a picnic area and made of pine — the wood that powered the eighties. It wasn't the pale untreated pinewood that's more popular today; our table was glossed to the colour of Irn-Bru and had large black knots in it. It was like eating our tea on a reclaimed wall from the inside of a Swedish sauna.

The front room was oblong with a big square window looking out onto the street and on the opposite wall a dark wood upright piano. Yvonne needed to practise, and before Mum could get round to buying a keyboard for her, Grandad heard of a friend of a friend who had a second-hand piano to sell, so there it stood, massive, dominating the relatively small room. There was always piles of stuff on the piano. Like an exercise bike that becomes a hanging rack for clothes, the piano became like a large shelf, covered with books, unopened post and general clutter. When the lid was open there'd often be one of our cats on it, casually stepping on the keys and accidentally playing a disjointed, mournful tune.

The squishy, pale-blue velvet sofa was opposite the gas fire and angled towards the telly in the corner. This was my spot, sitting on the floor, leaning against the sofa among a jumble of legs, my face shining with heat from the fire. It was in this position in this very room that I witnessed many historical moments, from Michael Jackson's 'Thriller' video when it was debuted on telly (my cousin Anthony came round specially to watch it with us and ape the dance routines), Bucks Fizz's skirt-ripping triumph at Eurovision and the Royal Wedding.

I was especially excited by the Royal Wedding. My mum and my nana absolutely loved the royals – every Christmas Day we'd watch the queen's speech and we couldn't talk or mess about in case a single syllable was missed. Mum and Nana would be nodding and murmuring their agreement with the queen, as if they were having a gossip with Liz over the back fence. Whenever the royals had troubles, Mum and Nana would discuss them as if talking about members of our own family, passing judgement on some of the seemingly sloppier members but always having sympathy with the queen.

The engagement of Charles and Diana took over the nation and everyone in our house was swept along with the excitement. I decided Diana might need some help with designing her dress, so I drew a picture of her in a huge pouffy frock with diamonds on and sent it to the Palace. I got a reply within a couple of weeks, on expensive, stiff, creamy-coloured paper with a red Buckingham Palace insignia on the top and on the envelope. I was beyond excited. Grandad, who seemed to have a lot of 'friends of friends', found another friend of a friend who worked at the local paper, the *Bolton Evening News*, and aged six I had my first taste of mega-stardom – I appeared on its smudgy black and white pages, proudly holding my letter from the Palace. In it the secretary to Lady Diana thanks me for the drawing. There I am, hair neatly pinned down in a side parting, forehead shining and grinning a shy smile. Pleased and proud as punch.

In the end Diana shunned my designs and opted to work instead with David and Elizabeth Emanuel, which I took on the chin. The dress was magnificent in a very eighties-princess way and I secretly thought that she'd been inspired by my pouffy big number.

We soon had our own wedding to plan, when Mum decided to marry Ken. He'd been her childhood sweetheart and once Mum, Yvonne and I had left the farm they rekindled their love. Ken was younger than Mum (only by a few months but she still took great pleasure in claiming she had a toy boy) and had been a bit of a wild lad. He had mousey-brown hair in a flick and a matching mousey moustache, olive skin and a gap-toothed smile. He loved to wear his keys attached by a ring to the belt loop of his jeans. As time went on and they became tenants in pubs the number of keys increased – cellar door key, pool table key, front door key, jukebox key, cigarette machine key, till key – all different shapes and sizes of keys hung from his belt in a massive bunch the size of a boxing glove; you could hear him coming for miles as he jangled along the corridors of the pub.

When we were all thrown together at School Street, Ken was kind and fun and his bad-boy rep melted away when he fell for Mum. He must've really loved her to take on not only Mum but six-year-old me and ten-year-old Yvonne.

My main memory of their wedding day was that for some reason I rebelled and refused to hold my hands in a ladylike manner for my individual photos. The photographer tried to cajole this seven-year-old bridesmaid to lay one hand gracefully over the other and then lean my head on them as if daydreaming some whimsical thoughts, but to no avail – there are photos of me with my chin resting firmly on two tightly clenched fists like a chess player trying to psych out an opponent.

Our dresses were beautiful and I loved them. We went to a local dressmaker and in the build-up had to endure many an awkward fitting, standing in vest and pants in the dressmaker's front room. The dresses were floor-length and made from floaty chiffon and were cream and pale green; I looked like a walkin' talkin', fist-clenchin' summer meadow.

In the photos Yvonne and I look our usual milky-skinned, pale selves, like we're haunting the photo ('in this example you can just make out the spirits of two little bridesmaids who choked to death a century before in the great confetti disaster of 1889'), and Mum looks serene in a satin cream number with headgear that looked part lacy pancake, part 1920s pilot's leather helmet.

The night before the big day I couldn't sleep, not from excitement but from mild agony. For some unknown reason my mum had snubbed the use of heated hair appliances (despite the eighties being the decade of the hot brush and crimpers) in favour of going back to Victorian times, and had created ringlets for us using 'rags'. These rags were metre-long, narrow strips of creamy fabric that were possibly the shredded bedsheets from a Crimean War field hospital.

Each 'rag' was folded in two and tied round a small section of the hair at the root. It then entwined, wrapped and encased the hair so I ended up going to bed with what looked like huge, white, cotton dreadlocks. They weren't the comfiest – whichever way you leaned your head on the pillow it felt like a small elf had grabbed a fistful of your hair at the scalp and was pulling it with all the strength its little elf arms could muster. Horrible. Still, the result was lovely and I had enough ringlets to make a Victorian weep with envy.

Being fitted for the bridesmaid dress served me well for the next big social event that lurked round the corner. For the Christmas play my primary school had decided to put on that Christmas classic *The Wizard of Oz* and I had been awarded the role of Toto, Dorothy's dog. I was very happy with this and, as an aficionado of the film, I knew I could do justice to the role of the small, sassy hound.

I would need an outfit, of course, in order to truly look the part.

Mum consulted the classified ads in the back of the *Bolton Evening News*, which was a bit like an eighties Amazon except everything was second-hand. Whatever you needed, you'd have a good chance of finding it in the back pages. Adverts selling second-hand skateboards, mattresses and food mixers sat along-side more for cars, cats, violins and walking boots.

Some items were 'free to a good home' and the rest fell into one of several categories: 'Under a Fiver', 'Under a Tenner' and all the way up to, if you were feeling flush, 'Under £100'.

Mum scoured the small ads and sure enough she found a second-hand dog costume. The lady who was selling it lived on a local estate and so one day after school we headed to her house to view the goods.

In the living room, as her three kids lounged on the sofa watching *Emmerdale Farm*, the lady produced the outfit with a flourish. It was conker brown, with shaggy fur and floppy ears. Embarrassed by having to change in front of the other kids, I crouched down behind the sofa and remained crouched there in my vest and pants until Mum held out the outfit, helped me step into it and zipped me up the back. I popped up the hood and that was it. It fit like a dream and I WAS Toto.

The play went down a storm. I remember building up my part, sliding around on my knees and enthusiastically yapping. The watching mums and dads started to laugh at this very vocal Toto and the more they chuckled the more I barked.

17. How Much for the Donkey?

We had real dogs to look after at Mum's and they came in a variety of shapes and sizes. Gemma was a beautiful setter-cross pup with a black, glossy coat, liquid brown eyes and the waggiest tail you'd ever seen. She also had a penchant for buggering off if someone accidentally left the front door ajar. One morning she escaped and Mum searched all day, only coming home when it went dark. Later that evening we got a call. Someone had found her dead by the side of Seven Stars Hill; she'd been hit by a car. We were absolutely distraught. I remember Mum crying. It took us all a long time to get over that.

We begged and pleaded for another puppy but I think Mum decided that the way forward was to get an older rescue dog that wouldn't have the energy to scarper and get squished. She contacted her mate Margaret from the local RSPCA and gave her a heads-up that we were on the lookout for a new four-legged friend.

Therefore, without any prior discussion with her family, Mum set in motion a repetitive chain of events that went like this:

We would rehome a middle-aged, whiskery dog that would last an average of five years. We'd of course absolutely love the dog but it became normal for us that we'd come home from school to see the dog's collar on the white circular dining table, which was the sign that they'd shuffled off this mortal coil.

After the tears, the sobbing and snotty hiccups had ceased we'd blow our noses and then beg and plead with Mum for a puppy.

Somehow Margaret would get wind of the latest pet vacancy at ours and would ring Mum with details of yet another whiskery old dog that desperately needed a home.

Each time she used the killer line 'Honestly, Jackie, he's lovely, and if we don't find him a home he's getting put down in the morning.' Unsurprisingly, that always clinched the deal. We'd end up with another death row dog.

We steadily worked our way through a variety of mutts, beginning with multicoloured Merl, named after the wizard Merlin, a knee-high mongrel who looked like he was fashioned from a thousand carpet offcuts. He had a black head, a white chest and greying ears and beard; his back was a brilliant mixture of brown, more grey and undercoat of black; and there were bright ginger layers all round his back legs. His coat was shaggy and rough and he had bright, smiling eyes.

He was no trouble and was Ken's best mate, following him round like a slightly shambolic shadow.

When we inevitably found Merlin's collar on the table we started begging as usual for a puppy, but I swear as soon as we said the word the phone rang. Yes, it was Margaret. Old dog . . . lovely personality . . . execution planned for tomorrow . . . blah blah.

So we then opened our arms to Scooby, a short stocky black terrier with a white tip on his tail, a white star on his chest and four white socks. He looked like the result of a romantic liaison between a rogue corgi and a Border collie.

Mum could be a sucker when it came to cute animals. There was an occasion at a local funfair when I almost persuaded her to buy me a donkey. I'm not even kidding. It was dusk and we'd been having a whale of a time, but now the fair was winding up. I spotted Holly, a small grey donkey, tethered to the side of the owner's horsebox on a break from giving rides. I went over to stroke her and all I can remember is feeling an instant connection with this donkey. I was convinced she was communicating to nine-year-old me, telling me through her snuffles and grunts that I was her saviour and could take her away from this life of drudgery. I looked deep into her dark-brown donkey eyes and knew we were meant to be together.

Mum came over and I explained all this. That I loved Holly (her name was stitched onto the browband of her bridle, by the way; I'm not psychic), that we were meant to be together. I don't know what I expected Mum to do; swagger up to the owner like Veruca Salt's dad, pull out a wad of fifties and declare 'Alreet, sunshine! How much for the donkey?'?

What she actually did was explain that we couldn't take Holly home. She was always the tougher parent – the eat your greens/ do your homework/get to bed parent. 'Darling,' she said gently in her broad Bolton accent, 'We can't take the donkey, where would we keep it? No, love, now come on, say goodbye to the donkey and let's head home, eh? Do you want some candyfloss?'

At this point I calmly accepted the fact that it wasn't meant to be and we went home. Not really! At this point I went into meltdown. I threw the biggest paddywack the world had seen. I cried, I wept, I begged, I sobbed and snotted and screamed and sweated and gulped and threw my arms round the donkey's neck and made her fur soggy with my hot tears. I hyperventi-lated, hiccupped, whimpered and wailed. It was actually pretty out of character for me. I'd learned from an early age that a tantrum achieves not what thou doth desire. In fact, it was so unlike me that Mum was compelled to go and ring Dad from a payphone and explain the state I'd got myself into. She asked him if we could get the donkey and if it could live at the farm. To which came the resounding reply 'No. Absolutely not.'

Once he'd said no, Mum seemed to snap out of the spell I'd cast with my hysterics and broke the news to me and dragged me away from Holly and into the car.

As always, given a bit of literal and emotional space from the incident, I now realise that when I decided to fixate on the donkey it was just stood there minding its own business. It wasn't trying to communicate with me. There was no connection. It couldn't move – it was tethered to a wagon – and I was just a curious distraction from the boredom of hanging around in the cold.

I'd eaten my own weight in sugar and my hysterics were most likely a result of a crashing candyfloss comedown.

I have warm memories of life with Mum and Ken at School Street; they were happy times. We didn't have much, and although it wasn't quite 'There were fifteen of us living in a crisp packet by t'side of the road but we were happy', I was aware, usually from ear-wagging on Mum and Ken's conversa-tions, that there wasn't money to spare.

We were lucky though – we still had holidays, driving down to Cornwall for camping trips with my 'Auntie' Carole (actually Mum's best friend) and 'Uncle' Trevor.

Mum and Carole had been friends since they were teenagers, both of them petite and back then having the same dark bobbed hair and an obsession with the Beatles, even wearing stockings with a pattern of tiny beetles – of the insect variety – scuttling up their calves.

Uncle Trevor, a short, handsome man with inky black hair and tache who died far too young, loved to fish and on one holiday took Ken out on a day trip with local fishermen. Trevor also loved to cook and I will never forget the smell or the taste of freshly caught Cornish mackerel being grilled over the hot coals of a barbecue on a sunny but windswept campsite. It's no exaggeration to say that although I've not exactly dedicated my life to finding mackerel as delicious, every time I order it in a restaurant I have Uncle Trevor's mackerel in mind and I'm always slightly disappointed that it never quite matches up. Is it that the fish all those years ago was a once-in-a-lifetime dish or have my tastebuds dulled at the same rate that my memory has become more rose-tinted?

We had a couple of trips like that, the grown-ups supping little bottles of imported beer round the glowing embers of the barbecue while Yvonne and I ran feral with our 'cousin' Laura, our hair knotting in the sea air.

One year they rocked up with a trailer tent, which to me might as well have been a spaceship. I was in awe. Up until then, our family had observed the five commandments of camping: 1)Thou shalt be missing a vital pole; 2) thou shalt curse the tangled-up guy lines and wonky tent pegs; 3) thou shalt argue with thy loved one during the putting-up of the tent; 4) it will start to rain/go dark during the tent erection; 5) thou must not crack open a small imported beer until the tent is up – it doesn't help.

No wonder then that, when Uncle Trevor's Sierra rolled serenely over the grass of the campsite and he reversed his trailer tent into their pitch, I was intrigued. We all gathered round while Trevor proudly demoed his new purchase. In my memory he pressed a big red button and, Wallace and Gromit invention style, the top of the innocuous-looking trailer sprang open and out exploded a ready-made massive tent, like a great big blue fabric vomit, where it settled, all ready and upright on the grass. I know now that there was a bit of prep and the odd tent peg to be hammered in, but to me then it was magical.

It was thanks to those holidays that I was nibbled by the camping bug and I still have the compulsion. These days I make my young family endure a few nights under canvas at a family-friendly music festival every year.

As festi time approaches I spend hours raiding the attic and garden shed for all the camping gear, stacking it all up and ticking items off my checklist, then my husband spends ages packing, squishing and brute-forcing bits of kit – gas camping stove, foldaway table, pillows, inflatable mattresses – into my car, then crowbarring the kids into the remaining gaps. We then drive to Dorset, to Camp Bestival, a weekend-long festival held in the magical shadow of Lulworth Castle.

Once we've parked up we unload all the gear and cart it all to the campsite, where I proceed to fall foul of each of the five camping commandments. It's also a tradition that I then almost ruin the weekend before it's started by shouting at all my children in turn, for getting under my feet/mithering/booting a footie full pelt at the half-erected tent/asking for a snack just as I'm on my knees wrestling a metal peg into submission.

In a neat reflection of the shift in attitude around women's and men's stereotypical roles in society, it's me who loves to put up the tent, usually with the help of two strapping youths I've flagged down. I love the fact that some fabric and poles can be brought together to make a place good enough to sleep in. All it takes is teamwork, a bit of elbow grease and some swearing.

I'm in my element camping; I love the sound of a zip in the morning, I love poking my head out of the flap, surveying the skies, hoping to see blue not grey. I'm at my happiest frying an egg on my camping stove, sitting on a picnic blanket, supping a plastic mug of tea.

A few years ago at Bestival we didn't camp, and instead hired a little motorhome all ready and parked on site, but it wasn't the same. Plus there was a slight hiccup with the route. Instead of typing Lulworth Castle into the satnav I put Ludlow Castle and slavishly followed its directions like a fool. I just glanced at the initial big map of the UK that pops up on screen before returning to the road-by-road directions and it looked about right – we were heading west so that'd do, I thought. But in the end it definitely didn't 'do'.

Instead of heading south-west to Dorset we drove north-west towards the edges of Shropshire. As we were nearing Ludlow I started to get a slight nauseous feeling in the very pit of my stomach. That bit that churns whenever you're late collecting a child from school or when you're six and you've smashed a dinner plate.

I was looking out for the usual yellow AA event road signs in vain; there were none, of course, because we were about to arrive at our destination – ONE HUNDRED AND FIFTY-FIVE MILES AWAY from where we were supposed to be.

Two miles to go and still not a single telltale sign of a nearby festival – no other cars packed with gear and kids, no increased traffic, no teenagers walking the last couple of miles on foot with their rucksacks stuffed.

It was at exactly the time that I started to get the sinking feeling that something had gone horribly wrong that the kids' tempers started to fray; they'd been cooped up in the car for four hours and were desperate to get out. 'Don't worry,' said

Ben cheerfully, 'We're there in a few minutes.' Little did he know of the horror that was about to unfold.

The satnav informed us we had reached our destination and we pulled up as instructed. But where were the security checks, the crowds, the cars, the funfair rides and huge circus tents in the distance? They weren't here. What was there was a castle and, before it, a street deserted save a couple of old dears heading into a tea shop.

I then uttered what would have been the standout line if this had been a movie, the kind of thing like, 'We're gonna need a bigger boat' and 'That's not a knife, this is a knife' – I turned to Ben and said, 'We're at the wrong castle.'

As the kids squabbled, unaware, I quickly corrected the satnav to Lulworth Castle; as it started to calculate the distance and time my head was spinning with wild thoughts and hopes – maybe we've just gone wrong by ten miles and before we know it we'll be sipping a beer by the motorhome, chortling at my minor mistake.

But my mistake was major. This became apparent when the satnav announced that our estimated time of arrival at Lulworth would be gone 11 p.m. It was currently 6 p.m.

The kids were so shocked they took it surprisingly well – they fell silent and must've sensed that this wasn't the time to whinge as Mummy was fully aware what a humongous mistake she'd made.

Ben also just murmured quiet words of support as I turned the car round and headed away from Ludlow and towards Lulworth. I gripped the steering wheel, teeth clenched, and bedded in for a long journey.

That was a low point. As was stopping off at a service station to change the children into their pyjamas in the grotty loos, hopscotching over puddles of pee.

It was at the services when I was queuing for a coffee that I got the phone call from a lovely lady from the festival reassuring me we would definitely be allowed on site no matter how late we arrived. She was so kind and I was so relieved that we wouldn't be missing the first night on site, another burden of guilt I couldn't bear on such an emotionally charged day, I burst into tears of gratefulness. As I sobbed, clutching my cappuccino, a lady's kind face hove into view and, seeing my tears, she offered . . . not a clean hankie to dry my tears but a Starbucks takeaway cup and a biro, and asked me for my autograph.

Many hours later we arrived at the festival gates and Ben unfolded his six-foot frame out of the human origami shape he'd performed in the back seat in between the two smaller sleeping children. We unloaded bags and kids into the motorhome and flaked out.

The next morning was bright and warm and our troubles of the day before melted away. The rest of the weekend was brilliant. Word spread round the festival staff about my monumental mess-up and it was possibly the best anecdote of the weekend and has gone down in history as part of the Camp Bestival legend. Every year since, Rob, the bloke who owns the festival, always quips as he passes me happily frying eggs outside the tent, that at least we 'Got the right castle this time.'

Back in 1980, decades before I knew how it felt to try your best to make your kids happy, I was the kid, six years old, and although things were a bit of a struggle money-wise I was cushioned from any stress by Mum's love and my own blossoming social life on the street.

Opposite our house was the 'half-circle' – smaller than a precinct but bigger than a regular pavement. Where School Street sprouted off to the right from Masefield Road on the left there were two houses marooned together in a no-man's-land, being half in each street. In front of these houses was the half-circle.

This was where we all played out. There was a boy called Paul who split open my head by lobbing a rock at it, a neighbour called Claire whose dad had the first official goatee beard I'd ever seen, and Neil who lived further down the road, whose dad had a penchant for argyle jumpers and who would come out to call him in for tea by standing at the garden gate and shouting at the top of his voice 'NNNEE-IIL', at which point we'd all fall to our knees on the cold pavement. That joke never got old.

I especially liked Claire because her fridge always had a can of that disgustingly delicious aerosol cream in it and I'd flip my head back like a pedal bin so she could fill my gaping gob with big sweet clouds of the stuff.

She'd also get a massive tub of margarine (a whopping catering-sized vat, big enough to bath a spaniel in) and scoop out a teaspoonful of marge, then roll the marge in the sugar dish and pop it in her mouth. A ballsy attitude to nutrition – not even bothering to eat food laden with sugar and fat, just rolling some fat in some sugar and chowing straight down.

The half-circle was our domain. If you crossed the road and went down a wide path between the houses you'd get to the park. It was the park where my sis Dot taught me how to ride my bike and where I once went when I decided to run away and start a new life after being told off. I packed three malted milk biscuits, an apple and some clean pants. I hid under the slide till dusk, then got cold and bored and went home for tea. Mum hid her relief very well and played it cool. Either that or she hadn't even noticed my dramatic exit.

18. A Case of Leprosy Perhaps?

Mum was always busy; she worked hard, often holding down a couple of jobs at a time.

I think a combination of her being busy and me wanting attention, coupled with my penchant for drama and play-acting, led to a really peculiar habit of mine that showed itself a few times when I was around six.

As I write this now it sounds completely mad and, to be fair, it was. But it did show a great deal of imagination and an impressive determination to avoid school.

On a regular morning, and it must've been winter because I remember it being dark outside, I would be sitting happily at the kitchen table/picnic bench eating my Ready-Brek. Then as soon as Mum left the kitchen I would pretend to have fainted. With no audience to witness it, I would simply lie down on my front on the cold lino and carefully arrange my limbs in a classic police chalk outline shape – head turned to side, one arm bent at the elbow, fist near face, other hand bent behind me, legs split in a running position. I'd clearly seen too much *Columbo* as I had perfected the 'how people land when they've been felled by a bullet/candlestick/desire to skip school for the morning' technique.

I would then close my eyes and breathe calmly and deeply to give the impression that I was unconscious. So far so normal – NOT!!

Mum would then re-enter the kitchen to find her youngest daughter laid prone on the floor and would let out a small yelp before gently gathering me up in her arms and sitting me at the table, as I started to 'come round'.

She'd always grab a blanket from somewhere (I don't know where from; this was way before the high-falutin' days of 'throws' – maybe she kept a special 'fainting blanket' to hand) and I remember nestling in her arms as I bravely fought my way back to full consciousness.

I have a daughter of similar age now and I'm pretty sure if she decided to do an Oscar-worthy performance of 'Girl faints unexpectedly' I'd smell a rat.

However, having just spoken to key witness number one (my mum), she's confirmed that she totally fell for my act. In fact, so convinced was she that I was actually fainting (remember, this happened more than once), she took me to see our family GP, the legendary Dr Parikh, a middle-aged Indian man whose manner was a grumpy mix of suspicious and slightly bored in equal measure.

I remember him sighing a lot during appointments, as though he was frustrated and had something more pressing to attend to than rashes, lumpy bits and listening to our wheezes and splutters.

It's as though his mind was elsewhere or he wished someone would at least come in with something a bit more exotic – a spot of leprosy perhaps – something to get his teeth into and test the knowledge he'd gained while slogging away at medical school.

Anyway, Mum would explain how she'd found me unconscious on the kitchen floor and he'd eye me sideways from underneath his thick dark lashes and shiny black hair-flick. He always wore a grey suit and I remember thinking he was so wise and important – the font of all medical knowledge, if a slightly bored and suspicious font. He'd check me over, but I imagine now that the whole time he knew there was nothing wrong with me apart from a severe case of dramaqueenius skiveus maximus. He knew I was faking it, wasting his time when he could be doing something much more interesting like being a secret agent or whatever it was he seemed to have his mind on.

I can't really remember my motivation for these faux faints but I'm guessing the cuddled-in-a-blanket-missing-school vibe was one I embraced.

If Dr Parikh thought these episodes were a tad OTT he was yet to experience the full potential of my imagination.

Having had two or three fainting trips, my six-year-old self obviously decided I needed a new act. And so it was that in the middle of a lesson at Masefield Junior I felt compelled to put my hand up to get the teacher's attention. The teacher looked at me, said 'Yes, Sarah?' and I replied 'Miss, I can't move my legs.'

What is fascinating is the absolute lack of planning that went into this; no thought of the consequences or why one maybe shouldn't fake paralysis for kicks. I didn't stop to think if it'd get me in trouble, I didn't plot how I would make it work, I just said it. It also illustrates the chutzpah six-year-old me had.

Once I'd alerted the teacher to the 'fact' that I couldn't move my legs, there was no going back: 'No, miss, I can't wiggle my toes – I can't feel my legs at all. Up to where, you say? Er, up to my waist . . . No, I definitely can't stand up.'

The teacher went to fetch our headmistress, the no-nonsense Mrs Edge, but even this formidable woman, all below-knee tweed skirts and neat, cropped salt and pepper hair, softened on seeing this poor stricken child sitting helplessly in her chair while her classmates gawped in wonder and awe.

Unsurprisingly, the teachers didn't try to force me to stand – I was clearly unable to BECAUSE WHAT SORT OF CHILD WOULD FAKE PARALYSIS?????

Mum was called to the school and she came to collect me. I remember being carried up the garden steps by her and a teacher, sedan-chair style, one on each side, holding me under my bottom. I was put on the pale-blue squashy sofa to relax while Mum rang the doctors. An appointment was made and back down the steps I was carried and we headed off to see Doctor Parikh.

Mum managed to carry me into the waiting area, then into the doctor's room. Dr Parikh at last had an exciting medical mystery to get his teeth into – the unexplained and sudden paralysis of a young girl. Except within seconds of me being carefully plonked on the plastic cushion of the chair in front of him he knew it was an elaborate scam. He checked me out and told Mum there was no physical reason why I couldn't walk. Mum, boosted by this, asked me to try to walk. To my eternal shame I took a few faltering steps, wobbling and unsure, like a real miracle had just happened before their very eyes. What was a real miracle was that I didn't get a wallop from Mum across the back of my (now recovered) legs for lying so outrageously. She was just so relieved that I was OK, and says now that she remembers thinking she had to laugh as I skipped across the car park to the car, magically cured, not even bothering to keep up the frailty act.

19. The Ghost of Toulouse-Lautrec

There was an annual event where my taste for drama came in handy: Bolton's legendary carnival. Every summer different pubs would design a float for the carnival and it would be all hands on deck as each pub competed to produce the best float with the most exciting, fun get-up for the cast of characters riding it. The floats would then take part in a procession alongside performers on foot performing circus tricks, and dancers in amazing outfits.

There would also be the May Queen, May Princesses and May pageboys, who I was completely fascinated by. In a tradition apparently dating back many centuries, the May Queen would lead the procession, officially signalling the beginning of spring.

I don't know how the royal party travelled along the route in the Middle Ages (or how they travel now, for that matter), but in 1982 the Little Lever Carnival Queen mainly travelled on the bonnet of a Vauxhall Cavalier. Imagine the elegance: a car decorated with dozens of white paper carnations, stapled to a white bedsheet that was tethered to the wing mirrors and then stretched over the front, held taut by trapping the front edge under the bonnet. The Queen would be sat on top of the sheet, legs tucked demurely to one side of the bonnet, wearing a beautiful frock – usually the second outing for a confirmation dress – a tiara perched on her head and wearing a satin sash.

Following behind her on other slow-moving cars were the rest of her entourage. Oh what I would've done to be crowned a Carnival Queen. Unfortunately, the chosen queen earned her coronation by racking up the most attendances at church and Sunday school, so I never had a chance. We only went to church on special occasions – when family members were hatched, matched or dispatched. I went to Sunday school twice when I was very small – I loved it the first time as we sat at little tables colouring in. The next week the teacher kept banging on about Jesus and I found it really boring – I refused to go again and that was the end of my Sunday school education.

Our float was from the Queen Anne pub. The carnival committee, which included the Lady Glades and the Buffs, would decide on a theme (themes varied but all required the participants – by day car mechanics, cleaners, supermarket workers – to dress in flamboyant costumes and dance around on the back of a wagon) and the locals would cobble together costumes, often with incredible results. Everything from hats to headdresses and floaty frocks to fake facial hair would be made, bought or borrowed.

The float itself was usually a flatbed wagon – a cab fixed to a trailer, driven by owner Sam at strolling speed along the carnival route with spectators waving and cheering from the pavement, as the convoy of brightly decorated lorries trundled past. From my position on the float, I'd wave and grin my gap-toothed smile at the crowds; I loved it. My sister Yvonne and I loved the outfits and it was always a real family affair with Nana, Grandad, Mum and Ken and our cousins Anthony and Tracy, the kids of Mum's late sister Vivien (a lovely, vivacious woman who'd died tragically young from an asthma attack) joining us aboard too.

The floats would do a two-mile circuit of the village and end up back at the pub, where everyone would hop off and celebrate what a brilliant day it had been.

Waving at the crowds (made up of the local population of the village) meant you were potentially making a complete buffoon of yourself in front of ex-lovers, your kid's head teacher, former bosses, people you hated from school – so unsurprisingly some Dutch courage was needed; riding on the carnival float therefore became quite a boozy affair – not that I realised; I just thought everyone was having a fabulous time, not getting gently sozzled.

One theme that allowed there to be an actual bar on the wagon – while most of the characters fell off it – was the Moulin Rouge float of 1981. Dressing up a lorry to recreate the legendary late-nineteenth-century Parisian cabaret club was no mean feat but they did it; gold and red fabric was draped along the edges of the wagon, the famous three Moulin Rouge wooden windmills were recreated with a bit of MDF, and a few large wooden beer barrels were stood on their ends and secured to the floor, creating a safe surface for drinks.

Bookending the whole scene was an upright piano at the tail end of the wagon and a small but apparently amply stocked wooden bar at the front, nailed into position behind the cab. My sister Yvonne and I, along with all the other young girls, wore can-can, multi-tiered dresses in rainbow hues, knocked up by the sewing-machine whizzes at Nana's dressmaking group. To a seven-year-old girl a long dress is a big tick anyway, but add frills and a feather in the hair and that right there is the dream costume thankyouverymuch.

My nana was in a slightly more grown-up can-can dress in black and red, with a lace choker embracing her slender neck. Randomly, my mum sported a black eyeliner beauty spot just above her lip and a French maid's outfit, the sort that is popular for fancy-dress fun between consenting adults.

I imagine there was a shortage of can-can dresses and so the theme was broadened to include any French-leaning outfit – there were a couple of chaps who were wearing Breton striped T-shirts and a string of onions. My Grandad Vince, however, surpassed everyone with his Toulouse-Lautrec. Added to his moustache was a beard, round wire-rimmed specs, derby hat and overcoat to recreate the look of the famous French artist. The *pièce de résistance* was Grandad's determination to make his interpretation historically correct. To get across Toulouse-Lautrec's diminutive stature he attached shoes to his knees and knelt on them so his overcoat came almost to his false feet.

This is hilarious for two reasons – 1) the kneeling-on-shoes thing will always be funny, and 2) my grandad was pretty little anyway and if the life-size ghost of Toulouse-Lautrec had appeared that day he'd have towered a good two inches over Grandad Vince – so there was really no need to make himself smaller and spend two hours shuffling around on his knees on a slow-moving wagon.

Another year, the theme was 'Turkish Delight' and the whole wagon was covered in yellow-painted cardboard to depict sand dunes with plywood palm trees dotted around.

I've always thought that theme came about after about thirty-two miles of sheer, dusky-pink tulle and salmon-pink satin somehow fell into the laps of the carnival committee and they leapt at the chance to use it. I imagine they worked through a number of pink themes – Inside the womb! Flamingoes! – before thankfully settling on the rather vague Aladdin-meets-*Arabian-Nights*-via-Bolton.

Every person involved was mummified in the pink tulle and satin – the men and boys wore harem pants made from it, with matching little cropped waistcoats revealing bare chests and turban-esque headdresses made from twisted tulle, while the women and girls wore more of the fabric fashioned into improvised bikini tops with harem pants and a strip of fabric round the forehead.

We had a ball – Grandad's moustache was waxed and curled up at the ends, giving him a touch of the 'Genie's' and both Nana and Mum managed to look impossibly glamorous. Ken, with his olive skin and boasting a beer belly at that point in its earliest infancy, managed to get away with the cropped waistcoat/ bare chest look better than most.

I'm not sure where the booze was stashed that year – reports suggesting it was inside a large wooden camel are unconfirmed. I do know that ninety per cent of the adults on board smoked, so they were playing a dangerous game, wrapped in so much flammable fabric atop a wagon with a full tank of diesel; one stray spark from a Regal Kingsize and we'd have all gone up in a fireball visible from Turkey itself.

I don't think health and safety was a thing in the days of our carnival. This was very apparent the following year; the theme was the sedate-sounding 'English country garden' but the carnival itself was anything but sedate.

The costumes were less bonkers than in previous years as we merely had to recreate a quintessential English garden party – imagine a *Downton* picnic on a lorry and you're there. All the women and girls had long, floral frocks on and luckily Yvonne and I still had our green and cream flowery bridesmaid dresses, so we wore those topped off with wide-brimmed flowery sun-hats.

Mum and Nana wore long dresses too and the men togged up in smart suits and top hats. Casual spectators would've drunk in the wonderful sight of the Queen Anne float approaching, bedecked in hundreds of multicoloured scrunched-up paper tissue roses, the party attendees sitting at white wrought-iron tables sipping 'tea' from fine china cups poured from delicate teapots. However, it wasn't really tea they were sipping but vodka! Outrageous. Getting smashed in plain sight. Wouldn't have happened on the Dowager Countess's watch.

This year we were appearing at the main Bolton carnival, so we were all very excited as it was a bigger affair and would take place a couple of miles away. The other difference was that we weren't on Sam's usual flatbed wagon, so instead of Sam driving it was a different bloke and a bigger, longer, curtain-sided lorry. These are the wagons with a roof held up by columns along the side and huge, thick plastic curtains that can be pulled along and fastened into place, creating a lorry that can protect its load from the elements.

Of course, on carnival day the curtains were open (after all, this was a charming village tradition, not people-smuggling) and were tightly concertina'd to the columns, acting as trellises for the dozens of roses wound round them for the occasion.

The carnival was fantastic – we waved, the crowds cheered, the grown-ups drank their special tea. It had been a spectacular debut for the Queen Anne.

Our new driver manoeuvred the float towards home and, as he did, we felt the first few spots of rain. It didn't cause any panic – this was Bolton, after all, where precipitation is a familiar companion – but then the rain started to get a little heavier. As it got heavier, the lorry went faster and the screams from us got louder.

The driver, on seeing the rain first spotting and then streaming across his windscreen, must've panicked and decided the best course of action was to get us home as quickly as possible. Either that or he wanted to get back home himself in time for *The Generation Game*.

Unfortunately, he simultaneously overestimated how much we disliked the rain and underestimated how difficult it is to remain upright on a fast-moving wagon, especially when you're half-cut from drinking vodka from teapots. He put his foot down, unable to hear our shouts over the roar of the wagon's engine. The sedate pace of Sam and his flatbed was a distant memory as the new guy hit an estimated top speed of . . . 20mph. We were all clinging on for dear life. What a sight it must've been – a bedraggled tea party lurching around on top of a wagon, bonnets flapping in the wind. Once we got our balance we dug in and clung onto whatever was nailed down, accepting that the new driver just wasn't quite au fait with the etiquette of driving a float.

Then we noticed he was manoeuvring towards the right and was actually pulling onto the dual carriageway. We all started screaming again and some of the men managed to bang on the back of the cab, but to no avail.

Luckily, once on the dual carriageway, the driver didn't go any faster, instead crawling along in the slow lane. Once we'd exited the dual carriageway, after much thumping on the cab and shouts of desperation from some of the women, he finally pulled over. After all that drama (combined with several gallons of booze), some of them desperately needed an emergency pee stop. The driver managed to find a big brick wall to stop next to and, windswept and traumatised but thankfully in one piece, several of the women clambered down from the wagon and over the wall. Squatting, they hurriedly tugged down their bloomers, wide-brimmed hats askew, giggling uncontrollably at the crazy predicament they'd found themselves in – and no doubt high on the adrenaline of surviving and the relief of emptying their bursting bladders. The men followed suit and then we all slowly trundled back home on the wagon.

20. Gumption

My grandparents were always organising fun stuff – they were after all the war generation and relished life, working hard and playing hard. They were among the millions of sun-seekers who took advantage of the introduction of cheaper package holidays in the seventies and jetted off every year to the Costas. I remember Nana always looked even more glamorous after a stint in the Spanish sunshine, her bronzed skin setting off her light-honey bouffant, her gold chain glistening on her tanned décolletage.

Buying gifts on holiday for the people back home was a real thing when I was growing up – we're not just talking a bottle of ouzo for the lady who minded the cat, but souvenirs for all the family. My grandparents would return laden with gifts for everyone: white T-shirts with hems shredded into long tassels round the bottom and the sleeves, which Yvonne and I considered to be the absolute height of fashion. Souvenir ashtrays, bottle-openers and miniature straw donkeys all made the journey home as well as duty-free Bell's whisky and cigs for Mum and

Ken. Holiday shopping became akin in stress levels to Christmas shopping, completely counteracting the whole point of getting away from it all and relaxing. One year before leaving for a week in Cyprus with Mum and Ken, Dad fished around in his jeans pocket and pulled out a crumpled fiver with a flourish. To my teenage self, these spends – once changed into the local currency – were to be used to buy my father a magnificent gift. I treated it as if I was a buyer for a billionaire businessman, on a mission to source Cypriot artefacts. Sadly, my time on holiday was slightly tainted by my stressful search for Dad's present. The hotel gift shop didn't sell anything he'd like and in the end, in last-minute desperation, I spent the whole lot on a bootleg copy of A *View to Kill* from a street vendor.

Both home and away my nana and grandad found ways to have fun. By 1980 Grandad was working as a forklift truck driver at Dobson and Barlows, a local engineering firm. With his friend Bob they set up Dobbies, a social club they started in the factory canteen so the workers could get together after clocking off.

The factory is long gone now but Dobbies is still going strong. It's no longer in the canteen but is a thriving members-only club with a venue of its own.

One of the biggest events Grandad and Bob set up for the club was the annual treasure hunt, which was hugely popular, with around forty teams taking part.

The treasure hunt involved several generations squeezing into the family car and setting off on a route around Bolton and out into the surrounding countryside of the Rossendale district, searching for answers to mystery clues. Grandad and Bob devised the whole thing and it was against the clock; they handed the competitors a printout that would be clutched by the co-driver as the cars screeched over the gravel of Dobbies' car park and out onto the road.

They were supposed to be a fun-filled activity for all the family, and that's how they started, but soon frustration would snowball into a stressful car chase around Bolton, gripping a crumpled sheet of A4 in your hand, shouting at the bored, hot kids in the back, being impatient with the grandparent also in the back, and the co-driver barking directions to the driver while trying to solve clues.

It's fair to say these treasure hunts were a test not only of the teams' intelligence, imagination and gumption but also of the marriages of the competitors. Uncle Trevor and Auntie Carole also used to take part and Mum now jokes that they came close to divorce at least twice during the event.

The clues would be pretty cryptic, occasionally involving foreign languages, literature, mathematics, history or geography, and led the players to a wide range of places where the answer would hopefully be found – a shop sign, the name of the vicar written on a church's noticeboard, a house number or type of tree.

The entry fee was a pound per car and the prize for being the first back to Dobbies with the most correct answers was all the entry money. That could be around forty quid, which of course in 1980 wasn't to be sniffed at – it could've bought you a three-bed house with change. I think the main prize, however, was pride; although I wouldn't know as we never won it – most of the cars would already be in the Dobbies car park by the time we returned, and the occupants would be on their third celebratory pint and the second helping of pasties and peas.

I guess it was a 1980s version of geocaching, but instead of using satellites and global positioning systems to find hidden containers anywhere in the world we used our wits and a rickety family motor around Bolton.

21. Cowgirl

Despite not living on the farm any more it was – and still remains – an important piece of the puzzle for me. As a teenager it was the place I'd escape to, to tell Gus all my troubles. For a while I'd stopped riding but I always came back to it. Even now if I don't sit on a horse for a while I get the urge to – the equestrian form of really craving a KFC every once in a while.

While Gus and I were on a serious break, Dad decided to loan him out to a local girl so he'd be ridden and get all the fuss he deserved. After a few months I started to find this really hard and I was desperate for him to be officially mine officially.

Christmas morning when I was at the farm there was a weird energy in the room, like Dad couldn't quite relax. In retrospect there was the air of an undercover operation, Dad and his wife communicating just with eyebrows and shrugs. Then Dad popped outside and a few minutes later there was a knock at the door and lo and behold there was Dad holding Gus, who had a red ribbon tied in a bow round his neck and a new hairdo, clipped up like he'd joined the Marines, dark brown coat shorn to reveal a velvety liver-coloured undercoat. He was sporting a new rug – navy blue with red piping round the edges and his name stitched on the bum in big red letters. It was a lovely surprise and I was so happy he was mine again.

There was no stopping us. Gus and I once again ruled the sandy paths and although things at school still weren't going smoothly, riding and school, both such big elements of my life, were about to combine in the most fantastic way.

In the third year of school every pupil had to take part in work experience. This involved spending time out of school and pretending to have a job, which generally involved looking busy, clock-watching and finding lunch break and home time the best bits of the day, so really preparing you for the real adult workplace. From filing and photocopying in an office to donning a hard hat and making tea on a building site, the jobs on offer were varied and sometimes depended on what your parents did for a living – if Mum was a dentist or Dad an accountant you'd maybe be able to do a stint working for them, including cushy transport to and from your new job in your parent's car.

I didn't need a lift to my work experience though; I provided my own wheels thankyouverymuch. Well, not actually wheels but hooves. One of the jobs available to me was to work at the local holiday kennels and cattery. It was situated on the country lane between the notorious Seven Stars dip and the sandy paths and I jumped at the chance to work there. Scooping up cat poo and walking dogs – what's not to love? This Holiday Inn for pets was fronted by a neat bungalow behind which was a square courtyard with each side lined with long, open-fronted sheds split into separate kennels by chicken wire, each with a bed and feed bowls in there for whatever dog or cat was holidaying there at that time.

One of the kennels had been converted and refurnished as our staffroom, which was where I hung out with the other young girls who worked there, eating our lunchtime butties and gossiping about boys. Well, they gossiped, I mainly listened wide-eyed to their chat about boys and their various sexual adventures. I often nearly choked on my ham barm.

Clearing up the cat poo wasn't the most fun but I absolutely loved walking the dogs. We'd take them out to the disused railway line that ran along the back of the kennels. We kept them on their leads to avoid losing them and occasionally it was the dogs who'd walk us, especially the big breeds. I remember once a pair of big, ginger Rhodesian Ridgebacks continually taking off with me, only pausing when I'd managed to dig my heels into the gravel or they stopped to sniff an interesting bush.

The absolutely best bit about the job though was that I rode Gus to work every day. The owners had a small paddock in front of the bungalow, next to their front garden. Dad knew them and they kindly agreed to let me keep Gus in there each day while I minded the moggies and pampered the pooches.

Saddling up for a day at work was the best – the closest I've come to being a cowgirl (my ultimate career ambition). All week I stayed at Dad's and every morning I'd put Gus's tack on, climb aboard and head off to the kennels with my lunch in my backpack.

There was something so gloriously old-fashioned about this, with serious whiffs of *Little House on the Prairie*. It was a wonderful way to start and end the working day and, hand on heart, if I was able to ride a horse into work and back every day now I'd absolutely love to. I can see it now, the outside of Radio 2 in central London looking like a saloon bar in the Wild West with a wooden post with various charges tethered to it – Vanessa Feltz's glamorous palomino pony with the flowing mane, Ken Bruce's stocky cob munching hay next to Jeremy Vine's leggy chestnut gelding.

Finishing my work experience at the kennels and getting back on the school bus was a sad jolt back to reality. To this day, every time I'm up north and drive past that place I smile to myself and remember how special it was. I don't know if the owners ever knew just how much it meant to me to ride Gus to and from their place every day.

Working at the kennels wasn't my only job as a teen. In between getting fired for dressing inappropriately while glass-collecting and becoming the world's most surly barmaid I managed to secure a Saturday job at Scotts Sports in Bolton town centre. Lord knows how. I can't remember the interview; I imagine there was just a shortage of grumpy sixteen-year-olds on the day they needed to fill the position. I must've shown enough enthusiasm for the gig. That was always a speciality of mine growing up – Girl Guide keenness only matched by the Famous Five en route to solve a mystery, even if that keenness would dissolve quicker than a sugar cube in lashings of ginger beer as soon as I'd been required to roll my sleeves up and get properly stuck into any activity. From helping Mum in the kitchen or garden to hobbies and work, my enthusiasm would always wane, and my job at Scotts Sports was no exception.

Every weekend I would get the bus into town and make my way over the pedestrianised precinct to the double-fronted store, over the way from the Early Learning Centre and round the corner from the glorious golden arches of McDonalds. My role was as head of the ladies' department, which wasn't as highfalutin as it sounds. The 'ladies' department' was basically a rack of women's jogging suits and a few bras. A lady would come in looking for some leisurewear and I would mooch at a snail's pace to rummage around for a size 12 in dusky pink or whatever she wanted in the stockroom downstairs before climbing back up the stairs many minutes later with her goods.

The stockroom was where I spent the vast majority of my time, hiding as the hours inched by, lazing around, flopped on the stacks of polythene-wrapped leggings and hoodies. When I wasn't blatantly avoiding work completely I was trying to look busy, rejigging the boxes of Reebok pumps. Of course I know now that the time would've gone much faster if I'd just thrown myself into my role at the shop. I also know now that when I'm confronted by a teenage assistant while out shopping not to expect too much, because if they've graduated from the Sara Cox School of Retail they'll not give a monkey's.

My retail career quickly segued back into one in hospitality – I had experience as a glass collector, after all, so I found a job working at a nightclub in town. At sixteen I was too young to work behind the bar, so I was the guest-list girl; just inside the door of the club was a sort of wooden lectern and I'd perch on a bar stool behind it, clutching a clipboard. The guest list would be attached to the clipboard and it was my job to check people's names against my printed-out list. I wasn't that busy, to be fair – this was Bolton, not Ibiza, so there weren't exactly queues of revellers desperate to get in. The Saturday night would rumble on; my hours were 9 p.m. till 2 a.m. and for the last half-hour of my shift I would largely be entertained by the security staff encouraging troublemakers to leave the premises. The club itself was up a flight of stairs just next to my seat, and by 1.30 a.m. the bouncers were living up to their names by literally bouncing people down to the bottom of the stairs, where they'd land in a sozzled, angry heap. Their girlfriends would come screeching down the stairs in a clatter of high heels and drag them the last few feet to the door and out onto the pavement.

It was a job where even I questioned if I was old enough to be doing it; I was only sixteen. Then again, I'd been around pubs all my life – from being a regular in the Queen Anne with Nana and Grandad to living above the Pineapple (more on which later) – and had seen more bar brawls than your average Wild West saloon. And I'd started drinking in pubs aged fifteen, using a borrowed driving licence to gain access to the hostelries of Leigh in Greater Manchester with my best friend Joanne where we'd guzzle Taboo and lemonade, syrupy drinks sweet enough to make your eyes fizz. Even so, the scenes at the end of the night at the club were more out of control and extreme than the boozy squabbles or testosterone-fuelled fisticuffs I would witness at the Pineapple and I was glad to leave my position at the idiot's landing spot after a few months.

22. Cool as Fook

Even though I'd moved from Boothstown back to Bolton for Mum and Ken to run the Conservative Club at Astley Bridge when I was twelve, I remained really close to my friend Joanne Lloyd, who I'd met at junior school there. Joanne lived in a busy bungalow with her two older brothers and her parents, who ran the family business.

Joanne's mum Gill was tall with a neat halo of mousey permed curls and a wide, full-lipped mouth and dad Fred was little, with ruddy cheeks and was rarely without his flat cap.

They both spoke in broad Mancunian accents that swung and stretched every other syllable – 'Jo- WAAAN' – and the entire Lloyd clan were always warm and welcoming and I loved them.

The bungalow was always full of activity. In the big kitchen there would be the wonderful mouth-watering whiff of crispy bacon that seemed to be constantly frying – Fred loved the stuff and his favourite thing was to pair it with beetroot in big butties.

I used to go round there and get swallowed up in the hustle and bustle of family life. Joanne's brothers – John, with his golden-blond hair, wide mouth and light-blue mischievous eyes like Joanne's, and the eldest, Anthony, dark-haired and handsome – would be forever banging and crashing round the house.

They both went straight into the family business after they left school, and worked hard and played hard too. When I was there after school the lads would bowl in from work, wolf their tea in minutes, then rummage through neatly washed and folded clothes, trying to find the right outfit to wear for their evening out, before slamming back out through the kitchen door and into the night, like two rougue-ish whirlwinds.

Joanne's mum used to ride when she was little and was determined for Joanne to follow in her footsteps, so she'd got Fred to knock up a little stable, tacked to the side of the bungalow like a bumbag round its waist and painted white. It was essentially a lean-to that was home to Joanne's little grey pony and took up the area at the top of their driveway, onto which was also squeezed an old blue horse trailer and their tan-coloured Mercedes estate. Joanne soon outgrew the pony and a new stable and field were rented a couple of miles away for her upgrade, a beautiful piebald gelding called Apache.

He and Joanne were quite a team and competed most weekends at horse shows, eventually qualifying for the Wembley Horse of the Year show, the Wimbledon of the showjumping world, when Apache was the ripe old age of twenty-one. Joanne was my riding hero; she was brave and gutsy and dedicated – trophies, rosettes and medals jostled for space on the walls alongside framed pics of Joanne and her ponies in mid-air, flying over brightly painted jumps, her plaited hair trailing behind her.

Joanne was always more daring than me. Whether it was on the netball court or whizzing downhill near some local lock-ups in our navy suede roller boots with the rainbow on the ankle, she was always faster, braver and stronger.

She was shy though and would blush bright strawberry-red if put on the spot. I was more confident socially, so we made a good team. We were also partners in crime and one time back when we were ten we were particularly naughty.

After a busy morning balancing the books, setting up the bars ready for opening, taking deliveries – rolling full barrels from the brewery's dray wagon down a massive wooden ramp into the cellar below the bar – and collecting the empties, stepdad Ken would come home from Boothstown Conservative Club. His commute was quick – he'd nip in through a door just past the snooker table, like exiting one world and entering a new one, a mustachioed Alice in Wonderland – from the excitement and hustle and bustle of the club and into the little two-up two-down that was latched onto the side like an afterthought. He'd get a brew and the jangling bunch of keys on the belt loop of his jeans would fall silent as he settled into his scuffed-up velvety armchair, where he'd flick through the paper and fill out a Spot the Ball coupon.

Inevitably tiredness would get the better of him and he'd snooze off. This is when ten-year-old me, with Joanne as my wing-woman, would creep silently towards him and, moving slowly, inching forwards, soundlessly extract two cigarettes from his packet of John Player Special that sat with a lighter on top on the unit next to his armchair. We'd replace the packet and slip the ciggies up our sleeve, then hotfoot it through the kitchen and out the back door, thrilled and scared in equal measure at our daring and our illegal bounty. We'd make our way to our junior school, which was closed for the school holidays, and sit concealed behind a low wall in the deserted playground. Before lighting the cigarettes we'd each put on a woolly glove (we shared a pair) to protect our fingers from the stink of the fags in case we were busted by my mum and our digits sniffed for evidence. We puffed on the ciggies, obviously hating the taste and coughing and spluttering but for some reason thinking it made us ever so grown-up and sophisticated. We'd leave the playground and eat a fistful of Polos and, having removed the gloves, we'd lick a mint and rub it onto our fingers as backup in case the smell had seeped through the wool.

All that effort to smoke a filthy fag!

When Joanne and I left junior school we started at the local comp, Bedford High School. Her brothers were still there then, holding court on the top deck of the bus. There was always a pecking order on the bus – the ultimate seats were upstairs at the back but it took years to work your way up to the heady heights of that position – you had to start downstairs with the mums, buggies and pensioners and gradually try your luck getting a seat upstairs, occasionally clambering up the terribly designed spiral staircase and peering over the handrail at the top, praying there'd be space in the very front seat so you didn't have to retreat and do the walk of shame, lurching back down the stairs to the mums 'n' buggies bit.

Upstairs very front was brilliant for two reasons – I used to love the slight vertiginous effect, looming over all we surveyed like Leo and Kate on the front of the *Titanic* but without the imminent disaster bit. It was also far enough from the kids at the back to be out of range of any missiles/insults they might fling. It was never too intimidating though and felt very much like the natural food chain on the bus, within which we first-years were definitely the snack-sized minnows at the bottom. To get attention from the fifth-formers was not good; at eleven years old the aim was to silently observe the wild behaviour of the older kids without them noticing you, so you'd slink quickly to your seat at the front and essentially melt into it to avoid catching their eye. From there you could ear-wag gleefully at their shenanigans, shouting, showing off and puffing on fags, without the risk of an empty Cherry Coke can ricocheting off your head.

Thanks to Joanne's older brothers, who ruled the back seat, we were given a leg-up and allowed, even as first-years, to sit in our spot upstairs at the front without too much trouble; bus seat nepotism was alive and well.

I had some great friends at that school – Olivia, whose mum bred West Highland Terriers and who was Amazonian with dark curls and a pretty snub nose perched on a round olive-skinned face; Joanne number two, who had white-blonde hair scraped into a high ponytail and was the first of our gang to get a bra, and red-headed, slender Lisa. I was happy there; I had good pals and most importantly I had Joanne number one. So you can imagine how devastated I was when Mum told me we were to leave Bedford High, the top deck and Joanne after the first term.

Mum and Ken wanted to move back to Bolton to run Astley Bridge Conservative Club, going where the work and opportunities were. When you're little you don't really have any choice in where you go; you just have to follow your clan wherever they roam. Of course, the grown-ups have their reasons, and as the child you just have to follow them; and before you know it you're the new girl at school all over again with a cracked funny bone and the head teacher carrying your lunch tray.

We were reassured that moving back to Bolton was going to be a good thing – we'd be about four miles from the farm, so closer to the rest of the family, and Astley Bridge Conservative Club was bigger and a new exciting prospect. We moved after three happy years in Boothstown, in the January of 1988 when I was thirteen and in the second year of big school. I was devastated to leave Joanne but I was happy to be back in Bolton. We'd also be trading in our two-up two-down for a sprawling three-up three-down; a wee terraced house not attached to the Conservative Club, as in Boothstown, but over the way, meaning Mum and Ken could keep work and home more separate than it's possible to with just a paper-thin wall between you and your customers.

I didn't know it then, but we'd stay in that area for the next decade or so, which for us was a long time. Looking back it's clear that from quite tough times at School Street, when Mum had done lots of casual cleaning and bar work to make ends meet (and Ken struggled to find any work at all), there's a clear upward arc as Mum and Ken grafted and grafted to improve all our lives. With each career move came more responsibilities, more ambitions for the places they managed, bigger homes to live in and more spare cash to spend on nice things.

It was hard though – I loved Bedford High School and was gutted to leave. I would miss my form teacher Mrs Pimlott, who was one of the best things about that school. Moving up from juniors to secondary is always pretty intimidating but Mrs Pimlott had been the perfect person to oversee that transition and had eased us from little to big school with her kindness. She had a name and a fashion sense that were more Hogwarts than northwest state school, sporting long, silky flowing skirts in swirling fuchsias and lilacs, teamed with acid-bright angora cardigans; she was like a tall, slender exotic bird. Her hair was cropped, spiky and peroxided and she had huge eyes with lashes of bobbly mascara so she looked like someone had squished two massive spiders on her face. She always seemed to be in a rush – she'd swirl into a classroom like she'd been blown in on a brisk breeze like an autumn leaf.

Even now, if my mascara goes lumpy I think of Mrs Pimlott. I loved her because she was kind and funny.

It's amazing the imprint teachers leave on you, good or bad; I was only at that school for a couple of terms but Mrs Pimlott crosses my mind regularly – as does, for different reasons, my maths teacher Mr Jones, who I still blame for my fear of numbers. He was strict and sarcastic, with cropped deep-red hair matching his ruddy complexion and maroon V-neck jumpers – he was like a walking talking Dulux colour chart for reds. He was left-handed and wrote on the blackboard with such vigour that his entire body moved. His right hand would ape his left, as if writing the exact same thing as the other on the board with invisible chalk.

He wasn't a tyrant or cruel, he just went so fast and was so scathing that I quickly fell behind, too intimidated to ask for help when I didn't understand something. My hatred and fear of maths was set; I couldn't do it. Maths is like a language – you just need to work it out to be able to speak it fluently – but in my very first year at secondary it became an indecipherable foreign tongue, and has remained one. We all knew that to be allowed to study A levels we had to achieve the holy grail of C or above in GCSE maths; it took me THREE attempts. By the final time I felt like that scene in *Elf* where Buddy is in the classroom towering over his classmates.

Teachers aside, Joanne and I were best friends and there was no getting away from the fact that I was about to move seven miles away from her. This resulted in me spending a lot of my teenage years on buses – I would catch one to Bolton town centre, then another one on to Boothstown for a thrill-filled night hanging out on the precinct in the drizzle with Joanne and our other pal Lisa.

This was 1989 when Manchester was the centre of the universe for bands and fashion and coolness. Until now music for me had been mainly what was played at family parties and get-togethers – my musical memories up until my teenage years are just random moments, scraps and snatches of songs providing the soundtrack to Cox clan moments. My Uncle Stan, the widower of my mum's sister, jiving with Mum to the strains of Bill Haley's 'Rock Around the Clock'; dancing to Status Quo at my older siblings' birthday parties at the farm (a sea of tight double denim swaying and swinging to 'Rockin' All Over the World', thumbs firmly hooked in jean belt loops); hanging off Yvonne's coat-tails as she played her Prince CDs; and, one of my earliest memories, my eldest sister Dot teaching me the words to Gloria Gaynor's 'I Will Survive' – even though I was only three or four she'd have me perform it in the bedroom we shared, a pocket-sized diva sashaying up and down the full length of the room in my lilac nylon nightie, giving it some welly for my audience of two (Yvonne was usually there), me channelling Gloria as she sang of triumph over heartbreak.

The whole Manchester thing was different though. This was something I could own, belong to, be part of the tribe. Homegrown talent, from bands like the Happy Mondays, Inspiral Carpets and the Stone Roses to clubs like the Hacienda and fashion labels like Red or Dead and John Richmond, flew the flag for the north-west and Manchester swapped the 'n' for a 'd' and became Madchester. We all wore Joe Bloggs jeans and Inspiral Carpets T-shirts with the cow face logo mooing 'Cool as Fook'.

We loved having our melons twisted and the band James

All the siblings together. For some reason I seem to be wearing an old lady's shower cap.

Here come the girls – cousin Tracy, Sis Dot, Yvonne. Me in tartan either giving a thumbs up or subtly picking my nose.

First day at work on the farm aged 9 months.

Clearly very pleased to be cuddling up to dad.

No Yvonne, you can't blow out the candles or make a wish until we've taken an awkward photo.

Mum and Merl the dog having a curl-off.

Dad not letting a broken ankle or health and safely concerns get in the way of driving half a tonne of tractor.

Nana showing Yvonne a thing or two about how to sit like a lady.

Late stepdad Ken who made my mum's smile as wide as his shirt collar.

You can tell from my hesitant smile that I'm already regretting the wonky plastic earrings.

Darling mum and my wonderful Nana.

Small but fearsome. Mum in full kickass landlady mode.

Sara pushed aside any thoughts of wild teenage parties and got on with brushing the cow.

Baby cow.

It's behind you!

Moments later the wagon mowed down the bull. Not really.

Dad wowed the show crowds with both his bull and his impressive sideburns.

Carnival king Vince with
his princess Jackie.

Only Nana was pleased
with the amount of
fabric she had been
given for her costume.

One naked flame and
we would've gone up
in seconds.

Photo booth
hilarity with Joanne.

Gus looking very handsome,
hoping to distract onlookers
from my inappropriate t-shirt.

The art of steering a horse
using only a rainbow jacket
and heavy fringe.

On Muffin with a very
leggy baby Gus.

Where are the breaks?
On Martini.

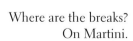

Ani and I trying to pull off the tricky Victorian dicky bow and espadrille look.

Beyond 80s : The perms, the patterns, the dungarees.

The embarrassing time Joanne and I got our hoop earrings tangled together in Ibiza.

What has a furry coat, pouts and wears trousers higher than Simon Cowell? Me in 1990 clearly.

'I've not got your bobbled beret, honest.'

Clare and I modelling in south Korea, one of us has probably just said something rude.

implored us to 'Sit Down'. We all wore Kickers boots and chunky black and white British Knights hi-top trainers, as clumsy and clumpy as strapping a couple of baby's car seats to your feet.

We girls sported spiral perms with fringes structured into a stiff vertical wave, cresting atop our heads. Impressive, slightly crispy monuments secured with layer after layer of hair-dryered Rock Hard hairspray. The boys cultivated hirsute 'curtains', their hair hanging limply down each side of the face as if they were wearing an open pamphlet like a hat, the spine stapled to their skulls along their centre parting.

Joanne and I loved going out – perms piled up and pins on our heads, we'd head into the centre of Leigh, a local town, and hit the pubs there, taking advantage of the rather lax attitude to the alcohol laws back then. Bouncers were likely to let you in if you walked up confidently enough and smiled. I became good at just strolling into a pub as if it was the most natural thing in the world – after all, I was a sophisticated eighteen-year-old, wasn't I? Err nope, you're sixteen, clutching a driver's licence borrowed from your mate's brother's girlfriend. Almost every time I fooled them with my faux confidence – either that or the bouncers were momentarily incapacitated by the cloud of Body Shop Dewberry scent I insisted on dousing myself with. We'd drink Taboo and lemonade – a drink sweeter than a thousand fluffy kitten gifs – thinking we looked sophisticated. If we wanted to switch it up we'd drink Mirage and lemonade, which was a bit dryer. We'd stand with our drinks, swaying about to whatever the local DJ on the decks was playing, getting gently sozzled.

It wasn't a pub crawl, more a pub loiter – we were so relieved to be let in that we didn't want to push our luck by leaving one place and trying to get into another in case we were refused.

We also went to clubs, cadging lifts from Ken on Saturday

nights to places like Angels in Burnley, Monroes in Blackburn and Pleasuredrome in Farnworth.

The latter was a vast open space with all the charm and intimacy of a Sports Direct off the A41, and the two others had speakers as big as garden sheds and no air con. In Monroes there'd be water dripping down from the low ceiling, landing on your face, down the back of your neck, on your head. Except it wasn't a leak, it was condensation from the hot clubbers dancing in the dry ice and strobe lights. It was recycled raver rain, a sweat storm. But we didn't care – we were there for the house music, we were cheesy quavers, we were ravers.

We loved house music with piano popped on top of thumping bass – I bought N-Joi's 'Anthem' on 12-inch and played it non-stop on rotation with Nomad's echoey 'I Wanna Give You Devotion'. We followed our favourite – DJ Welly – and we saw 808 State play a gig at the G-Mex in Manchester with MC Tunes.

I wore my raver uniform: red Puffa coat with a Vicks Rave-a Rub sweater, denim shorts and thick black tights, the look bookended with my long perm and Kickers boots.

At chucking-out time we'd fall out the club's front doors and into the cold, faces pink with exertion, ears buzzing and hair wet with sweat (some our own, but mainly other people's) and look for a lift home.

These clubs were massively popular in the north-west and there was always a good chance there'd be people there from Bolton and somehow we'd find them.

The raving community was kind – we were part of a move-ment that believed there was no space for bad vibes, just good music and a coming together.

Having said that, my blood does now run slightly cold at the thought of Joanne and me piling into a stranger's car to get a lift home, slamming the door of the 'scooby-doo' (XR2) behind us and putting our sixteen-year-old lives into the hands of lads only a year or so older than us. I don't mean we were in danger of being attacked, more that after a night of clubbing maybe a teenage boy wouldn't be the best driver. But we always got home in one piece, possibly thanks to good luck more than good judgement.

Occasionally we'd venture with some pals to Blackpool, the Vegas of the north. We'd go to the Zone, which was on the seafront and always had a huge queue to get in. Back then the longer the club queue the more I wanted to go. Which is in sharp contrast to now. I can't queue at all now. I'm allergic. My indignation swells and my breathing becomes shallow. In London you see fools queuing around the block, waiting for a table at the latest Vietnamese café because their pho is to die for. Nah, you're OK, I'll go home and make an omelette. Eateries are now essentially the new clubs, people desperate to get into the latest place.

Back in 1990 though it was all about the clubs – and we'd think nothing of queuing outside of the Zone in Blackpool for an hour or so, huddled together for warmth like penguins. We'd go into a vegetative, meditative state, inducing in ourselves an out-of-body experience to escape the reality of the chill that was seeping into our bones, the brutally cold wind from the Irish Sea whipping around us.

I lost a pale pink Kickers boot at an Inspiral Carpets concert at the now defunct GMEX venue. It was July, the hot summer of 1990, and I was sixteen. Joanne and I were driven to Manchester by Mum and we ran from the car, up the wide steps and through the huge glass doors and through to the gig. We were so excited, but alas we found ourselves at the back of twelve thousand equally excited fans, bobbing about, curtains swinging, the heady scent of Lemon Hooch filling the air.

We set about slowly pushing ourselves through the crowd, steadily working our way towards the stage, but a few metres from the front we were blocked by an impenetrable wall of Manc teen. Our method of apologising sheepishly and looking a few feet in front of us as if trying to reach invisible friends just up ahead stopped working. We could see our heroes now – with one determined push, surely we could get to the front? This was when I came up with, to quote Baldrick, a cunning plan.

If I utilised all the skills I was currently learning in Drama GCSE then maybe I could feign illness – after all, I had form from my Dr Parikh days. Obviously no one wants a teen with a spiral perm vomiting on them at a gig, so sure enough, with Joanne playing the role of 'concerned friend', one arm round my shoulders, the other gently tapping people on the back and gesticulating at me, mouthing the classic line 'Let us through, she's gonna be sick,' we started to push through the throng.

It was working!! The crowd started to part as people got the gist of what was happening. It was packed near the front but somehow, even while being carried on the current of the mosh pit, flowing right or left a couple of feet, pushed by the swell of the crowd, still a path to the barriers at the very front was opening up. I was doing my best bilious grimace – cheeks puffed out, eyes slightly rolling, my tongue lolling from my mouth occasionally – while Joanne gently ushered me to the front. People were looking really concerned. Not only were they moving out of our way but now they were pointing at us, obviously signalling to someone that we needed help. Oh no. This had gone too far. We felt a backfire approaching. We'd done so well to get to the front but as we neared the barriers just in front of the stage, we saw that everyone was now signalling to the security staff, who were standing there waiting to help us. We managed to glance up at the band at close range for possibly two seconds before the big security guys in luminous jackets grabbed an arm each and hauled us over the barriers, plucking us to safety. To add to the humiliation, as we were birthed out of the crowd, the suction as we emerged pulled off one of my boots. Security delivered a mortified Joanne and a limping one-shoed me to the St John Ambulance set up at the side of the stage in a small marquee.

After ten minutes of politely sipping water from a plastic cup and reassuring the lovely ambulance crew over the deafening din of the gig happening mere metres away that my nausea had subsided, we were released like rehabilitated otters from a wildlife sanctuary and shuffled off forlornly to resume our position at the back of the crowd. By some miracle, the Kickers boot had been spat out by the undulating crowd and was duly returned to me by security.

I'm pretty sure there must be some ancient Chinese proverb along the lines of 'She who hopes to gain from feigning sickness is doomed to lose face and shoe.'

Joanne and I were thick as thieves. She would come on family holidays with us; Yvonne was always either at uni or hiking in the Himalayas, so it'd be me, Mum, stepdad Ken and Joanne.

Mum and Ken worked long hours – our accommodation was often connected to the licensed premises they ran, so there wasn't much escape from the hubbub; bar deliveries would arrive just as we'd sit down for tea, the hours were long and spent dashing around and Mum and Ken were permanently stressed and knackered. No wonder they grabbed the chance to seek out some sunshine.

It was long before the convenience of online booking and Mum and I would make the pilgrimage to Bolton town centre, sitting patiently at the travel agent's desk while she tapped away at her keyboard, squinting at the screen of her monitor, which was in those days the size of a shipping container. It was an exhausting experience that took hours – we'd ask a question – 'Is there a sandy beach?' and she'd launch into another eighteen minutes of continuous typing and bashing of the return button, peering at the flickering screen, grimacing, ho-humming, then eventually answering 'Yes. Well, it's four kilometres away. And shingle.'

After what felt like days she'd eventually come up with the flight itinerary and accommodation.

Well, kind of. Mum and Ken used to plump for the sort of holidays that had an exciting element of surprise – we never knew where we'd be staying, just that it was self-catering and guaranteed to be three-star or above.

So it was essentially a lottery and where we ended up was in the lap of the Greek gods. Or possibly the Majorcan ones.

We weren't well off, so if we wanted to go on holiday somewhere hot we could only really afford this kind of deal, where apartment owners and holiday companies found a clever way to make sure their accommodation wasn't left with any empty units – by slashing prices and bunging those brave enough to take a punt wherever was available.

I loved that about Mum and Ken – they were pretty gung-ho about the whole thing. We still laugh now about the transfers from the airport to the apartments, peering nervously out of the windows of the coach. Occasionally there'd be a cement mixer beside a half-built reception area and you could feel everyone hold their breath as the rep from the travel company held aloft her clipboard, grabbed the crackly microphone and announced the names of the holidaymakers who were doomed to stay at

Los Apartamentos Derrelicta. We'd all be silently praying our names wouldn't be read out, and would sigh with relief as the coach pulled away, leaving the unlucky ones standing with their suitcases in a cloud of diesel fumes and brick dust.

We were fortunate and always seemed to end up in nice enough apartments – 'basic but clean', as Mum would say.

One year Joanne and I noticed an army of ants marching along our balcony and making their way in single file through our bedroom towards the kitchen. We came up with an ingenious way to stop them – Mum came in to find Joanne and me on our hands and knees by the patio doors, giggling like mad, wielding a tube of toothpaste each as we squeezed out along the linoleum floor a minty barrier to stop – or indeed stick – the ants in their tracks. It was like an ant-size version of the Great Wall of China, a fluoride-filled fortification that remained there for the rest of the holiday.

Ant infestations and cement mixers are a world away from some of the lovely five-star places my own kids have stayed at. Although having said that, my kids don't live in a luxury bubble when it comes to travel – they've loved a half-term break in a slightly mouldy-smelling, three-star, dog-friendly place on the Isle of Wight, been constantly drizzled on in Devon, nearly blown away in Cardigan Bay, and their favourite hols have probably been cheap and cheerful all-inclusives, running around in the sun with a gang of their newly made mates, smiles bright pink from the non-stop strawberry slushies and wall-to-wall chicken nuggets for dinner in the buffet restaurant.

Going away with Joanne was brilliant for me, and easier for Mum and Ken as she was a playmate for me. Though there were rules about how much we could actually play – when we went to Ibiza we were fourteen years old, too young to go to the proper clubs but too old to hang out with Mum and Ken, so we were allowed to frequent the local strip of bars a few minutes' walk from the apartments.

We felt terribly grown up and would carefully tether our perms up into ponytails high on top of our heads in the classic 'pineapple' style. Our curls would be looking particularly blonde because every day we'd sit in the blazing sunshine trying to lighten our locks with lemon halves – skived from the barman at the pool bar – which we'd squeeze directly onto our hot, pink scalps. We had to keep our heads dipped slightly back and didn't dare look down in case the juice ran off our foreheads and into our eyes, and we would gather an extensive collection of lemon pips and pith that got tangled into our hair. Not to mention the constant threat of wasps, circling our heads, attracted by the sweet citrusy smell.

Once we'd washed away the fruit from our scalps, we would slip on our floral culottes and Kickers and hit the town.

This was during the Italia 90 World Cup, which captured a lot of people's imaginations – it featured the infamous England semi-final match when Gazza burst into tears at being booked and the team crashed out on penalties against West Germany – so wherever we went big screens were showing the matches. It was also at the very height of the Madchester era, so whoever we chatted to – always people our age, seemingly also marooned between their parents and the real clubs – I'd tell them I was from Manchester. Straining to be heard over the cheesy Euro-house music at the half-deserted, neon-blue-lit bars, I would revel in my 'Mancunian' status, proud to be able to say I was from the current capital of cool. I'd even try to slip in a bit of a nasal Manc twang to add to the effect. Sadly, Joanne would always helpfully remind me in front of our new friends that I wasn't actually from Manchester, I was from Bolton.

She did it from pure mischief, to wind me up and bring me down a peg or two. In fact, though, since then Bolton, which historically was part of Lancashire, has been reclassified as Greater Manchester, so I was right all along – in your face, old pal!! I'm from Greater Madchester, cool as fook!

23. Molten Hot Chips

I was always very happy to be going abroad on holiday, apartment lottery or not, because it'd be fair to say we had a wide variety of holidays in the UK that . . . varied in their fabulousness.

I can't remember ever holidaying with Dad, although before I was born he and Mum had trips with the eldest kids to Venice – there are lovely faded photos of the twins Dot and David, aged about five, looking very sweet in matching pale-blue dungaree shorts, chubby hands holding ice-cream cones, in some beautiful Venetian plaza.

I'm guessing that when three became five and then the farm became busier, holidays weren't a priority – farmers rarely get to go away and leave their land and livestock. I've never lain on a hot beach with Dad or paddled in the sea. The only pool I've swum in with him isn't an infinity one overlooking a Caribbean island, or even at a waterpark in the Med, but at Bury Baths.

*   *   *

Most Saturday mornings when I was little Dad would take Yvonne and me swimming. Although it's not really accurate to say we went 'swimming' – really we went 'clinging' as we spent approximately eighty per cent of the time clinging to Dad, our arms wrapped round his neck like we'd just been tossed from the deck of a ship into a churning sea and were going to drown at any moment.

Of course now, thanks to my own children, I know how intense it is to be clung to like that, trying to peel their skinny little arms from round your neck; and I empathise with Dad when I remember him also trying to loosen our vice-like grips from round his windpipe. I was never very confident in the water but I also think I relished being attached to him like a whelk; it was a chance for me to slightly regress and be carried by him, be his baby again. I felt protected and safe in his arms.

The pool was always busy, full of screams and splashing. There would be other dads and their kids – maybe they were all the Saturday fathers – bobbing around in the pool like a big broken-family soup, trying their best to spend quality time with their kids. You see them still on a Saturday at the cinema, the park and Pizza Express, studying their offspring's faces, wondering how they got so grown up, mourning the daily mini-milestones they're missing.

Luckily for us we were, Dad included, always at the farm so he was never just a Saturday father. He just took us swimming as part of our family routine. I loved being with Dad and though he was never overly demonstrative, never overly cuddly or gushy, he showed his love for us by letting us half-throttle him at Bury Baths every Saturday morning.

The cherry on the cake was the paper cone of molten-hot chips we always got from the café afterwards, which we (famished in the way only swimming can make you) devoured, burning our tongues. We would wash them down with vending-machine hot chocolate, our sopping wet hair hanging in rat-tails down our backs and making our sweaters soggy.

The closest we came to a holiday in those times was visiting Dad's friend Jim on the Isle of Arran. The three of us, Dad, Yvonne and me, set off at dawn and rumbled up towards Scotland in Dad's wagon, which was fully loaded up with a tower of straw on the back for Jim and, in the cab, a tower of ham butties for us, all wrapped in foil.

Like Hansel and Gretel we left behind us a trail of bright yellow straw, fluttering along the motorway, loosened and freed from the bales as the load was buffeted by the wind as Dad roared along the M6.

We drove all the way up through Cumbria, skirting Dumfries, bypassing Glasgow and taking in the views of the Trossachs National Park, until we arrived eight hours later in Ardrossan. It was summertime and still light as we passed the little fishing boats bobbing around in the port and finally arrived at the more industrial ferry terminal.

The trip on the ferry was exciting – Yvonne and I sat in hushed reverence so Dad could concentrate as he edged the wagon and the tower of straw onto the ramp and into the belly of the ferry before we clambered down from the cab and he jumped down, his work boots landing with a clatter on the metal floor, hitching up his jeans at the same time. We cadged a can of Lilt and some crisps at the on-deck cafe from Dad, and docked at Brodick just under an hour later, Yvonne and I trans-fixed by the grey-blue water of the Firth of Clyde rolling by.

We unloaded the wagon and wound our way through Arran's country lanes, hugging the coastline, brushing against the hedge-rows, no doubt depositing some of Jim's straw in the odd low-hanging tree branch. We arrived at Jim's and, before the straw was unloaded into the barn, the kettle was put on for a journey debrief and general catch-up. We spent the night there, then next morning it was up and at 'em. Jim took us in his jeep with his collie dog up to the top fields to check out his herd of commercial cattle, which means a mixture of beef breeds bred for fattening, as opposed to seed stock like Dad's, which is a herd of one breed that is nurtured to a high pedigree standard.

With a few bursts of barely decipherable instructions Jim had the dog fetch the cattle closer so Dad could check them out. It was a bright but blustery day and as we walked across the field I realised we were on a clifftop, looking out beyond the cattle to the rolling sea below. I found it amazing that these cattle grazed so close to the cliff edge, just a couple of strings of barbed wire separating them from a sheer drop and certain death.

We headed back to the farmyard and, before setting off on our return journey, drove in Jim's jeep down to the coast and watched seals lounging on the rocks in the distance. After our whirlwind visit it was time to set off, back on the ferry and towards home, which was obviously quicker because the wagon was empty and, as my dad was fond of saying, it's all downhill from Scotland.

I returned to Scotland a few years later with Mum, Ken and Yvonne. It was August 1987. I know this because it was the month that Yvonne turned seventeen and therefore gained her provisional driving licence. It was decided that the best course of action to mark this milestone occasion would be to embark on a very long car journey, with Yvonne using the high roads and low roads of Scotland to practise her blossoming skills at the wheel. Ken would drive for the majority of the journey, then once off the motorways Yvonne would whip out her magnetic L plates, whack them on the car, and the adventure would truly begin as she attempted to negotiate the smaller B roads.

Our weapon of choice was Mum and Ken's Renault 12. A car that if you saw it now, it'd be vintage, charming and slightly kooky. It'd be driven round Brighton by a girl wearing a polka-dot headscarf and her hipster boyfriend with a beard, both in their ironic cowboy boots. They'd be sipping turmeric lattes and listening to Beck. But in 1987 it was just a regular, and occasionally rubbish, car.

I'd always had an issue with the way this car looked – the shape was just strange. The bonnet looked a little too long and was flattened at the front, like a harmonica that had been accidentally stamped on. Moving round to the rear, the back end sloped downwards at a horrible angle like it was giving up on life. It looked like it had been fed, rear bumper first, into a car crusher but the owner had had second thoughts and dragged it out again.

I think I'd harboured ill feeling about this car since the day it bit me – a few years before, when I was eight, we were loading up the car to head out on an errand. I was round the back of it, generally getting under Mum's feet as she was busy wanging on at Ken about something or other. We were running late as usual – looking back we often resembled the family from *The Fast Show*, the ones holding lots of bags or equipment and always legging it through airports, bus stations and shopping centres yelling 'Sorry! Excuse me!'

We were almost ready to set off and I was still leaning on the back of the car when, in a hurry, Ken slammed the boot shut with considerable force. Unfortunately, my finger was still there. To be precise, my wedding-ring finger was now trapped in the boot of the car. I did what anybody would do in this situation, and screamed. A blood-curdling screech of a scream; the sort of scream that awakens every primeval instinct in a mum and makes them drop whatever they're doing and run to their offspring. On seeing my finger Mum also started screaming. All of this wasn't really helping Ken, who had the unenviable task of finding the key to unlock the boot of the car. You see, for some unfathomable reason, in those days boots locked automatically when you closed them and you needed a key to open them. For any whippersnappers reading, this was centuries before it was possible to unlock cars remotely with a fob and millennia before the magic of a keyless start.

What we had on our hands (or my finger) was a perfect storm. The automatically locking car boot and Ken's penchant for keeping dozens of keys on a ring attached to his belt loop meant that, as Mum and I screamed and his stepdaughter's finger went on being mangled, he went panic-blind – jangling the keys madly, frantically searching for the small boot key but he couldn't see it. The more we screamed, Mum helpfully shrieking 'UNLOCK IT!', the more the keys jangled. It felt like I was trapped for ever but it must've been only a few seconds until Ken found the key and, with shaking hands, opened the boot and released my poor rapidly purpling finger.

I lost more than just respect for the car with the stupid automatically locking boot that day. I also lost my fingernail.

Fair to say from then on I hated that car. Still, I sometimes didn't fancy walking to school in the rain so I would occasionally harangue Ken into giving me a lift, but because I didn't want any friends to spot me arriving in this misshapen motor, with breathtaking cheek, summoning up all the ungratefulness only a child can muster, I'd duck down out of sight in the passenger seat, pretending to tie my shoelaces, before doing an SAS commando roll out of the car and onto the pavement.

Fast-forward a few years and we were loading up the Renault 12 outside our little house in Astley Bridge preparing for our Highland adventure, the entire car interior looking like a shambolic version of Tetris.

A neighbour who lived a few doors away on the neat row of tiny terraced houses was a car mechanic; Jimmy was a stout, muscular man with bright green eyes, a booming voice, broad Bolton burr and a scar where a cleft lip had been fixed, which just added to his charm.

He had a nice wife and a couple of preschool kids who were often shyly hiding behind his legs when he knocked to chat to Mum and Ken. Before our epic journey Jimmy checked out the now slightly decrepit Renault and gave us the all-clear for going to Scotland in it.

We set off late afternoon, nosing our overstuffed car into the Friday traffic, heading north. Mum and Ken had planned to head to a static caravan park in Fort Augustus, just south of Loch Ness, some 360 miles from home and a six-and-a-half-hour journey. We didn't want to attempt the journey in one fell swoop – we were in no rush and we didn't want to push our luck with the Renault – so we scheduled a stop in York, a mere ninety minutes away from home, arriving as darkness fell at a B&B bungalow run by an elderly couple, every inch of every wall covered in floral wallpaper and framed family photos and the faint smell of lamb chops.

Next morning we hit the road early, Ken at the wheel, Mum juggling her many roles – co-driver, map-reader, peacekeeper, caterer ('Another custard cream, Ken?') and general commentator, in which role she critiqued selfish manoeuvres by other road-users, mused on the purpose of interestingly shaped buildings in the distance and pointed out roadkill ('Aww . . . Badger').

She was also the DJ in charge of the entertainment, which was mainly Radio 1 – Mum absolutely loved Simon Bates's mid-morning show with its emotionally charged feature 'Our Tune', where Simon's usually light-entertainment voice would drop to a deep baritone as he read out listeners' stories, adding gravitas and solemnity to the tear-stained tales, which always featured heartbreak, occasionally death, sometimes unrequited love and – if it was a really juicy one – all three.

When Mum wasn't sniffling along or openly sobbing to heart-wrenching radio features she'd pop on a tape – and the song that soundtracked that entire trip was Queen's 'Another One Bites The Dust'. I will always remember it playing as Yvonne and I lounged about in the back seat, all tangled limbs and Vimto smiles, occasional squabbles breaking out, Mum shifting round in her seat to referee if things got too physical. That song would be blaring out with Ken on percussion in the driver's seat, beating out the drum rhythm on the steering wheel as he picked his way through the winding country lanes. The more we squab-bled, the harder Ken hit the steering wheel, beating out the 'Dum dum dum – another one bites the dust . . .' in time.

The journey up to Fort Augustus was painstakingly slow because August 1987 was wetter than average for Scotland and indeed it felt like for the entire week we had a cartoon raincloud following us, hovering just above the Renault wherever we drove. The car was steamed up and cramped, the roads were treach-erous and there were two teenagers folded up in the back, by turn reading, snoozing, arguing over Travel Connect 4, munching biscuits and complaining of boredom. I wondered what in Ken's head was the 'one' in 'Another One Bites The Dust'? His freedom? His prime? Happiness? Patience?

Mum and Ken had given up smoking a few years before but Ken had struggled and so had switched from cigarettes to thin Hamlet cigars, in the beginning just smoking a couple a day – surely better than a twenty-pack of cigs, he reasoned – but inevitably his intake crept up to a dozen or so.

I always worried about their smoking but of course at thirteen you can't always find the right words to vocalise your worries and concerns, so instead I'd just grumble and gripe, fanning the air in front of my face at every opportunity.

The switch from cigs to cigars always seemed like madness to me – I thought that if anything, cigars, even thin ones, must be worse than regular cigarettes. Like saying 'I'm giving up juggling knives, it's too dangerous – instead I'm going to juggle live grenades.'

Every hour or so, the stress of the journey would take its toll and we'd pull over for Ken's smoke break. If the rain had eased to a light mizzle we'd all get out for a stretch and to lean against a soggy lichen-covered boulder and take in some of the beautiful views.

Yvonne would occasionally get a turn behind the wheel, which considerably slowed down what was already a pretty sedate journey. Ken would go in the passenger seat to guide her and Mum would be demoted to the back seat with me, which was actually quite nice as I got to cuddle up to her and make myself comfortable on her ample jumper bumps.

Despite getting Mum to myself in the back, it was during the stints of Yvonne driving that I would be at my most grumpy because we couldn't have any music on and we couldn't talk in case we distracted her and she sent us plummeting off a mountainside.

I was jealous because she was getting lots of praise and was the centre of attention – a position I was used to occupying.

With every correct indication and snippet of praise from the front of the car I'd roll my eyes and huff and puff, muttering my displeasure at the snail's pace and lack of Radio 1. I remember thinking 'I hope she crashes' – alarming to think a car accident involving my loved ones seemed preferable to the torture of my sister getting a bit of a fuss.

The car was so steamed up I couldn't make out the rolling green outside; it just looked like there was a bright green tea towel flapping around outside the window. After what felt like an eternity we arrived at our static caravan on a site in Fort Augustus, where moods lightened even as the skies above darkened with a fresh batch of good Scottish rain to pelt down on us.

The caravan was lovely – furnished in fifteen shades of beige – but the whole week was so wet we barely had the chance to unpack the swingball. It all went by in a bit of a blur – I just know it involved a lot of Connect 4, rainstorms, more of Yvonne's driving practice, scampi and 2p penny-pushers at the campsite's small arcade.

With some relief on all our parts, our final day rolled round and we packed up the Renault.

Mum wanted to take a different route home and stop off at Fort William. Which was where the car, which had until then been performing like a dream, decided to give up the ghost. No amount of coaxing could bring it back to life and Ken, after half an hour of looking at the engine, scratching his head, giving something a waggle and then shouting to, um, to try the ignition, finally admitted defeat, slammed shut the bonnet and went to call the RAC.

And so it was we arrived back home in style at 3 a.m., the entire row of terraced houses illuminated by the blue lights of the RAC wagon; all of us were snoozing, squished into the huge warm cab, the little red Renault strapped onto the back like a felled deer on a hunter's truck.

The next day our mechanic neighbour Jimmy called round and Mum thought she'd pull him up. 'Hey, Jimmy, I thought you said the car was all right?' 'I said the car would get you to Scotland,' he replied. 'I never said it'd get you back.'

24. Bob and the Beanstalk

On the farm there was always a new arrival to look forward to meeting. Waifs and strays would rock up – a flock of twenty guineafowl one day, who landed in the yard and decided to make it their home, sleeping in the rafters of the cattle sheds, waddling quietly around the farm during the day, chattering quietly among themselves like a group of day-trippers round a National Trust property. Another stray was the appropriately named Max – who the vet said was the biggest Alsatian he'd ever seen. He was malnourished and mistreated when he first arrived, in need of some serious TLC. He had a shiny dark coat along his back, with thick, brush-like blond fur across his broad chest that continued under his belly and along the underside of his always-wagging tail. He was huge, with paws the size of side plates and a massive head, out of which lolled a wide tongue, the colour of boiled ham and the shape of a size twelve shoe insole.

He was physically massive but even his impressive size was dwarfed by his personality – Max was one of the most loving dogs we ever had. He was a rescue dog and had come to us weighing roughly half what he should've done. Whatever sins past humans had inflicted on him, he obviously didn't blame us for he was the sweetest soppiest hound ever, always on the lookout for affection. In fact, he was so soft that I wondered if maybe his past owners had maltreated him for not shaping up as a guard dog; he looked the part, though, and definitely sounded it too, with a ground-shaking woof and an intense stare that quickly melted into a dreamy-eyed gaze whenever he recognised a familiar face. When I'd arrive at the farm he'd come lolloping over and nearly knock me down by leaning his full weight on me, wanting a cuddle. He was always panting and a long stalactite of drool was often suspended from each side of his huge mouth and shiny black lips. We knew to duck and cover to avoid being splatted whenever he shook his head, as the dribble would cast out from him in long gluey strings.

The farmhouse was often freezing inside until the fire had been lit (in fact, before we had central heating, frost would settle on the inside of the windows), and Max made an excellent furry duvet to cuddle under on the floor while watching telly. When he'd get up you'd be left covered in a thin blanket of his moulted hair and possibly a couple of his calling cards – damp spots of drool.

Max formed a partnership with the Jack Russell Sally, who was all white except a choc-chip-coloured patch on her tail and a caramel-coloured ear. Sally was supposed to be a tough little farm dog but since she had arrived as a tiny puppy, able to curl up neatly into the size of a bagel, she had been treated like a princess. She loved nothing more than being in Dad's lap, whether he was driving about in his bashed-up old Daihatsu jeep or sitting in his leather armchair in front of the fire.

Sally, however, was no princess when it came to ratting and

loved snuffling after them, like her forebear Benji had. Together Max and Sally made the greatest partnership since Scooby Doo and Scrappy – and they were similar in proportions. Sally was fearless when it came to protecting the house – whenever a car pulled up into the yard she'd scramble up and at 'em, yapping her head off and obviously feeling especially brave because always following a few feet behind would be the biggest Alsatian the vet had ever seen.

The vet was Bob Potts. Of all the characters who came up to the farm, Bob was one of the most memorable. He was a large man, with a bulbous nose and a windburnt face, a close-knit web of spindly purple veins blanketing his ruddy cheeks. His small eyes were bright and sheltered beneath huge eyebrows like two black marbles under a couple of pan-scourers. His sideburns were wire wool, as was the hair that stuck out from the rim of his flat cap. Bob Potts spoke in the broadest Bolton accent, thick with dropped aitches and dialect. He also talked very loudly, in a booming voice people usually reserve for very old deaf ladies or foreigners. Being within chatting range of him was like standing behind the engine of a 747 taxiing for take-off.

Considering he spent the majority of his time at the business end of cows Bob was exceedingly well turned out, always in an olive-green trilby and tweed suit tucked into wellies – topped off, if he was planning on doing a bit of bovine puppetry, with a big green rubber apron and a disposable plastic opera glove going up beyond the elbow. The outfit sounds a bit *Toad of Toad Hall*, I know, but he was a big enough build and personality to carry it off.

'AYE UP, LEN,' he'd holler at my dad, and I'd hide behind the kitchen door, peeking through the crack of the hinge, fascinated and terrified in equal measure. He'd always clock me and try to speak gently but it was physically impossible for him.

His big red face would lower to mine and he'd boom 'WHO'S THIS THEN?', stray whiskers from his sideburns twitching as he spoke, me frozen to the spot. I remember one winter he pointed out the crusty sleeve of my dressing gown, which was stiff with dried snot – for a few nights I'd been cleverly utilising the right sleeve as an emergency hankie and it now resembled a piece of pale-green armour, a vambrace of germs. Mum came to my rescue and ushered me away, and once out of sight she whipped off my dressing gown and bunged it in the wash.

Whenever Dad said he'd have to call the vet Mum would secretly hope it would be Ian, one of Bob's partners in the vet practice, who according to Mum was tall, handsome, blond and always wore Old Spice aftershave. I love the idea of Mum being one of the many farmers' wives who'd quickly run a brush through their hair and sashay across the yard in the hope of seeing (and smelling) Ian, only to be met by the more senior partner Bob and his bristles.

To me, Bob was like some giant who'd clambered down from a beanstalk, but to Dad he was a friend and a loyal, dependable vet. When you run a small farm with a few dozen head of cattle it's a business but it's also a passion. Dad knew all the cattle by name, not just by a number on an ear tag. He cared for each cow or bull and wanted to keep them well. Bob knew this and would always do his best to help out Dad, rattling up the farm lane in his green Land Rover Defender at all times of day and night.

According to Mum, one windy day in March 1974 he'd been up to give one of the cows a check-over and a jab and, as he headed across the yard, he spotted Mum. Bob took one look at her and said in his usual broad, sonic-boom-bothering voice, 'BY 'ECK, JACKIE, YOU'RE IN CALF AGAIN!', which shocked

Mum because only that morning she'd made an appointment with Dr Parikh as she suspected she was may be pregnant. And indeed, despite her not showing at all, Bob turned out to be right – she was six weeks gone with me. It seems somehow fitting that the man who was responsible for Dad's prize cattle was also the one to detect the existence of the last offspring to be added to Dad's personal herd.

25. Feather Carpet

In the same way that downing a few pints at a family barbecue before driving your kids home sans seatbelt, them sliding around in the back of the car while you chuffed on a delicious fag in the front, became outmoded as we became more educated about the dangers, then so did many farming methods. Dad had to move with the times and by the early eighties it was becoming increasingly obvious through the media and people's shopping habits that keeping battery hens was no longer the done thing. Along with boys getting perms and the Reynolds Girls, battery-hen farming was soon to be consigned to the eighties rubbish bin for ever more, and quite rightly.

Before the general population turned to the belief that it was the basic right of animals to be able to live a life free of distress and pain and be able to turn around in their living space, egg farmers kept their hens in battery cages. Different times, as they say.

Dad's laying hens were kept in the long wooden sheds that were turned over to the Christmas turkeys after the egg business ended. These sheds were narrow, squat buildings about a hundred metres in length and looked like the wooden dorm blocks you see in army barracks in old war movies. Inside the sheds the 'batteries' were stacked three high and ran the full length of the shed in four long rows. Seeing as each battery was essentially a wire cube with a floor the size of a tabloid newspaper and there would be three hens in each cage, that meant a lot of chickens.

The first thing that hit you when you slid aside the huge wooden doors on their runners was the smell. Hen muck has a sour scent to it and it was carried through the air on a gently swirling snowstorm of dirt, dust and tiny feathers. To this day if I'm out in the sticks and get a whiff of a chicken farm as I'm driving along, my nose wrinkles and I know what it is right away. After the smell came the deafening noise. Hundreds of hens make a racket and it wasn't a contented hubbub, more of a pained cacophony.

Of all the spooky, smelly or noisy places on the farm, I found the hen sheds the worst. It was a real attack on the senses – the noise, the stink, the dust. Walking among the stacks of hens was so scary; the floor a springy carpet of compacted reddish-brown feathers and muck, their beady eyes watching you, the constant moving as they lurched and flapped, trying to get purchase and stand comfortably on their wire floors.

Underneath each cage was a metal shelf like an in-box on an office desk and the droppings would drop down between the bars and land there. The floor of the cage slanted downwards, allowing any eggs to roll to the front of the wire and through a small gap, where they came to rest in a curved metal lip, ready to be collected – which was another job that really scared me; I'd have to close my little fingers on a still-warm egg and try to whip it away before a hen strained to peck at my soft knuckles. The design of the crates was actually genius in some ways but, as we now know, the hens weren't living, they were merely existing.

Back in the seventies and eighties though, attitudes to animals were very different. They were seen by consumers and farmers alike as commodities to be used, discarded and replaced and Dad was only one of thousands of people who farmed this way.

Changing times and a broader awareness of the hellish effects on animals means that, in the UK at least, battery, veal crate and sow stalls have all been resigned to history. Just as women are now allowed to vote and we don't shove kids up chimneys any more, we now know more about animal welfare and allow hens to live and lay in much better conditions.

26. Genie from a Bottle

I look back on most of the farm dogs with a warm glow of love. I have happy memories of being tiny and cuddling huge Spud, the lurcher/collie cross, my arms slung round his neck, face buried in his thick black fur with the garland of white round his neck – him wolflike, the Akela to my scruffy Mowgli.

Sally snoozing on my lap, Dad's gun dog Brin, a beautiful, sleek short-haired German pointer, docile and sweet, resting his heavy head on my lap wanting some fuss.

Even Radge, caking me in stench every time he threw himself at my legs, desperate for affection, and, most recently Jed, Dad's loyal black Lab with a tail so waggy it looked like it was wagging him.

There is one dog, though, who holds no happy memories for me. Nero was a rescue dog who arrived at the farm looking in good shape physically but who, we were soon to learn, hadn't recovered mentally from the abuse he'd suffered at the hands of his former owners.

Nero was a Rottweiler, 140lbs of muscle with a shiny black

coat and a tan muzzle, neck and eyebrows. He was chained up in the yard and was one of our 'second-chance dogs' – we had a few over the years for whom the farm was to hopefully be their second chance at happiness. His backstory was pretty grim, according to his rescuers. He'd been abused horribly. He was owned by criminals who wanted to use him to attack the police, so they used to wear fake police uniforms and beat him, instilling in Nero a deep hatred of anyone in a uniform. Whenever our local bobby used to pop up to the farm Nero would go mad. He'd be wrestled into the porch but even then he'd throw himself against the door and the window, trying to get to him. He'd bark furiously, his breath misting up the glass, drool smudging the window as he shoved his face against it.

He was a damaged dog and we were aware we had to treat him differently – apparently big dogs who are troubled don't like to be stared at directly in the eyes as they see it as a challenge, a confrontation. I was always scared of accidentally locking eyes with him, as if he was a Hollywood star and me a mere assistant.

When he was on the chain I'd make sure I'd stay beyond its reach as I went back and forth filling up water buckets, always keeping myself aware of where he was.

Avoiding him was harder in the house, where he obviously wasn't on a chain, but I just tried to stay out of his way.

One chilly afternoon, though, I'd ridden Gus and done my chores so decided that I deserved a little break. Dad was mooching about in the yard, so I was alone in the house. I helped myself to a couple of malted milks. These were the biscuits that we always had at the farm, small sweet rectangular things showing a raised scene of a biscuit cow and calf grazing in a biscuit field. I always particularly enjoyed that the biscuits were a confectionery representation of Dad's fields.

I was so engrossed in getting to the sofa without the biscuits sliding off their plate that I didn't even notice Nero was lying in the corner of the living room. It says something about the deliciousness of malted milk biscuits that they stopped me from spotting a whopping beast of a dog just a few feet away.

I flopped onto the leather sofa, still watching the plate of biscuits, and swung my legs up onto the seat next to me.

Like a canine genie from a bottle, Nero appeared from nowhere.

He was massive but it wasn't his size that intimidated me, despite his head alone being the size of a Nissan Micra. I was used to big dogs – Max and Spud were definitely bigger and I'd cuddled and fussed over them, but Nero was to cuddling what loose bowels are to scuba-diving. It wasn't his size but his fearsome reputation – I sensed from Dad that he didn't entirely trust Nero and there was a general consensus that the dog was very much a work in progress.

So there he was, wide as a bison, big brown eyes staring intently at me, then at the malted milks. His glare switched from the biscuits and back to me several times as if he was weighing up which to eat first, like scones on a cake stand. Any other dog would've been gently shoved away or I would've shared a bit of biscuit with them, but with Nero I was frozen to the spot like someone had stitched the rear of my jodhpurs to the chesterfield. I quickly ran through my options – scream for Dad, make a run for it, shout at Nero, ignore him and just eat my biscuits – but each one ended with the same conclusion – I'd be torn to pieces by a furious Rottweiler.

Meanwhile, Nero intensified the stand-off by inching slightly closer to me so I could feel his broad chest pushing up against my legs. And then the worst bit. He made a deep, low noise – a growl that came from the very pit of his soul. It wasn't loud and was in fact more petrifying for its quietness, like it was our little secret. The teachers I always feared were the ones who'd tell you off with an intense hoarse whisper rather than the shouty ones.

In the end I decided I had to escape and in one smooth move threw the plate and with it the biscuits onto the carpet. As Nero moved towards it I leapt over the back of the low sofa, out the door and into the kitchen, shutting the dog and the malted milks in the living room.

I was so relieved – and seriously shook up. I'd grown up around big dogs, animals that given half a chance would literally make a meal out of local cats, rats, other dogs, but I always knew they'd never hurt me.

In fact, the only other animal that I'd been really wary of on the farm was Leeroy the giant goat. What a force they could've been if they'd teamed up: the goat and the Rottweiler, the Phil and Grant Mitchell of the farmyard, demanding malted milks with menaces.

If we had our suspicions that Nero was slightly unhinged then sadly we were to be proved right. One day Dad was up in the field with Nero, fixing some fencing, when he saw a Land Rover bumping up the farm lane. It was Jack Henry, Dad's good mate, popping up to the farm to have a brew and look at Dad's new bull. Spotting Dad, Jack stopped the Land Rover, got out and walked up the field to meet him.

Dad blames himself but I think it all happened so quickly it would've been impossible to stop. As Jack approached, Nero's hackles rose up all along his spine like a mohican and he stood across Dad, blocking Jack off and – he thought – protecting Dad from this stranger. Before Dad could stop him, Jack reached over Nero to shake hands and Nero launched himself at Jack, tearing at his wrist. Dad managed to get Nero off, kicking him away, but an ambulance had to be called and poor Jack taken off to be patched up. It was a shocker. Nero had to be destroyed and Dad's wife was devastated. I think we'd all hoped Nero could be fixed, but the legacy of his abuse shadowed him for the rest of his short life.

Rottweilers as a breed have often been the subject of press campaigns over the years but, as far as I'm concerned, a dog isn't born bad, it's made bad. Having said that, would I ever have a Rottweiler myself? Nope. Nero left his mark on me for sure and I'm lucky I escaped physically if not mentally unscathed.

27. Fern Britton was a Cow

Starting from long before I 'helped design' Lady Diana's wedding dress, there had been a long line of doe-eyed Dianas on the farm – of the bovine persuasion. Dad bred Hereford cattle, a breed native to the UK, from – spoiler alert – Herefordshire, where the breed evolved. There are mentions of Herefords by agricultural authors as far back as 1600. The breed is thought to be founded on the draught ox descended from the small red cattle of Roman Britain, mixed with a large Welsh breed popular along the border of Wales and England. Love that a fruity Welsh loverboyo used to pop over the border to romance the hot red herd, or some slinky scarlet lady cow scarpered to Wales to find her big, as they'd say there, 'golygus' bull.

Herefords are a gentle breed, not highly strung; they're calm, kind, solid, long-lashed and bonnie. If Fern Britton was a cow she'd be a Hereford.

They're so placid in fact that as a little girl I would often be plonked on Dad's prize bull after a successful showing season.

In the garden, with the bounty won that summer – cups, trophies, rosettes, all laid out in front of the bull – a photo would be taken as a memento of the family's achievement. For the last pic, for a bit of fun, I would be sat on the bull's back, grinning over a ton of twitching, muscular prime pedigree beef.

However, before the heady days of rosettes and accolades, in the early sixties when Dad moved on to Grundy Fold Farm from his dad's farm, he had a 'starter pack' of cattle – a mish-mash of commercial breeds, good for beef but not for the show ring.

Once Dad had settled on the farm he decided he wanted to start a proper pedigree herd, so he took himself off to a Hereford sale over the Pennines in York. Mum put a call in to the school and my brother David was given special dispensation from the headmaster to have a day off to accompany Dad to the sale – after all, Dad was purchasing what would be the beginnings of a herd that one day David would take over, so it was seen as work experience.

I don't think that'd wash these days. Taking one of my kids to Radio 2 with me because they fancied being a DJ one day would probably not get past the head teacher.

That day Dad came home from the cattle sale with two heifers. These were the seeds from which his whole herd would blossom. Two Eves who just needed an Adam. The Adam came in the form of a young bull Dad bought privately from a farmer called Sam Woods, who became a trusted seller. Sam, who lived in Blackburn, brought over the young bull, a fine polled Hereford lad called Halesdown Dermot, and the beginning of Dad's first herd sparked to life. Dermot was introduced to the heifers, and I imagine Dad lit a few scented candles, popped on a Barry White LP, and left them to it. The heifers were sisters and both were called Diana.

Diana 1 and Diana 2. So not confusing at all. All pedigree cattle have by law to be registered before they're sixty days old, so they were already both named (after their mothers) by the time Dad bought them. There were three people in this marriage and that suited them just fine. Dermot (like my radio buddy O'Leary) was obviously a charmer and he set to work creating 'Masefield Herefords', the herd being named not after the farm but after the area.

Masefield Herefords at its height would have forty cows with calves at heel plus the main stock bull, as well as maybe a dozen or so young bulls at any one time. Although it's a more modest size now, the herd is still going strong today, half a century later.

Hereford farmers name their animals alphabetically, each year bringing the next letter, like car registrations. It's always exciting when a letter comes round that you can really do something with – out there somewhere there's a young bull called Isaac and a cow called Lola, named after two of my kids. Let's just pretend they're out there anyway, and not in a burger or Bolognese.

Along with the cattle there were pigs. Dad had dozens of Large Whites – huge white pigs with pretty, slightly dished faces and big pink erect ears. I was only young when Dad had the pigs and the sows seemed to me the size of a two-seater sofa. My main memory is of sitting on the barn floor in my dungarees, my bottom cushioned by a thick bed of clean straw, clutching tiny squirming piglets on my lap, their sweet little pale snouts the colour of strawberry milkshake.

I remember becoming vaguely aware of what their final destination was when Dad loaded them up in the wagon a couple of months later. I felt so sad for these wee pigs – they were no longer tiny and as cute, but I felt the injustice of their premature deaths keenly. 'Dad, pleeeeease don't take them,' I begged. Dad didn't want to leave me at home, getting under Mum's feet, moping around and sulking, so he took me to the slaughterhouse with the pigs. I must've exhausted myself with my histrionics because I'd fallen asleep before we even got there. All I remember is waking up chilly, with a rumbling tummy, in the silent, cold cab of the cattle wagon parked back home. After this trip Dad wasn't quite so keen to, in Iron Maiden's words 'Bring his daughter to the slaughter' and I never again asked if I could accompany him.

28. Up in Smoke

The farm was a busy, bustling place. From spring to mid-autumn (if the weather was kind) the cattle would be out in the fields. Summer was all about keeping one eye on the pregnant cows for calving and the other on the skies for haymaking.

All year round the pigs and laying hens kept ticking over. Winter, when the weather turned bad, was when the cattle came in. The wet fields would get churned up by the herd standing at the gates, mooing mournfully, protesting at the wet, wanting to come in to the dry. Once in their pens the hard work really began. Feeding up happened twice a day and the work of mucking out all those different sheds was pretty much constant. Add to this the odd casualty that called for a visit from Bob the vet, plus foot-trimming, worming, occasional escapes . . . running a farm isn't a job, it's a vocation. A challenge. Twenty-four hours a day, seven days a week. Plus us five kids running round. Busy with a capital insane.

* * *

Dad had never been afraid of graft, though, and he worked to build up his herd over the following years until a cold November night in 1981, when all his hard work went up in flames. Literally.

It was a Saturday evening. I was living at School Street by then and so at the farm was just Dad and the older kids. Everyone had just finished their tea and was settling down in front of the telly for the night when there was a hammering at the door of the farmhouse. It was a lad called Ian, who was the brother of one of Rob's pals, raising the alarm – the barn was on fire.

Everyone scrambled into their wellies and ran up top to the barn. I can only imagine the panic as they raced across the garden and turned a right onto the lane to run up past the main cattle sheds to the barn. It was a beautiful old traditional Dutch-style building, with a high roof made from old timber and the lower sections from huge long logs, sleepers reclaimed from railway lines. The main body of the barn was full of the hay that had to last until late spring, when the cows could at last kick up their heels out in the fields and have a pick of grass with the warm sunshine on their backs.

The fire had to be stopped. At the nearest side as you approached, underneath the loft, were three stables, two of them containing young bulls and the third holding Muffin, my pony Gus's mum. With Dad shouting instructions, he and the kids swung open the stable doors and shooed all the animals out. Muffin clattered onto the lane, desperate to escape the flames, which had begun to lick around the old timber at the rear of the building.

There had been a huge blaze that afternoon in Bolton Town Hall, which was connected to the historic Albert Halls, and so all local fire crews were in attendance there. No regular engines were available and eventually two army engines, Green Goddesses, roared up the lane and fought the flames. They managed to put it out in minutes. The damage was minimal; just a few bales were damaged.

Dad and the animals had a lucky escape that night.

The next night their luck ran out.

The local lad who the police eventually collared for the crime had returned. Nobody knew why. It wasn't a grudge against our family – his brother was pals with David. So was it a fascination with fire? He never gave a reason.

Whatever his motivation, the bastard set light to the barn again.

It took hold. There were two terrible differences now from the evening before: it was a blustery night and the wind was against them. It fanned the fire, blowing over the fields towards the barn, pushing the hungry flames through the bales, the heat rampaging at speed, eating up the wood, devouring the straw stacks, heading up to the roof.

It was also later in the evening than the previous night, so no one was out to stumble upon the fire and raise the alarm. It had time to burn.

By the time Dad knew about it the barn was fully ablaze, flames roaring up into the pitch-black winter sky. In no time four fire engines were speeding up the bumpy lane and fire-fighters spilling out, ready to do battle. But this time, although the animals again escaped, the barn couldn't be saved.

Dad was helpless. He had to stand there and watch as his beautiful barn burned.

Inside the barn was all of Dad's hay and straw he'd harvested in the summer. It was his only means of feeding and bedding his livestock and it had all gone up. A whole winter's worth of food up in smoke. Balancing the books on a farm is a delicate business as it is; having such a valuable asset wiped out like that was absolutely devastating. The firefighters had to stay for a week to keep dampening down the fire. The hay was good quality and dry, so it kept reigniting. They cut open and spread out the blackened bales, dragging out the hay and straw over the gravelly lane, thinning it into a still-smoking carpet. It smouldered for days, the acrid smell drifting over the fields and the estate.

A handful of cattle who were temporarily homeless kept having to be shooed away from the thick blackened tapestry of hay; it was ruined, so they weren't eating it; they kept lying on it because it was so warm.

The barn fire nearly finished Dad's business off and his career as a farmer was almost snuffed out before it had even begun. He had to buy in fodder for the cattle to replace the hay lost in the fire. My brother Robert remembers this time vividly, the sounds and the smell of the fire – awful stuff. He says it was lucky that Dad had lots of hens – they ate only eggs and chicken for about six months after the fire. It was only because of those hens that Dad managed to feed the family through the winter.

If the kitchen was the heart of the farmhouse, then the barn was the beating heart of the farm – it's the thing that stands solid, crucial to the survival of a smallholding. It feeds and homes the animals. It is storage and it is shelter. It's hard to comprehend and it's hard to forgive when someone is callous and cruel enough to rip out the heart of a place like that.

Eventually, after a nerve-shredding wait and lots of investigation, the insurance paid out and Dad was able to start piecing together the barn area. The blackened skeleton that remained was removed and in its place was built a more modern structure, half grey breeze block, half pale tinder slats, with huge bright blue sliding doors. The new barn of course lacked the charm of the original, but I have lovely memories of playing in it with my buddies, lounging on the bales gossiping with my pony-riding pals. It's still there today, breezy and well lit, and it echoes with the laughter and banter of over thirty haymaking seasons and with the squeals of my own kids from the times they've spent in there, leaping from stack to stack of the bales.

29. Martini – Shaken and Scared

Until Gus was mature enough for me to ride, Dad acquired a small, pretty mare called Martini. She was dun – pale beige with a flowing, long, darker mane and tail. Like with most of the animals that weren't bred on the farm, I don't know where she came from but I heard rumours that Dad's mate's daughter couldn't handle her so Dad got her for a knock-down price. I presume that I was expected to get in the saddle and show Martini she didn't shake or stir me; basically I was to be the one to take charge of this little asbo pony and knock her into shape.

Problem was, I was six. I also wasn't brave enough to act as some sort of screw in a horsey borstal. Martini and I got off to a shaky start; she wouldn't go forwards or backwards – in fact, she wouldn't move at all. When she did decide to move it was usually sideways, always an alarming manoeuvre on horseback unless you're deliberately doing a jaunty dressage display. The ponies at the riding school were like being on a merry-go-round, happy to just follow the bum in front, so to be confronted with a pony with attitude was alarming. I was scared of her – in the world of ponies she was no Shire (and retiring type, lol) but I was only a wee scrap of a thing and she was stroppy and, compared to me, massive and strong.

All these issues were taken into consideration and it was decided that the best course of action would be for me to have a few lessons on Martini to slowly build up my confidence so we could begin a new and everlasting friendship. Only joking! Instead it was decided that I should be locked in a field with her.

Yes, classic. Read any respected psychology studies and they'll clearly state that the best way to deal with something you're frightened of is to be locked in a field with it.

I'm surprised Relate don't just welcome warring couples into their therapy room and then show them out of another door leading straight to a paddock, in which they'll be locked until they've sorted out their differences.

Anyway, I was plonked into Martini's saddle and led into the field. Once there, my dad's wife swung the big gate closed, bolting it shut.

If this was a Hollywood movie, Martini and I would've stayed in the field and there would've been tears (me), bucking (Martini), falling off (me), snorting (Martini) and determined grimaces (both) – then after a montage of all this, possibly to the *Friends* theme tune, I would've horse-whispered the heck out of Martini and we'd be best friends, galloping up to and jumping over the locked gate, sailing over in slow motion.

What actually happened was Martini and I remained parked in the same position, right next to the gate where we'd been deposited, and I wept. I cried my eyes out. I was cold and frightened and it was getting dark.

Some kids are fearless on a pony – put them on anything and they'll cling on, boss it and eventually win it over. I just wasn't that kid though. I hated falling off and I found it scary when a pony played up.

I felt a complete failure, like I'd let Dad down. I knew I'd messed up but to me it wasn't altogether clear how it was my fault; I was scared of a pony I hadn't asked for and was now being punished, which to my six-year-old (and to be honest, 43-year-old) mind seemed rather unfair. Anyway, I busied myself with the kind of gulpy, hiccuppy crying that small children favour for what felt like for ever but was probably less than half an hour.

Eventually my dad's wife came stomping out, dark permed hair quivering with fury, face thunderous, naturally disappointed that the cunning plan hadn't worked and that locking a frightened child in a field with a pony hadn't turned out to be the best way to resolve confidence issues.

Martini's time on the farm soon came to an end and she left as promptly as she'd arrived, hopefully to a braver kid who'd do her justice.

Over the years my confidence in the saddle has fluctuated but the highs – hours with my best mate Gus, as an adult competing in charity horse races – and the literal lows – facefuls of dirt and a couple of fractures – have all been worth it.

At the age of fifteen, I had outgrown Gus; the famous Cox legs had truly sprouted and my limbs dangled way past his rotund belly. If I wanted to keep riding him I'd have had to wear roller skates so my feet didn't drag along the ground. There's something peculiarly humiliating about riding a pony that's too small; you feel cartoonish and ridiculous. It probably also reminded me of being the tall girl on the little bike with stabilisers. It's a similar feeling to when you outgrow your trousers and they become half-mast.

The answer was Chantel – a beautiful bay mare, tall, elegant and sweet-natured, with the build and breeding of a racehorse but the personality of a yoga teacher. I arranged to have her on loan for a while, but our time together was to be sadly cut short.

One of the worst times of year for riders is the couple of weeks leading up to Bonfire Night, when fireworks go on sale. As you can probably imagine, small explosives and horses mix as well as fun runs and minefields, so I was always wary in the build-up to the fifth of November. Young ne'er-do-wells were fond of setting off fireworks at all times of day and night and the loud bangs echoing round the skies were terrifying for horses and their riders. Still, poor Chantel couldn't be confined to barracks for the whole of October, so one afternoon we set off from the farm, squeezing through the blue iron gate and down the path and into the estate. We'd barely been out for five minutes when someone let off a banger in a nearby street. The loud crack that it made either terrified Chantel or she thought it was a starter pistol because she set off at high speed away from the noise, along the road. Mercifully the road was quiet but I had no idea what was round the corner. At any minute a car could appear and we could career into it. And Chantel was carting me off towards a T-junction that opened up onto a busier road. I had to stop her.

I can remember the sound of her metal shoes clattering along the tarmac. When a horse gets the bit between their teeth and decides they want to leg it, you can't just pull on the reins and pray. You have to take emergency action. There's one surefire way to stop them, though it's not without its risks. If something is running really fast in a straight line the best way to slow them down is to turn them in ever-decreasing circles until they've nowhere left to go and have to stop.

Problem is, turning a racehorse-sized mare in a narrow road is a bit like turning a high-speed conga line in a corridor; it's easy to crash. Which is what Chantel and I did. I quickly grabbed the right rein close to her bit and, using all my strength, pulled on it and hauled her round to the right; we managed to circle in a clockwise direction and she slowed down, but then in all the drama, as she was coming to a stop, she tripped up the kerb. She stood there panting, her neck sticky with sweat, but we were in one piece at least, and I hopped off and led her slowly back to the farm. We'd soon discover she was so lame she had to be retired from being ridden.

I've never enjoyed a firework since. OK, not really.

Riding stayed with me throughout my teens and, in various forms, up to the present day. Even while waiting to hear if I'd got my first job in telly on *The Girlie Show*, I was working as a groom for a married couple in Bolton called Mark and Joanne – he was my optician and a keen showjumper and competed every weekend while Joanne cheered from the sidelines. My duties included loading and unloading the horses from the wagon, tacking them up and untacking them – just general grooming duties, but I loved it.

I think they slipped me a few quid but I didn't do it for the hard cash, I did it for the thrill of the whole thing – watching the classes, being around the camaraderie of the shows and smelling of sweet, sweaty horse when they'd drop me off home after a long day helping out.

I'm sure it was during an eye test that our shared passion for riding came up, and I'm pleased it did. I was in flux at the time, managing to combine the two careers of mediocre model and slightly sulky barmaid while approaching the brow of an exciting rollercoaster-ride few years, and this would turn out to be my last chance for a while to get down and dirty with my four-hoofed friends. I remember Joanne telling some of the other riders at the shows that I wasn't going to be grooming any more as I'd got a job in showbiz and them laughing, fascinated that the quiet knock-kneed girl sweeping out the horsebox was going to be on the telly.

30. Leather, Lace and Fishnet

When I was seventeen, running in parallel with my life with horses was real life, and the move from Smithills Secondary School to Canon Slade School's sixth form was looming. I was about to switch from being a small fish in a big pond to being in a slightly smaller pond, but any pond is intimidating to a fish with self-confidence issues, so my nerves about starting this new chapter were off the scale.

As well as worrying about making friends and fitting in, I was in a spin of contradictory emotions about the fact that at my new school we could wear our own clothes. So mind-blown was I about the heavenly release from the constraints of uniform that I absolutely could not get my head around this. The dress code at the sixth form was actually a little stricter than your average college as it was connected to a Church of England school and had an overall much tighter grip on its pupils than my old school ever had. It was decreed that jeans wouldn't be allowed, or leggings. I was soon to discover they upheld these uniform rules so fervently that I imagined they thought denim was the devil's work and, to be fair, with the parallel jeans I used to sport, like two wide windsocks completely concealing my Kickers boots, giving the impression I hovered rather than walked, they weren't far wrong. As for leggings, I think society would benefit as a whole if they were outlawed nationally.

With my faithful jeans and black leggings no longer options, I floundered. I wanted to look smart and stylish, so went shopping for some day-to-day A level essentials, flashing my Clipper Card and travelling not to Rodeo Drive, baby, but to Bolton town centre. I hit the shops (Etam, Mark One) and, after refuelling at Greggs, bussed it home, pretty confident I'd sorted out my look.

The first day rolled around and Mum ran me to school as I was sick with nerves – my history of being a new girl was riddled with negative experiences and I hated the prospect of having to make a first impression to dozens of fellow students that could potentially set the tone for the rest of that first term. The only consolation was that, even though the majority of pupils would've come from the fifth form of the school into its sixth form, today was still a nerve-wracking transition for everyone.

Back then Canon Slade school was a huge creamy-brick building with a squat two-storey sixth form tagged on at the end like an afterthought.

As I walked towards the double doors of the sixth form I looked down at my outfit and was suddenly racked with doubt. Not surprising really – for reasons that to this day elude me, I'd settled on a pair of Baileys-coloured slacks and a cream buttoned-up cardigan with pale pink and blue chunky flowers knitted onto the front and round the neck. The effect was less cool college kid and more born-again Christian working part-time at the library.

As I was new to the school, aside from a couple of Smithills lads the first day of sixth form was literally the first time my new schoolmates had clapped eyes on me. The first impression of me must have been baffling – who was this Sunday school teacher who'd been shipped in from 1950s Alabama?

I walked into the common room and although it wasn't quite like a stranger walking into a rough locals' pub – jukebox falling silent, pool balls stopping on the ripped baize – it felt like it. As the door swung shut behind me the membrane that had caused my fashion-blindness fell away from my eyes and I could see clearly and instantly that I looked all wrong.

I was met by a vast array of better dressed pupils: in the goth corner was a sea of black miniskirts and thick tights, baggy jumpers and Doc Martens; the drama gang wore floaty ankle-length floral skirts, polo necks and an air of importance; and the lads wore the kind of pastel-coloured chinos that are favoured now by David Cameron on his Devon hollibobs but which back then were bafflingly passable for teenage boys.

Safe to say, the next day I upped my game and stopped dressing like a florist from *Midsomer Murders*.

In fact, I moved a little too much in the opposite direction and a few weeks later I was hauled before the head of sixth form for flouting the uniform code. Mr Dyson could've been Mr Bean's older brother – he had dark bushy brows and rubbery lips that, when displeased, would contort and twist like they were trying to wriggle free from his face.

With his wild wiry hair, greying at the temples, he always looked dishevelled, as if instead of travelling to school by car or bus like the other teachers, his preferred method of transport was hurricane. He always seemed to wear the same grey checked suit that looked like he'd buttoned it up wrong, with his tie skew-whiff and tattered too-long trouser hems catching the bottom of his battered brogues. Ironically, though, he was a stickler for smart uniform.

For all I know, away from school Mr Dyson was a lovely

bloke – maybe he was a popular member of a pub quiz team, collected toby jugs, enjoyed charades and cooking Mexican cuisine for his family, was keen on yoga or his favourite film was *The Commitments*.

To me, though, he was just my head of sixth form, devoid of personality, compassion or human emotion. A teacherbot and my arch-nemesis for the couple of years I was at Canon Slade.

After a couple of run-ins about my trousers being too tight he was constantly on the lookout to check I'd fallen in line with the dress code. Whenever he'd encounter me in the corridors he'd quickly and surreptitiously scan me for uniform contravention. One day I was wearing ski pants, a curious fashion long since consigned to history's style sin bin. They were fitted trousers, often with an elasticated waist, and at the end of each leg had a thick fabric stirrup worn under the arch of the foot to keep the trouser leg stretched and taut. I've never been skiing but I imagine the foot stirrup is the only similarity between ski pants and actual skiwear, as the flimsy black numbers I enjoyed wearing in the early nineties surely weren't suitable for any kind of sport. Except perhaps darts.

Mr Dyson's eyes settled on my ski pants and he ordered me to his office for wearing leggings. Once inside, after the usual lecture about how rules are rules, I played my best hand; I popped off my shoe, exposing the fabric stirrup that was to save me. A simple strip in a stretchy polyester/Lycra mix was all that lay between me and a right rollicking.

Triumphantly I flashed the bottom of my trousers, showing that I wasn't actually wearing leggings at all but SKI PANTS! In your face, Dyson! Mwahaha.

I watched him gaze at the stirrups and waited for his face to crumple as he realised that on this occasion he was beat. Maybe he'd use his hankie as a surrender flag?

Instead he said, 'They're still leggings,' and sent me home to change.

Despite my battle with Mr Dyson I did enjoy my time at sixth form. I liked my chosen subjects, English Literature, English Language (we were convinced our two English teachers were secretly in love, Mr Jones and Mrs Smith; he had big square specs, matching mousey beard and floppy hair), Geography and Theatre Studies. Especially that last one. In my second year a new pupil arrived who was so good at drama you could see the teacher's eyes shine with excitement; like pirates opening a treasure chest, they knew they'd found something special. And they had; the girl with the broad accent, white-blonde hair and penchant for blocky heels and chunky knitwear was Maxine Peake, now an award-winning actor of both stage and screen. I like to think that I can take some credit for her career success – surely watching my faltering performance of a *Medea* soliloquy inspired her to try even harder.

During my time at Canon Slade I started to wear glasses, having obviously inherited not only my mum's knobbly knees and jumper bumps but also her less-than-perfect vision. I was actually quite thrilled that I was officially slightly short-sighted; during my 'faux fainting' years I'd always tried to cheat at colour-blindness tests, pretending I couldn't make out the number nine or the letter T written in different shades to the background colour. I was desperate to be officially declared medically lacking or different in some way – oh to be diagnosed as having something as exotic and exciting as colour-blindness! It never happened, though – the opticians always saw through my lame attempts to fake it. I clearly wasn't the first kid – and probably not the last – to try to fool them.

Imagine my excitement when a decade later it was revealed that I needed to wear glasses when I needed to see the whiteboard in class and for driving. A lovely tortoiseshell pair were picked out and I was absolutely thrilled. The only issue was that my mum came with me and with the two-for-one deal on offer she thought it'd be a great idea if, like her, I had one pair with 'react-to-light' lenses, which automatically darken when subjected to bright sunshine but when indoors remain clear. The only problem was that they never darkened quite enough to look cool like sunglasses and they took ages to lighten up when I came back in from outdoors, meaning that when I lost my regular pair and had to wear the react-to-light ones, I spent the majority of my time in lessons looking like a Roy Orbison tribute act.

Despite my unusual look, I had some really lovely pals at sixth form. Take Sonja, who was fully obsessed with Madonna and lived in a huge, higgledy-piggledy three-storey house. Sonja's room was on the third floor so her mum, to save her voice, kept a big brass handbell at the bottom of the stairs to ring when she needed Sonja to come down to the phone when one of us rang her.

Sonja with her poker-straight, long dark-blonde hair, who would pause and widen her eyes while pursing her lips to add extra va-va-voom to the nugget of juicy gossip she was about to impart, the facial equivalent of rolling out a red carpet for her salacious titbit to make its grand entrance.

And there was lots of gossip – Sonja came out in the first year, which we all found extremely exciting. We all threw ourselves into the big gay adventure that followed. Like Mickey Mouse in *Fantasia*, Sonja was at the centre while we all swirled around, engulfed by the excitement of her love life – late-night phone calls, bitter break-ups and passionate make-ups. We loved it. We'd all troop off to Blackpool to drink in gay bars with her, feeling ever so worldly. We loved the drama – listening, rapt, in the common room as she laid out all of her complicated affairs on the communal table and painstakingly untangled them for us like dozens of balls of wool.

Sonja's audience was made up of myself and Rebecca, who had huge brown eyes, a gap in her front teeth and dark wavy hair that reached down to her bottom. She worshipped Prince and I still can't hear 'Diamonds and Pearls' without thinking of her.

There was also Louise, crow-black, poker-straight hair, a penchant for thin black velvet chokers and as sarcastic as she was straight-talking. Think Wednesday Addams with excellent liquid eye-liner.

We'd all go to 'Flesh' at the legendary Haçienda on a Wednesday night. By now it was 1993 and the halcyon days of the club were behind it, but Flesh was still special – an intoxicating mix of gay men, lesbians, drag queens and party girls. We were the latter, drawn partly by the music, the style, the crazy crowd bedecked in leather, lace and fishnet, but mainly because we felt safe there; it was less intimidating than in the more alpha-male days of old. One of the night's promoters, Paul Cons, has been quoted as saying 'This isn't Madchester any more – it's Gaychester.'

Flesh was fun, inclusive, friendly. It throbbed with personality and slight craziness. I could wear what I wanted, even be, as the *Sun* newspaper would say, 'scantily clad' without feeling like it was a meat market – once we'd run the gauntlet past the slavering bulldog bouncers.

One week as I danced I was approached by an older girl, who slipped a flyer into my hand – she was scouting for people to be in the audience of *Dance Energy*, a 'yoof' music show on BBC2 hosted by a DJ called Normski. I went along to the recording, so somewhere there is footage of an eighteen-year-old me dancing self-consciously in the background in a starkly lit studio wearing my faux-leopard jacket.

I absolutely loved the girls I was friends with, but I found them complicated. The sands of friendship would always be shifting and from day to day you'd never know where you stood. I'd literally wave goodbye to my friends on a Thursday afternoon and we'd be all smiles and everything hunky-dory, then the next time I'd see them, on Friday morning, there'd be a frosty silence shrouding their table in the common room and they would be cool with me, exchanging knowing glances with each other. It was like starring in a soap opera where no one ever gave me the scripts.

Each day I'd walk in not knowing whether I'd be met by smiles or silence and I found it mentally exhausting. I'd been put through the mangle by the bullies at secondary school so I was extra-sensitive to animosity. Of course these girls weren't being horrible on purpose – everyone at this age was just busy working out who they were and what they were about and that involved sometimes nudging the weakest chick from the nest if they needed more space. They certainly weren't bullies, just helpless passengers clinging on a runaway chariot of their own hormones.

And I was weak – I always felt frustrated by my cowardliness, for not being able just to blurt out how I felt, stick up for myself, push back a little when people tried to intimidate me. Instead I shrank away from confrontation. I've always been familiar with the feeling of pushing my head into the sand. This is what I did with the girls – I didn't fit in with them so I slowly melted away, out of their grasp, away from their drama.

31. Plaque in the Attic

Luckily I was put out of my misery by meeting Ani, a lad in the year below me who became my first love. Ani was many things – charming, hilarious, witty and kind – and he had what I saw as the perfect family which, I'm now slightly ashamed to say, I was very in awe of and envied. I was happy at home but things weren't always easy; Mum was busy and stressed and life above the pub wasn't the most relaxing. By comparison, Ani's house was a stone-covered cottage down a country lane and his dad Jeff was an art teacher, all slightly wild grey wavy hair, slouchy jeans and Birkenstocks, hippy vibes with a bit of edge. Jeff loved to hang out with us in the kitchen, taking the mickey, cracking gags while tall gangly Ani warmed his arse on the Aga.

My mum used to laugh because customers at her pub would say to her, 'Hey, Jackie, I saw your daughters earlier, walking hand in hand.' Yvonne was away at this point, so she knew the 'daughter' in question was in fact Ani. He had straight dark-blond hair that fell below his shoulders and from the back, with his long legs and willowy figure, could easily be mistaken for a girl.

His face, though, was handsome, with bright, kind eyes and full lips, which he often gently chewed on while chatting, as if mulling over his next quip.

He was a really lovely lad with a lovely family. His mum was a petite yet formidable woman called Val, who had sharply bobbed hair and was a lawyer. She was faintly terrifying because she seemed to be able to look into my very soul whenever she asked what we'd been up to. I thought she was awesome though; she was always kind to me and the deep love she felt for her sons always shone from her, even when she was interrogating us on what time we'd got in and where we'd been. I thought at the time that they were the perfect family, even though we all know that doesn't actually exist.

Ani – a nickname acquired at birth when his toddler brother Jeremy couldn't pronounce Antony – had a bunch of brilliant friends and they quickly became my friends too. I'd found my tribe. Boys seemed a lot less complicated than girls and I loved being one of the lads. You'd never meet up after college to find that one of them was inexplicably not talking to you. The worst they'd do was nick your seat when you went to the loo and tell you when you came back that you'd been 'taxed'.

There were about eight of us who hung out and, from sixth form to when I eventually left for London at twenty, they were a big part of my life. The lads were hilarious, sarcastic, daft and strangely caring in a gruff way. There was a uniform – baggy jeans and Karrimor or Berghaus Gore-tex jackets, the latter designed for mountaineering, though the only expeditions they were used for were hanging around the chippy and scouting for magic mushroom patches on the playing fields.

No one really went by their given names, instead preferring a bastardisation of their surname – Braddy, Middy, Briggy, Fitz

– and Fads, who answered to this name even though it stood for 'Fat and dopey shit'. He wasn't particularly fat (although he did, as my dad would say, 'Have enough cover on him') and wasn't dopey, more affable. I think it speaks volumes about his lack of insecurity that he not only answered to the name but found it humorous.

We looked out for each other and smoked, played *Street Fighter III* and listened to the Kinks and the Orb in the attic of Phil's massive house in Bolton. Phil had dark floppy hair framing huge round eyes that looked too big for his slender face and he had a fine patter in hippy-leaning pseudo-philosophy. He paid homage to those years in the attic by getting the *Screamadelica* album cover tattooed on his upper arm – we played that Primal Scream record to death.

Phil's parents very much took the view that if their son was going to get up to the usual teen behaviour they'd rather he did it under their roof. And they let all his mates in too.

I spent so many hours in Phil's attic with the lads that there should be some sort of plaque there commemorating the formative years that occurred under that roof among a gang of pals, laughing and nobbing about.

I'm still grateful to those lads for, if not quite taking me under their wing, at least letting me be part of their crew. Growing up on the farm I was always comfortable in the company of men – from the lads helping out at haymaking to my big brothers and their friends to trips with Dad in his wagon, chatting to the geezers at the depots – I admired their uncomplicated friendships with each other, the easy conversations, the relaxed banter. It's no real shock that after slipping away from the dramas of my girlfriends I felt relieved to be hanging out with Ani, Phil and the rest of the lads.

*   *   *

My relationship with Ani lasted about three years and could be tempestuous – I loved the bones of him but I was immature, despite being a year older than him, and I think I found this 'love' lark a little overwhelming. I was insecure and jealous, easily threatened if he spoke to other girls, even though his behaviour was always exemplary. I was just daft and young. For a huge part of the relationship, my sulks aside, there was a lot of laughter and fun times. He was a brilliant, gentle, good lad and the perfect person to do some growing up with; together we trod that awkward path between teenagerdom and adulthood, navigating the bumps along the way. I consider myself very lucky that my first love was such a sorted person.

32. Molehills

During this time I lived about a quarter of a mile away from Phil above a pub called the Pineapple Inn. It was a stone building on the corner of Blackburn Road and a massive dual carriageway called Moss Bank Way. I've no idea why it was called the Pineapple but I always thought it was a strange name for a pub.

The public area was on the ground floor and consisted of two rooms – the smarter room, with old-fashioned table lamps on the deep windowsills and floral-covered seats, and the games room. The bar was in the middle, separating the two. There was a narrow corridor that ran between the two rooms and, running off that, the doors to the backyard and the loos, which were opposite the public coin-operated phone.

Mum and Ken were tenants in the pub, employed by the brewery who owned the bricks and mortar. Mum was landlady and Ken was the landlord – he was mild-mannered and definitely the good cop in there while Mum was, not bad cop but definitely badass cop. Lads who were pratting about and generally misbehaving would quiver as the small shadow of Mum fell across them. Everyone loved my mum and the minute she told someone to behave, they did. She may have been belly-button height to most of the big bruisers but they still did as she told them.

The games room consisted of a pool table in the far corner next to the dartboard and next to that the fruit machine and jukebox. Men would come in here for a pint on the way home from work and it was fine if they had mucky work clothes on as this room wasn't posh like the other, 'best', room. There were maroon faux-leather banquettes with matching seats, wipe-clean in case grease, booze or blood got spilled. The tabletops had a shiny dappled bronze effect, with thousands of tiny indents on the surface, perfect for collecting drips of bitter or tiny flakes of fag ash. These of course were the days of smoking in pubs. People complain that now pubs smell of stale beer and farts, but at least that can't give you cancer. Well, I don't think so. Fart cancer sounds bad.

Each table had a large tin ashtray gifted by the breweries, emblazoned with 'Tetleys' or 'Guinness' or whatever. By the end of the night, if it was busy, they'd be close to overflowing, piled high with little molehills of grey ash and dozens of cigar-ette butts, some glossy with transferred lipstick.

When I was working a shift at the pub one of the jobs I hated most was 'doing the ashtrays' – I'd walk around with a little red plastic bucket and a paintbrush. I'd decant the contents of the ashtray into the bucket at arm's length to avoid the grey cloud that would billow up into my face, then whizz the paintbrush around the tray to dislodge any last traces of ash so they could be piled up and taken to be soaked in the big metal, trough-like sinks. At the end of each shift all the glasses were loaded into the massive glass-washers behind the bar, whose scalding hot steam would rush up into your face; the jukebox and fruit machine were unplugged and fell silent and dark. I loved the pub when it was closed; it was like a sleeping beast – dark, calm, subdued. It was so spacious and as I unstacked the clean ashtrays and put them out on the tables I'd always play the same song on the jukebox – Bjork's 'Violently Happy'.

When the pub was in full swing, though, all the action happened in this more relaxed games room, the pool table and the customers being looked down upon by framed black and white photos of former Bolton Wanderers players, whole squads surveying them like the ancient ancestors looking down in *Mulan*.

If you could make your way through the smoke to the jukebox you could put on a tune, but only if you beat Wayne to it. Wayne was one of the regulars – he was a heavyset biker dude, complete with a ZZ Top beard that looked out of place on his young face, which was topped off with a red bandana tied on his head. He sported pale jeans and a black leather waistcoat over a T-shirt.

Wayne's favourite song on the jukebox was Meatloaf's 'I'd Do Anything For Love'. Inexplicably, the version on the jukebox was the album version, which was a face-melting twelve minutes long. He'd put his three plays to good use by selecting this song for each one, which resulted in an ear-spanking thirty-six minutes of Meatloaf. You'd always know when Wayne was in because 'I'd Do Anything For Love' would be blasting out of the jukebox; it was his walk-on music, as well as his sitting-down-drinking-beer music, popping-to-the-loo music and walk-off music for when he slipped into his biker jacket and left the pub. He certainly got his quid's worth.

Whatever was playing on the jukebox had to battle to be heard above the general pub hubbub that increased with every hour and every unit of alcohol consumed. There were some real characters in the pub, like Dave the stonemason, who by day fashioned gravestones from big blocks of granite and by night enjoyed a banter and a pint of bitter. He was a big bloke, ruddy-faced with clouds of grey hair and matching tache. On his arm was always his lovely pocket-sized partner Freda, small and curvy like a Russian stacking doll, with a big laugh and tight silver perm.

Next to them were Michael and Marlene, a couple who I thought were very glamorous; she was well-spoken, in her fifties, with expensive-looking blonde hair cut in a flattering short bob. She was very stylish and had a touch of the Helen Mirrens about her. Michael was a few years younger and his hair was receding, but he still had a decent covering of tight auburn curls that ran in a wide strip round the back of his head and a runway that carpeted the top of his head. He was a trim bloke and an alpha male – chest thrust out like someone had just put an ice-cube down his back, fond of wearing a lambswool V-neck in maroon or baby blue set off by a fine gold chain round his neck and a gold Rolex. He was a bit of a twinkly-eyed rogue – a former bad boy, past his battling days but a good bloke to have about if you needed an extra pair of hands or, rather fists. He had a gift – he could always sense when there was discord in the air. The secret signal to the rest of us that trouble was afoot was when Michael calmly took off his watch and put it on the bar so it wasn't damaged in the anticipated melee.

The Pineapple wasn't generally rough, to be fair, but there'd be occasional trouble. Too much booze combined with the posturing of the young and stupid sometimes led to fights. One morning Mum was wiping down the radiator next to the pool table, which would normally be the cleaner's job. I asked her what she was doing and she replied matter-of-factly, 'They were bloody battling last night and blood got splashed on the bloody radiator' – she said it in the casual manner of someone discussing the weather at a bus stop. That was a bit of an eye-opener – poor Mum having to do that, plus some poor bugger was waking up with a radiator imprint on their face.

There'd also be parties sometimes, big, rowdy, drunken affairs that meant loads of people and new faces flocking in to wave off a mate. But they weren't for a pal who was emigrating or off on a gap year backpacking round Oz; they were for someone who was off to prison. Their date for sentencing was imminent and they would be having a pre-nick knees-up. Inevitably we'd see the same crowd again, usually a few months later, when their mate was released.

Twice there was fighting during my shift and Mum shouted at me to call the police – usually Michael, Ken and a couple of locals would have managed to shove the troublemakers through the front door and out into the street, bolting it shut behind them, but then the idiots would hang around outside, trying to boot the front door in or threatening to put the windows through.

I can't remember feeling scared – I found the process massively exciting.

999 operator (serious and professional): 'Which service do you need?'

Me (squeaky and secretly thrilled): 'Police please!'

I was harbouring some small shreds of ambition to join the force (mainly because I wanted to be in the mounted division – another bid at finding a career that involved me sitting on a horse for large parts of it) and to me just making this call made me feel a step closer. I mean I was literally part of a live police operation!

Police operator (gruff and calm): 'You're through to the police, what's the situation please?'

Me (excited and pumped but now fully aware that I'm basically IN THE POLICE so trying to rein in the squeakiness): 'Yes, there are three people trying to kick down the front door of me mum's pub . . .'

Within minutes we'd hear the sirens, the lads outside would usually scarper and the games room would be bathed in a blue glow as the flashing lights shone through the gaps in the curtains. The local constabulary would be there, rounding up any remaining idiots who were either too drunk or too stupid to run off, or both. I used to love the police officers. They'd come in for a statement from Mum and Ken, pink-cheeked with adrenaline from sorting out the troublemakers outside in the cold, and I'd hang about, giving the bar an extra wipe down, ears wagging.

Once the police had left, there'd be a lengthy lock-in for a major debrief where the drama was discussed over a few bevvies until the wee small hours. Discussed and perhaps built up a bit – by the end there had probably been thirty-five assailants, six helicopters and a samurai sword fight on the pool table.

On the whole, though, the Pineapple was just a regular pub. These few thrilling instances of sirens and shouting aside, most of the noise came from the frantic thumping of the thick end of the pool cues against the floor in celebration of a good shot, a rumbling noise that could be clearly heard upstairs in our living quarters.

The pool table was put to good use by me and my friends; on occasion we'd sneak in after hours to play pool and eke out the last minutes of our night out while Mum and Ken slept upstairs.

Through a large black door next to the pool table was the entrance to our home; a cold, sterile white corridor led to our back door and the stairs that took us up away from the smells and (most of) the sounds of the pub and into the peace of the upstairs living quarters. The set-up was, to say the least, bizarre, as if each room was a dice that'd been shaken in a giant's hand and tossed onto a table, settling in a higgledy-piggledy pattern.

Mum and Ken's bedroom didn't have its own entrance, so to get to my bedroom I had to walk through theirs. The only bathroom was an en suite that was also attached to their room, meaning they had no privacy at all, their supposedly private inner sanctum racking up roughly the same footfall as Oxford Street on the last Saturday before Christmas. This was when I was between the ages of seventeen and twenty and my social life was in full bloom, so I'd often be coming home at all times of night, walking tipsily through their bedroom as they slept, clattering around in the bathroom.

Being a parent now, I can see how annoying that was. It's annoying enough having to shoo my kids out of my bedroom and they're pretty small, but great big galumphing teens trampling through my room? No thanks.

There was a spare box room that served as an office and had a sash window, and on sunny summer days I would climb out and onto the flat roof to sunbathe. Like a burglar obsessed with soft furnishings, I would squeeze through the open window with armfuls of cushions and towels to lie on. I'd lie there on the roof of the pub, which was about half the size of a squash court with a two-foot-high wall running round the edge, and sunbathe like I was kicking back in the French Riviera, never mind the traffic of the major dual carriageway rumbling past a few feet below as I lay there in my bikini. When the sun went in, so did I. I'd always have to shower because my skin would be covered in tiny black flecks of dust and pollution from the traffic roaring by below that had settled on my skin, sticking to the slick of Mum's leftover Hawaiian Tropic I'd slathered on.

The lounge was at the front of the building and looked out through big sash windows over the traffic outside, and it was here I'd lie prone on the sofa, psyching myself up for a shift at the pub. I'd work on a Sunday night, starting my shift at 8 p.m. and – thanks to Sunday opening hours – finishing at 11 p.m., getting thirty quid from Mum for my efforts. In one way it's kinda jammy to live above your place of work – no schlepping around in the cold, no missing the bus to work, no shelling out for taxis home – but the downside was you could always hear the sound of the pub. I know this made it difficult for Mum and Ken to switch off. I, on the other hand, was so good at switching off that my problem was switching back on again. I'd lie on the sofa on a Sunday evening until one minute to eight; if I heard the beginning of the *Heartbeat* theme I knew I was late and I'd have to scarper downstairs before the phone trilled – Mum, calling from downstairs to chivvy me along.

I didn't really blossom as a barmaid. I hated having to work, though of course I loved the cash. I could and still can pour a decent pint and was pretty good at the maths, I just couldn't be bothered to make an effort with the social side – the banter with the customers that Mum was so good at, taking an interest, making small talk. Ironically, I'd probably make a brilliant barmaid now – I love talking to people and I'm naturally nosey, a combination that means I can talk for hours on the radio. When I've been asked how I sound so cheery when I'm broadcasting early or late, live on the wireless, I often put it down to Mum's example – no matter what was going on in her personal life or if she was tired or fed up, she'd have to put it behind her, pop on her lippy, run a comb through her hair and get behind that bar, and that's what I do on the radio (but without the lipstick – and sometimes without brushing my hair).

Most of the customers found me quite stroppy, and a few used to ask me outright why I was so miserable.

To them I was this studenty-looking girl, different from them in my vintage striped polo necks and tight cords. My hair was long and straight, not permed, and I wore no make-up, unlike the women who had made an effort and put their face on to come out for a Sunday night in the pub.

It didn't help that I've always had what's now called a 'resting bitch face', so even when I'm happy as not only Larry but his equally jubilant brothers Barry and Harry, if I'm not grinning then my mouth naturally curves down slightly, making me look like I've just smelled some very off pâté. My whole life I've been helpfully advised by builders and random men (always men!) to 'Smile' because 'it might never happen' when I've dared walk past them without a rictus grin plastered on my face. My sister Yvonne has the same facial issues, which didn't help our already fractious relationship because we'd both think the other was giving them a dirty look. I've got into arguments at school about it, all because I naturally look so miffed. When I start working with a new person now I always warn them I'm not furious, it's JUST MY FACE. The irony is that on the whole I'm not a glass-half-empty but a glass-overfloweth kinda gal. I'm annoyingly positive. Of course, I didn't know all this about myself at the age of seventeen as I stood there pouring pints of mild behind the bar, and the customers didn't know it either. It was just shyness and immaturity, but I guess it came across as arrogance, and to them I was simply a mystery wrapped in a snooty cow.

33. Grey Mafia

I should've been used to being behind the bar – I'd already worked for Mum for years. I started back in Boothstown, where Mum and Ken ran the Conservative Club. Being about ten years old, I was only back-room staff. They had a big upstairs room where people would throw wedding receptions and retirement parties and, as the guests couldn't live on warm Chardonnay alone, Mum would do the catering. I loved helping her.

I would spend hours finessing a large plate of crudités and salad; I was famous (in our house anyway) for the intricate arrangements of cherry tomatoes I would produce on huge foil platters, creating fabulous patterns with fresh veg, a mandala made entirely of your five-a-day.

I loved being Mum's sous chef and going with her to collect the hot pasties from Carrs, a famous Bolton pastie shop. We'd go in Mum's little Austin Metro hatchback and she'd put the big plastic tray of pasties in the boot. The heat from the pasties would steam up all the windows of the little car and the incredible smell of the buttery shortcrust pastry, potatoes and beef would fill the car so it was like we were driving along in a pastie on wheels.

I would wipe the drool from my chin with crossed fingers, hoping for a cat to run out, causing Mum to slam on, hurling the pasties forward and breaking one in two so we could have half each, but it never happened. It was torture.

Mum would dish out the pasties with steaming pale mushy peas. I still love Carrs pasties; I always have some in the freezer and served them at my wedding reception a few years ago and they went down a storm.

From Boothstown we moved to Astley Bridge in Bolton, where Mum and Ken took over as steward and stewardess of the Conservative Club there. I used to work there too, promoted from tomato artist to the dizzy heights of glass collector.

It was during these years that I used to joke that I was raised by Post-it notes. Every afternoon when I got home from school, Mum and Ken would be at work and in their place would be a paper trail of yellow squares instructing me what I needed to do.

They were always in Mum's big writing – she writes as she talks: loudly. From chores ('Sarah please wipe up' – stuck to the draining board) to instructions ('please feed dog') and the nicer ones ('Chilli for tea, zap in mic') and then at the end of this yellow informational bunting 'Luv you' – 'love' spelled in that colloquial way that she still does now, much to the amusement of my kids. As a working mum I now fully appreciate the luv she showed by leaving those notes. Even in absentia she was still looking after me. She worked really hard but she made sure I didn't come home to an empty, cold house. It was warm and lit against the winter dusk and those notes showed she loved me and she was there with me, in paper form. Now I do the same for my teenage daughter in the modern version of Post-it notes, texts. Her phone buzzes with my maternal love – checking what time she's home, dinner instructions, homework nudges, signed off with a 'Love You'.

Mum and Ken worked hard at Astley Bridge Conservative Club, which was a red-brick cube with a blue stripe round the top and one round its middle, like an iced cake. The building squatted beside a flagpole just a few metres away from our front door. The only thing separating it from Moss Bank Way, a busy dual carriageway, was its square car park, tucked in the front of it like a napkin.

Mum and Ken ran the club on a day-to-day basis, serving behind the bar, keeping the cellar ticking over and doing the books, but it was actually ruled with an iron fist by 'the committee'.

The committee were a gang of elderly men who were retired and clearly missed the cut and thrust of industry. Instead of spending the autumn of their years travelling, playing bridge or trying Pilates they instead became a kind of grey mafia, wielding their power over my mum with all the vim and vigour they should've saved for a crown green bowling ball.

Like the mafia they were all well turned out, in smart grey suits, and had glamorous septuagenarian wives on their gold cufflinked arms, who were the twinset and pearls crew. Also like the mafia, they revelled in their notoriety and could be ruthless smiling assassins, the cabaret lights glinting off their dentures as they grinned at you before stabbing you in the back.

Mum and Ken worked all the hours God sent at that place but never felt they got the recognition or respect they deserved from the committee, who would often override their decisions. The customers and staff all loved Mum and Ken, though, and that's what mattered to them.

* * *

Downstairs in the club was a large, smart room with plush seats and pale soft furnishings, and the sports room, which was huge, containing two full-size snooker tables, always with clouds of ciggie smoke hanging over clusters of men gathered around the tables in pastel V-neck jumpers.

The rooms were separated by the hallway, from where you could walk up the sweeping blue swirly-carpeted staircase past a huge gold-framed photograph of Queen Elizabeth II (the 1960s glam brunette version) and into the upstairs concert room.

This was where all the glitz and glamour happened. During the week it lay quiet and still but at the weekends it sprang into life. It was a large oblong room with all the seating favouring a large stage, painted black, at the end with a well-sprung dark wood dance floor in front of it and a long bar running along one side and windows along the other.

Weekends it would be packed with customers dressed up to the nines; women in their best dresses and jewellery, hair blow-dried to glossy perfection, lipsticked and powdered to the max. There really was an air of old-school Hollywood glamour about the place – sure, a lot of the customers were of a more impressive vintage than any bottle on the wine list, but they could still turn on the glitz come Saturday and Sunday nights.

The man in charge of making sure everything went with a swing was Paul the compère; in his early fifties, he had hair dyed jet black and sported a shiny black shirt that was tucked in at the bottom to gently wrestle his slight paunch into submission, and unbuttoned enough at the top to show a suggestion of manly chest hair to thrill the laydeez.

On Saturdays and Sundays before the evening's live entertainment commenced, Paul would wheel an old-fashioned bingo ball out onto the stage. It looked like a wire globe with a handle to turn it at one end and multicoloured balls in the middle.

Everyone would produce the bingo cards they'd purchased on the way in and it was eyes down for a couple of games before the cabaret began.

I thought Paul was awesome – he commanded the stage, striding up and down, warming up the audience before the other acts came on. He was a TV repair man by day but by night he was a star – a club singer and minor celebrity in his own right. Paul always had a touch of the Vegas about him – Astley Bridge Conservative Club was his Caesars Palace.

Paul always included Bruce Springsteen's 'Dancing in the Dark', The Searchers' 'Love Potion Number Nine' and Elvis's 'Suspicious Minds' in his set, accompanied by the house band, a couple of blokes on keyboard and drums.

Paul would break a sweat by the first chorus, face red, veins in his forehead throbbing with the strain of conjuring up the Boss and the King in one set.

Once Paul had done the opening song and patted down his brow, he'd introduce the first performer – maybe a female singer in a sparkly trouser suit and big hair, singing everything from Tyler to Turner, a local stand-up telling jokes about the missus and her mum – 'Take my mother-in-law – no, really, take her, please' – or a magician pulling stuff out of a hat.

Refreshment in between sets could be found at the bar, where Mum and her staff did their best to keep the booze flowing. Sometimes Mum would do pasties and peas to help soak up the drinks. By the end of the evening the room would be swinging and a lot of couples would take to the dance floor as Paul closed the evening, busting a gut to give it some welly on stage with another couple of big songs before the main lights went up, pint pots and Slim Jims were drained and the audience wobbled unsteadily down the stairs and out to their waiting minicabs.

Peter Kay always says his toughest audience is playing in

Bolton, his home town – everyone loves him but the funny stuff he says is almost too familiar to a local audience. I know what he means – cabaret nights at the Connie Club were basically the Phoenix Club.

My job at the Connie Club, because at fifteen I was too young to work behind the bar, was stacking the empty glasses in great swaying towers in my arms, squeezing between the seats at the weekends when it was busy, trying to appear invisible to avoid a stand-up making a wisecrack about me.

I enjoyed it – I loved having a few quid in my pocket and loved watching Mum run the upstairs bar like a conductor directing an orchestra. She kept everyone happy, customers and her bar staff, darting around, a blur of streaked permed hair and coral lipstick. At the weekends she was in charge of the big bar upstairs while Ken ran the downstairs rooms. Mum knew all the customers by what they drank, like Dad might tell his cattle apart by a dark patch of fur near their eye or a very curly face. 'You know, Jim,' she'd say, 'half a mild,' or sometimes it'd be 'Jenny, frizzy hair, G&T.' I worked hard, the glasses smelled of stale booze dregs and the main room upstairs was smoky and noisy. On cabaret nights it was always rammed and I'd spend the whole night running back and forth with armfuls of glasses, loading and unloading the glass-washing machines, replenishing the shelves with clean glasses.

My undoing here wasn't to be my work ethic but my dress sense. Or, some may argue, lack of sense when it came to how I dressed. I had the attitude of a regular fifteen-year-old, wearing my budding sexuality with a casual nonchalance. I had long slim legs up to my armpits and long dark-blonde hair down my back but wasn't really aware of how I looked. The bullying at school had undermined my confidence and I didn't realise that I was blossoming into a pretty young thang. This fact hadn't escaped the notice of the committee wives, though, and my mum was convinced that they had a hand, or rather a voice, in my dismissal.

For my part, I didn't see anything wrong with the outfits I wore but this was the reason the committee gave when they went over my mum's head and sacked me. My offence? Wearing hot pants. It remains one of my favourite sentences – 'I was fired for wearing hot pants.'

The committee dealt with it by informing my mum after a meeting that I was no longer employed as a glass collector. I love that nestled among the usual business to be discussed in the meeting – profit margins, proposed renovation of ladies' toilets – were me and my hot pants.

I loved hot pants and used to sport them with thick black tights, chunky shoes, a white shirt with a black sweater over the top and shirt cuffs pulled out in the dandy style that was all the rage in 1989. I thought I looked marvellous but I probably looked like a weird Dickensian pageboy.

What was the crime exactly? Malicious flashing of thigh? Distraction by hot pant? I did my job well enough but I imagine the committee wives with their crispy duck décolletages didn't appreciate someone on the cusp of fruitful womanhood bending over tables in front of their old husbands and jeopardising their blood pressure. I was completely oblivious to all this; I was just trying to reach the empty glasses.

We laugh about it now but back then Mum was fuming at the treatment we got from the committee and it soured her relationship with them beyond repair. A year or so later we left Hotpantgate and the committee behind when Mum and Ken decided to go for tenancy at the Pineapple pub, approximately 100 yards away, where I would go on to become the world's sulkiest barmaid.

34. Running on Fumes

It was just before we left the Connie Club that I started to learn how to drive – after the Scotland débâcle we'd finally scrapped the Renault 12 and were now the proud owners of a shiny second-hand Austin Metro in navy blue. This was to be my ticket to the highways and byways of Bolton, my ticket to freedom.

My teacher was a man called Derek who also drove an Austin Metro, which was clearly the car to be driving in the very early nineties. Derek was a nice enough chap who made cheesy quips and laughed too loudly at his own jokes, his guffaw escaping from underneath his neat black moustache. He would pull up outside our terraced house and toot the horn of his little red car, which was plastered in L-plates and had paintwork decorated with ads for his driving school. Every time I got in the car he'd reach in his top pocket for a little tin of breath mints, which were small, round and white. Barely able to suppress his chortling in anticipation of the joke he was about to tell, he'd hold out the mints and ask, 'Do you want an E?' Without fail I'd politely decline and he'd burst into fits of laughter before popping a mint in his mouth and needlessly reassuring me they weren't actually Ecstasy tablets.

It was the rave era and Ecstasy was occasionally hitting the headlines and this was Derek's peculiar attempt to be down with the kids. Still, he was patient and relaxed and, recreational drug quips aside, he was a good teacher.

Mum was keen to help me pass my driving exam because the fewer the lessons and the fewer the tests the less it all cost. Plus once I could drive, just as I'd be free of having to beg her for lifts she'd be free of being begged to run a one-woman taxi service. Thanks to Dad I'd been able to drive a tractor since the age of twelve, so I think I had already fine-tuned my spatial awareness and confidence with manoeuvring a vehicle. Plus a David Brown tractor was massive compared to a Metro, so how hard could it be?

In fact, not very hard as it happened. I loved driving and I'm forever grateful to Mum for her patience, bravery and generosity in donating both her time and hard-earned cash to the cause. It seems completely mad to me that anybody would be willing to sit in the passenger seat as their teenage offspring takes charge of one and a half tons of metal, commandeering it around the roads among other cars filled with people, but that's what she did and what loads of parents do – and what I'll be doing at some point. Eek.

So Mum and I would set off for a twenty-minute pootle in the Metro – out onto the dual carriageway to do a circuit of Astley Bridge, Mum only occasionally slamming her own right foot down on a non-existent brake pedal in the passenger foot-well, her instinct to survive overriding the fact she was in the wrong seat. We'd return home to Manley Terrace and Mum had a wee victory catchphrase she loved to yell as we turned in to the street – 'Slowly into Manley!' she'd exclaim as we rolled round the corner and came to a halt outside the house.

Dad used to let me have the odd go in the jeep on the lane, where I'd bunny-hop the car along because I couldn't master the clutch control; he'd claim I didn't have petrol in it but 'kangaroo juice' because of the big uncontrollable leaps we'd make. The tractor and the jeep, but mainly Mum and Derek's hard work, meant that after eleven lessons I passed my test. I was so thrilled. I loved driving and still do; I've always loved the open road. Maybe I link long journeys back to Dad and the only time I got him all to myself, when we were out in the wagon.

When we go up north or drive for a UK holiday now, it's me who does the majority of the driving. Once the kids are set up with their own in-car entertainments, I pop Jeremy Vine on and I'm off. With my wagon-driving genes, I want to get as many miles under my belt as possible before stopping for anything as indulgent as a loo stop or leg-stretch, though eventually I have to give in to the demands of my family. It's on those journeys that I always think I could do with one of 'Len's Ham Pockets'.

Once I'd passed my test I was allowed to use Mum's Metro. All I had to do was follow the three golden rules – keep the car tidy, absolutely no smoking in the car, and always keep the petrol topped up.

Rule one was regularly flouted, rule two only very occasionally, but sadly rule three, due to lack of funds and common sense, was impossible to obey.

There would be many times when I'd get a rollicking because I'd left the car, in Mum's words, 'running on fumes', which was bad for the engine and for Mum's mental health. I got away with a lot. I only hope there are some crumbs of comfort for Mum in the fact that all this annoying teen behaviour is now being inflicted on me by my own daughter – yes, it's started already, the mess, the 'borrowing'/losing of my stuff. The universe is dishing up a steaming hotpot of *Schadenfreude* for my mum now as I'm left picking up after my offspring and picking my battles. As Elton John sings, 'It's the circle of life'.

Despite me making it run on fumes the Metro still managed to get me to Ani's house one New Year's Eve, when sadly it was to meet its demise.

On my way home to get ready to go out and celebrate, I turned right out of a small road. It was dusk, light was fading and the light-coloured car seemed to come out of nowhere; I just remember that in the split second before impact we had eye contact. I noticed she had her hair neatly wrapped in big Velcro rollers. She walloped straight into the driver's side with an ear-splitting crunch, pushing me and the Metro a few feet up the road. I was lucky for two reasons: she wasn't going fast and she ploughed into the middle of the side of the car, so the stronger bit between the front and back doors took the full force of the impact. If she'd hit the driver's door it would've been a different story.

I managed to get out of the Metro but it was a write-off – the roof had buckled upwards when the impact had crunched into the side. I felt terrible for the girl, who was en route home from the hairdressers prepped to hit the town for New Year's Eve. She and the police were very nice; it was my fault but it was an easy mistake to make when visibility was low. Mum arrived and burst into tears when she saw the state of her car – it did look pretty bad. I didn't even get shouted at; she was just relieved I was in one piece. She hugged me so tight I'm sure she dislodged a kidney.

It's moments like these with Mum that have made an

indelible mark on me and my parenting style. My kids know I shout, I snap, I rant, I grimace, but they also know that all I want is for them to be OK and that when it comes down to it, they're my number one. Mum worked hard and loved us so much and I feel more and more, as my kids grow, that as close as I was to Dad it was Mum who was always there. Like you don't notice air but you breathe it, Mum was always there even if I didn't always notice.

By night, barmaid, by day, average A level student. I got four A levels and left sixth form, but not before the leavers' do at a local hotel. Everyone wore their best frocks and black tie. It was to be a huge bash and I wore a long white John Richmond dress that was V-neck, clingy and sheer, like a T-shirt that had got mangled in the wash and ended up ankle-length and with a split. On my feet I sported some red espadrille wedges from Red or Dead, one of the coolest labels of the time. I felt lovely and thought I looked OK too. I wore my straight, dark-blonde hair down and just a bit of make-up. When I look at pictures from that night I think I look gorgeous but I was never terribly confident in myself – I still hung out with my crew of lads, was more comfortable in jeans and trainers, and the marks left on my psyche by bullies in the years before were deep and ingrained, so I didn't trust people easily, especially some of the girls at sixth form, who always seemed to have a snide remark bubbling just under the surface of their fake lip-glossed smiles.

I was right to be wary; some of these girls had come up with a mini awards ceremony that was to happen during the evening – it had the usual prom king and prom queen awards but then they announced the next award – the 'I love myself, somebody has to' award – oof! I thought, that's a bit cruel. I wouldn't want to be on the receiving end of THAT accolade. Then they read my name out and everything went a bit slow-motion: the look of anger on Ani's face, people's heads swivelling to see my reaction as my face burned with humiliation. I remember my head swimming as I went up to the stage to collect the award that nobody wanted; I was mortified – if they thought I was vain and loved myself they couldn't have been more wrong.

Making my way back from the stage compounded all my feelings about sixth form and the cruel, shallow, bitter clans of girls who could make people feel rubbish about themselves with a click of their French-manicured nails. If that's what they needed to do to validate their own feelings of lack of self-worth then they were the weak ones, not me.

Many years later when I became the 'Pretty Polly girl' – a modelling contract with the hosiery firm that in the nineties was quite a big deal – I felt like it was a bit of a fairytale ending, this ugly duckling becoming a 30-denier swan; it was a big two fingers sticking up at the bullies who made fun of me for everything from having long skinny legs and big lips to daring to look nice at the leavers' ball. Here I was suddenly being celebrated for the things that I was previously mercilessly teased for – not bad for a rubber-lipped crazy-legged crane who loved herself because someone had to.

35. Rhymes with Carer

I waved goodbye to sixth form in 1993 aged eighteen. I wondered what to do next. I had the whole summer to decide. My sister Yvonne was studying for a degree but I didn't much fancy following in her footsteps – from what she said she was constantly skint and she had holes in her shoes and there was fifteen of them living in a biscuit tin eating potatoes. Or something like that. I flirted with the idea of being a journalist and if my arm had been twisted I probably would've tried to study media somewhere.

Luckily fate stepped in and my plans changed, thanks – ironically enough – to Yvonne. Despite not feeling particularly inspired by my sister's uni experience, I wasn't daft, so when she went on a placement as part of her French degree to work in Paris and when she invited me to visit, I leapt at the chance.

I flew to Paris Charles de Gaulle and found my way to Yvonne's place, on the third floor of a narrow grey brick building in Montmartre. The apartment was too small to swing a *chat* in but I loved it. High ceilings, cream walls with ornate cornicing, wooden floors and a tiny wrought-iron balcony pinned on the front like a nose piercing.

This was the first time I actually started to realise there was life beyond Bolton; up until then Yvonne's need to backpack, InterRail and see the world was beyond my comprehension. Bolton had everything you could ever wish for, I'd thought; why would you want to leave? It was massive, all our family was there, it had a Body Shop and a Greggs and a drive-thru McDonalds was planned for nearby. It was Utopia.

During her uni holidays Yvonne was always off – from teaching English in Russia to travelling round China and Hong Kong, trekking in Nepal and surfing in Hawaii while I stayed in Bolton, working at the pub and hanging out in Phil's attic.

So Paris was a real eye-opener. Yvonne had a job to go to every day, working at the French Electricity Board, leaving me in the apartment armed with a door key and a metro map. This was before the days of mobile phones – nowadays you could pop any destination into Google Maps and your iPhone could basically be your nanny and tour guide all day, but back then I really was on my own.

I set off into the streets of Paris with only a very light smattering of GCSE French and a gung-ho attitude. Every morning I popped to the same patisserie for a pain au chocolate to eat en route. I insisted on ordering it in my pidgin French and every morning the same stroppy woman who served me replied in cross English, fury etched on her brow as if I'd just spat on her best blouse. But I loved the whole experience. Munching my breakfast, I'd set off on my adventures – art galleries and mooching along the banks of the Seine. None of it fazed me and I began to think maybe there was something in this travel lark. In Paris as I strode along I could've been anyone, not just a sulky barmaid.

At night-time Yvonne would whizz me out on the town and

we'd go for dins and dancing. At this distance from home she and I reinvented our relationship; we were no longer squabbling sisters but friends hanging out. In cabs Yvonne would direct the cabbie and get chatting to them and invariably they'd think she was French-Canadian – her grasp of the lingo was so good they presumed it was her first language. I remember feeling proud as punch of my sophisticated sis. She took me to her favourite restaurants and made me taste mouthfuls of beef that melted on my tongue, washed down with deep red wine. We blagged our way into Les Bains Douches, the city's coolest nightspot, where we danced – and shared a drink, seeing as they were fifty pounds a pop.

I was only there for a few days but it was life-changing. I felt like a veil had been removed from my eyes and suddenly I could see the big wide world out there that was mine for the taking – all you needed was a couple of quid for a train ticket and enough chutzpah to find your way around a bit. Then, on my last day in Paris, something happened that set me on the road to where I am today, though of course I didn't know that at the time.

I was out window-shopping, wandering around the city in the late spring sunshine. Career-wise I had no idea really what I wanted to do; I was ready and willing to be blown in any direction, like a feather. Fate happened to waft me into a small boutique, where I looked at the rails of clothes I couldn't afford. I felt the shop assistant sidle up to me from his perch behind the till.

He looked at me closely – he was a petite, slender guy with a huge flick of peroxide hair over one eye. In a strong French accent he asked "Ave you ever thought of being a model?'

Now, that line has got to be up there on the 'Lines that should make alarm bells ring' list, alongside 'Will you help me find my puppy?'

I fought the instinct to karate-chop him in the windpipe as he didn't seem remotely predatory – he hadn't exactly whipped a leopardskin rug out and asked me to get naked on it.

What he did whip out was a business card with the name of a Parisian model agency on it. He told me to call them as, according to him, I ''ad a very strong look for ze moment'.

I must confess I was surprised as I wasn't swimming in self-confidence, but, like a lot of girls, I'd occasionally wondered to myself if with my slender figure and decent height I'd be able to model – the nineties were the decade of the supermodel and I rather fancied not getting out of bed for less than ten grand thankyouverymuch.

Every year since I was about thirteen, for my birthday treat my mum and I had gone to Clothes Show Live at the Birmingham NEC when the TV fashion juggernaut rolled into town every December. It was the ultimate girls' day out and we loved it. The huge aircraft-hangar-sized exhibition space was taken over by clothes stalls, shoe shops, hairdressing demos, catwalk shows and modelling agencies scouting for the next big thing.

Models One, Select Models – all the biggies – had stands with people holding clipboards, subtly scanning the crowds of girls mooching around, hoping to spot a cheekbone you could slice cheese on or someone sporting an overstuffed sofa where their lips should be. These scouts were looking not for ready-made supermodels but for potential; in the right hands that gangly fourteen-year-old with the knock knees and lank hair could be on the cover of *Elle* and the catwalks of Milan within six months.

I was that gangly fourteen-year-old at the NEC but I was clearly yet to blossom even to the potential stage – no matter how many times I walked past the scouts they failed to spot my model good looks! I cringe now as I remember trying my best to nonchalantly sashay past the Models One stand, bracing myself, convinced that any second I would feel a hand grab at my arm as a clipboard-wielding person with an edgy haircut and a flick of eyeliner would stop me to pluck me from my Bolton life and catapult me to fame and fortune as I became the next Kate, Naomi or Linda.

If I'd told Mum she probably would've marched me up there, blinded as she was (and still is) by maternal love, believing I'm beautiful. Even now when I ask her opinion on an outfit she still proudly proclaims, as she's done since I was a teen, that I'd 'Look good in a bin bag.'

So this Parisian encounter was really rather exciting. To me the chance to model wasn't exciting because I was particularly passionate about fashion – rather, it would give me something to do other than become a university student. The clock was ticking on my summer and I'd need to decide what I wanted to do; a contract with a modelling agent could provide the perfect distraction for a couple of years.

I rang the agency that evening and it was decided that as I was leaving Paris the next morning I would go to their sister agency back home. MMA – Manchester Model Agency – was situated on the second floor of a beautiful Edwardian baroque building on the stylish St Ann's Square. The agency was run by an incredibly glamorous woman named Mavis who had a fondness for dusky pink, its hue liberally slathered over all the walls and soft furnishings in the waiting area. She had poker-straight, creamy blonde hair, with a fringe framing twinkly bright eyes. She was in her early fifties and behind the sweet, candy-pink-lipsticked smile she was clearly a tough businesswoman, managing to run her independent agency despite competition from other huge local agencies.

She wore half-moon glasses on a gold chain round her neck

and she'd pop these on her nose in order to peer closely at whomever she was chatting to. You always felt like she was scanning your face, weighing up strengths and weaknesses in your features. It took me back to being in the ring at the cattle shows, except this time it was me being studied, not the cow at the end of the rope I was holding. Like the cows, I would also be judged against the specimen next to me – was she thinner, taller, more eye-catching, more unique? The best of breed?

The first time I met Mavis, I waited with sweaty palms until she came out, introduced herself, and had a good nosey at my face. She thought I had potential and said she would allow me onto her 'modelling course', which involved me paying £150 for make-up and beauty tutorials and a photoshoot, the pics from which would be the beginning of a portfolio that could then be used to get work. I'd read enough articles in *Just Seventeen* to know that paying for a shoot was actually not necessary and that a reputable agency wouldn't expect any money up front – but I didn't care; I liked Mavis and found it all very exciting, plus she'd recoup the costs of the shoot from my first earning as a model – I mean it was fine, £150 wouldn't make much of a dent in 10k anyway.

The shoot was set up with a local photographer and as instructed I duly turned up to his Manchester studio clutching a bag of various 'looks' – including a clingy black party dress that we shot in a dimly lit studio like I was in the spotlight on stage at a smoky jazz club with my hair in big, bouncy curls, and a more casual striped polo neck and velvet trews combo that I wore while being photographed leaning nonchalantly on the railings of a bridge stretching over the Manchester Ship Canal, staring moodily down the lens.

After a long day of posing for pictures we had enough to put together a composite card, a postcard featuring several shots of me in various poses and moods – cheeky grin to sultry sulk – plus my name and measurements. These cards could then be posted out to potential clients and left behind at castings. The photos were also put into my portfolio – a big black book that would soon hopefully contain magazine pages of my photoshoots but for now just had my test shots in it.

The day arrived when I was to go in and collect my composite cards. I was well excited. The photos looked great to me, black and white shots arranged in a little collage with my measurements written in white on a black background in the bottom left corner: bust 34, waist 23, hips 34 and, above that, my name in bigger letters. Except . . . hang on. That's not my name. My name was Sarah. With an h. Rhymes with carer. But the name in gleaming white print on my new, very expensive cards was Sara, no h. My h had been haccidentally dropped.

I knew there was no way I could afford to get them redone. Of course, nowadays, being all growed up and knowing my rights, I would simply demand they be redone with my name spelled correctly as it was their mix-up. But at eighteen I just accepted that I would now be known, for work anyway, as Sara Cox.

I'm pleased in retrospect that I was too young and daft to get the spelling corrected. I still work under the dropped h and my maiden name now. There's something rather lovely about there being two of me. There's the Sarah that my family and friends know, which means the Sarah written in birthday cards from my mum is different to the Sara that's occasionally fallen prey to hideous articles in the *Daily Mail*. It's easier to distance myself from any hurtful comments if it's work Sara instead of me, mummy, wife, daughter, sister, friend Sarah. So I owe a big thank you to whichever Manchester printer managed to spell my name wrongly all those years ago.

36. Pretending to Fish

So I was now Sara Cox, model. I had my cards, my portfolio and a landline. I was good to go. Watch your backs, Kate et al. All I needed to do was wait by the phone above the Pineapple pub and attend castings when the calls came in and I'd be on my way.

Our phone line, sadly, was shared with the payphone in the pub, so sometimes when I was talking to MMA I'd get a half-cut customer downstairs interrupting, all confused because they'd be trying to order a taxi into town and could hear people talking on the line. No matter. I rang MMA most mornings, checking in and asking if there were any castings going on. Usually the answer would be a resounding 'Nope' from the booker Georgina, a pretty glossy-haired brunette who manned the phones and was Mavis's right-hand woman and all the models' protective big sis.

Sometimes I'd pop into Manchester and swing by the agency instead. It was easy to spot models once I'd become one of them; they'd always be smoking and carrying a portfolio in their arms – they're an awkwardly big size, too big to go in a regular bag

– and would be wearing black, straight hair not troubled by perm and face largely untroubled by make-up.

It seemed as I walked through Manchester that every third girl was a model, and that was the problem; the city had a handful of big agencies, a lot of models and very few jobs. It was hugely competitive. Manchester is a very cool city but it wasn't the capital of the fashion world – that was the actual capital. Unable to just uproot and move to London, I joined the dozens of girls at every casting. Sometimes it'd be a mixed casting with the male models. We'd all be herded into the back room at MMA and, once cocooned in the dusky pink womb with the dusky pink carpets and walls to wait, it always struck me how different the male and female models were. All the girls would be clustered together in little groups talking about how fat, short or spotty they were. Bear in mind the average size was an 8, the average height 5' 9" and the skin was the dewy fresh stuff usually sported by your average nineteen-year-old.

Still. The girls loved to put themselves down. The boys, however, jostled for position in front of the row of illuminated mirrors in the back room, slicking down their hair, pouting at their reflections and generally loving themselves. To quote my mum, if they'd been made of chocolate they would've eaten themselves.

They had no insecurities, unlike us girls, who held our own self-criticism Olympics every time we gathered together.

The casting would begin and one by one we'd be called out to walk down the pink-carpeted catwalk in front of Mavis and the client. Again, faintly reminiscent of the cattle sales I'd frequented just a few years before, except instead of wellies I'd be wearing pointy ankle boots.

It was always slightly awkward because the catwalk must've only been about two metres long. It was a T-shape, so you'd walk out and turn right along the top of the T, then hang a sharp left and head down towards the end, but it was so short you always felt as if you might walk right off the end – more gangplank than catwalk.

The lucky ones would be shortlisted and the rest would be dismissed, heading back out into the Manchester drizzle, clutching our books and sparking up a consolatory ciggie.

My first job was for the cover of not *Vogue* but a travel brochure for a local firm. I went to a tiny studio on the outskirts of town, where I was slathered in fake tan, my hair gelled back off my face as if wet and heavy eyeliner applied. I had to wear a foul, Versace-style strapless one-piece costume that was patterned with big gold swirls. I was instructed to pose with my hands on my head as if I was being held at gunpoint and to close my eyes as if luxuriating in the glare of the hot Mediterranean sun rather than shivering in a draughty studio in Ancoats. The photographer was middle-aged and grumpy, barking instructions at me and clearly frustrated by my amateurish attempts to pose and pout.

I remember getting home that night knackered; holding an unnatural position while trying not to shiver was surprisingly tiring. It wasn't a very jolly or glamorous introduction to the world of modelling but that was probably for the best – it was at least a realistic introduction to modelling. I got paid maybe £80 for that shoot, which to me was riches, at least three shifts at the pub. When the brochure came out I still put it in my book – a cover is a cover, after all – but it wasn't the best; I didn't look like a hot Spanish señorita but more like I'd popped my mum's old cossie on and smeared gravy browning on me.

Other scraps of work came, including me prancing around in pigtails and checked shirts, pretending to fish by a pond for a fashion shoot in *My Guy* magazine, but on the whole I lounged around at home waiting for the phone to ring.

I drove Mum barmy; she'd come upstairs from working lunch-time in the pub and I wouldn't have lifted a finger all morning. Not one dish would be washed – instead I'd be watching telly and painting my nails, because of course a spot of self-maintenance is hugely important when you're a top model. 'Sarah, can you wipe up please?' she'd ask through gritted teeth. 'I can't, Mum,' I'd explain slowly, waggling my fingers at her, 'I'm DOING MY NAILS.' I'd say it as if it demanded the same understanding as 'Sorry Mum, I can't, I'm on a conference call with the UN about solving world poverty.'

Mum was surprisingly patient with me – this overgrown teen-ager lolling about like a long-limbed sloth while she continued to zip around like, as she used to say, a 'blue-arsed fly'. She'd remark, 'If you were any more laid-back you'd be horizontal.'

I was still working some shifts behind the bar, so at least I wasn't cadging money from her – I was earning enough to get into Manchester occasionally for castings and a mooch around Afflecks Palace, a grand building containing a slightly musty-smelling, multi-level indoor market, housing stall after stall of fabulous stuff and tantalising tat – a mixture of new young designers, second-hand clothes, entire stores stacked with indigo blue jeans and stalls selling crazy shoes in experimental materials like spiky black rubber stilettos and cherry-red platforms with smiley faces or glow-in-the-dark plastic bows on the toes, more like works of art than footwear.

Afflecks Palace was a Manc mecca. Like goths to a flame, students, indie kids and floppy-haired ravers made the pilgrimage from all over the north-west, collectively swooning at how cool it was – the exposed pipework, the sleepy-eyed stallholders sucking on roll-ups, the facial piercings, poster shops, display cabinets of bongs and poppers, vinyl stores, tattoo parlour, the mosaic on the wall outside stating 'On the sixth day God created

Manchester' – all of it was achingly cool, something that always made and still makes me feel completely out of my depth. The cooler a place was the more I used to feel myself shrink into my shoes. I've always had trouble blending into my surroundings if those surroundings aren't a farm or cattle show, and both those things are admittedly pretty niche.

I've always been more comfortable in my scruffs and my footwear of choice is wellies, trainers or boots over a heel any day. In fact, I've never been able to slink about in heels – I can't physically stand up or walk in them. I'm convinced I'm missing the gene that allows one to sashay in a towering heel. Instead I walk with the wide-legged gait of a cowboy who's had his usual boots nicked and has been forced to pop on a Jimmy Choo. The fact I chose to stick with modelling for two years – the one career where you're absolutely required to dress up and walk confidently in heels – proves just how determined I was to avoid getting a proper job.

Although I still can't walk the walk I'm getting better at talking the talk and not being intimidated; I can now throw my shoulders back and meet people's gaze with confidence – largely because one of the joys of growing up is you don't give as much of a monkey's about what people think of you, and also you're a little more cynical about the perception of cool. I now don't think anybody is all that 'cool' – once you've reached your forties you're wise enough to know we're all racked with the same insecurities and anxieties. Everyone is blagging it, just running around like ants in an anthill.

Back then, though, at eighteen, I always felt awkward, like a baby giraffe in a Puffa coat. I'd stroll around Afflecks Palace, clanging up and down the industrial metal stairways, my pub money burning a hole in the pocket of my flared jeans.

I bought quite a few interesting pieces there, and by interesting I mean hideous and by pieces I mean abominations to fashion – like a battered, dark-brown leather men's blazer with a paisley lining that came with a Ventolin inhaler still in the inside pocket. I wore this with pale denim parallel jeans – I basically dressed like Terry from *Minder*. Another beauty, purchased during my college years but still worn, was a second-hand faux fur leopard-print jacket that had alternating panels of tufty fake fur and flaking leather. It was tatty but I liked it. I must have looked like Bet Lynch after she'd been run over by a council gritter.

At one point during my A levels I lived back at the farm for a few months with Dad and his now wife and used to drive Dad's banged-up Daihatsu jeep – a deep-green bone-rattler with no windows in the back and a bench seat running along the sides in the rear, a real farm vehicle. I used to go and collect Ani and our mates and squeeze about six lads into that jeep, occasionally moving a bag of cattle feed that Dad had left in the back to make room.

I remember relishing the funny looks I'd get at traffic lights when the occupants of the car next to me would spot not a flat-cap-wearing farmer type but an eighteen-year-old girl in a leopard-print faux fur coat and round, pale-pink John Lennon glasses. I loved that jeep and I only mention that it was banged-up because it was me that banged it into the disused milking shed when reversing at high speed out of the farmyard one night after a row, fuelled by diesel (the jeep) and teenage angst (me). Sorry, Dad.

I only managed a few months at the farm before returning to my mum, tail tucked firmly between my legs. I loved being with Dad, I liked making a fire every night and didn't even mind the extra housework chores I had to muck in with – but it wasn't meant to be.

The old two's company, three's a crowd thing really resonated at the time. I for one loved living at the farm and for the first couple of weeks it was great, but then the cracks started to appear: some were subtle (frosty silences, being ignored) and some not so much (Lulu's latest hit single 'Independence' being played loudly and repeatedly on the battered hi-fi in the lounge).

I tried to be a helpful, positive member of the household – essentially I kept my head down – but it proved too much and Dad conceded that it was best if I left. I agreed – I loved Dad so much but I could see he was sad to be caught in the middle of the two women in his life and I didn't want to cause him any more grief. I moved back to Mum's.

My mum wasn't remotely surprised that I came back to my cushy life with her – you don't know what you've got till it's gone and all that. I returned to her bosom and lapped up her unconditional love, Post-it notes, central heating and packet chilli con carne, perhaps fully appreciating for the first time what side my barmcake was buttered on.

I'd always been a fully paid-up member of the daddy's girl club but things in life aren't black and white. As a teenager I think I viewed my family members as you would characters in a film – there were goodies and baddies. Dad was always the goodie and Mum, a lot of the time, though my guilty fingers falter over the keyboard as I type, was the baddie: setting rules, daring to ask for help around the house, demanding a little appreciation. How very dare she.

Now I see it all very differently because I've learned that in life there are no T-Birds and Scorpions; nothing is as simple as the Rebel Alliance and the Empire. What I gradually learned

as I grew up was that nobody is perfect: the people I idolised
– Dad – had their faults and the ones I clashed with – Mum
– usually had my best interests at heart. I think you only begin
to accept people and their insecurities, bad tempers, vulnera-
bilities, frustrations and sadnesses after you've lived a bit and
realise that none of us really know what we're doing.

I always presumed my parents had all the answers – they
were adults! Their actions should be controlled and considered,
not influenced by emotions or anxieties – they were my parents!

Of course, now I'm a mum I realise that when you become
a parent there is no miraculous moment where the brainwaves
alter and a switch in our soul is flicked from floundering young
person to responsible, 'together' adult. I was just the same old
me, picking my way through the puddles of life, only now with
a newborn baby in my arms.

The only thing that changed with me when I had my first
child (beyond of course the whole feeling-love-stronger-and-
more-potent-than-the-whiffiest-Christmas-cheese thing) was that
suddenly I would cry at sad newspaper stories and gravy adverts.

And I realised that it's not advisable to spontaneously jump
on a bouncy castle post-partum without first nipping to the loo.

Over my teenage years the picture I'd held in my head of
my siblings and parents began to change, the outline of each
person shifting and fading, the people I love and their personalities blending in to one another like a smudged pencil drawing
– who was on my side, who I trusted the most – and now they're
just my family and, I imagine, as complicated as all other families – loving, often hilarious, occasionally irritating, but always
loyal.

My modelling career didn't exactly take off.

I did a lot of shifts at the pub, interspersed with the occasional casting. I did a summer photoshoot for *Just Seventeen*, wearing cut-off dungarees and checked shirts, wielding rods and nets, perching on a wicker picnic basket as if I was off for a day fishing by a river. I was happy, though. Magazine fashion shoots barely paid sixpence, plus the agency would take their twenty-five per cent too, but they were fantastic for building up your portfolio. Work bred work; the more evidence of different shoots, the more 'looks' you could demonstrate, the more experienced you became. Mavis had explained to me during our first meeting that I had an 'editorial' look, which meant a unique, more quirky look. You were deemed to have either an editorial or a 'commercial' look, which was all teeth and eyes – think toothpaste adverts and girls next door. Editorial was seen as more high fashion – staring moodily out from the style pages of glossy magazines, stalking up and down catwalks, big-money ad campaigns, *Vogue* covers.

Those of us who were declared editorial were quite smug about it, but it was the commercial girls who'd make cash – big-money jobs for shampoo, cars, breakfast cereal. It was unlikely us editorial girls would make our millions; in fact, we'd be lucky to make our thousands.

It's the lucky few who get a spectacular breakthrough due to sheer luck or from just being so striking and perfect to photograph – the Mosses, the Campbells – then there's the layer underneath – the girls who eke out good careers by constantly working, magazine shoots and catwalk work, on rotation round all the big shows every February at New York Fashion Week, then London and Paris.

They make good money for braving the whirling, non-stop fashion juggernaut – racing from one show to the next, face and hair being scrubbed clean in between each one so they are a new, fresh canvas for the next designer's whims and follies.

The rest of us realise fairly early on that it's not really a viable long-term career. If modelling was a crème brûlée then the crunchy, delicious caramelised bit at the top would be the models with a successful, sustainable 'buy a flat in London and have savings' career and the rest of us would be the custard.

Hopes of *Vogue* covers and private jets to Bajan bikini shoots evaporate within the first couple of months, when you keep finding yourself squished into a clammy room in Manchester with two dozen equally pretty girls waiting to walk out onto a tiny catwalk to be barely glanced at by a couple of bored-looking clients.

The good news is, once we'd got over our delusions of grandeur the real fun began. Most of the models I knew just did it to escape real work, to get drunk in exotic faraway places, to avoid university and escape their home towns. After all, that's why I did it. I'd had vague and varied career ambitions that had been mulled over and mostly discarded: vet (too much studying, not clever enough), mounted police (not brave enough, bad at running, lifelong fear of knives) and journalist (this one I still harboured, loosely believing that one day I'd return to a place of education to study media and journalism); but for now I was very happy to spend a couple of years treading water before being forced to grow up.

The biggest photographic job I did in the UK was for Boots tights. They were looking for someone with very slender hips rather than any hint of womanliness and from the front my hips had about the width and shapeliness of a stick of gum. They wanted to shoot for some hosiery packaging – imagine that! My wonky legs gracing the packages of tights in every Boots store! Rows and rows of tights with me on them. Beyond exciting. The new line they were launching were 'suspender tights', which sounded like something a structural engineer might use on a railway bridge and were about as sexy.

They wanted to save ladies the faff involved with attaching stockings to suspender belts by making tights with areas cut out on the thighs, revealing flesh and creating the illusion that they were complicated lingerie.

If you were in a dimly lit room and squinting a bit, it would almost certainly look like the lady was wearing stockings and suspenders. It'd only be once you approached/flicked on a light that you'd realise they were tights with bits missing and the woman would be revealed to be a lazy slut too slothful to bother to attach real stockings to a suspender belt. Sure, hooking up the real thing is akin to a *Krypton Factor* puzzle and you need to remove a vertebra to twist adequately enough to fasten the rear ones, but any women worth her salt knows it's worth it for the pleasure of feeling like you're wearing a racehorse's bridle round the top of your legs.

On these charming suspender tights' packaging would be just a close-up, not of my face but of my pelvic area. But that didn't stop my mum buying a few pairs as souvenirs of my stratospheric rise through the ranks of hosiery modelling. These tights never really took off; in fact, I imagine Mum was probably responsible for about forty per cent of the overall sales.

I also modelled some over-the-knee socks and my face WAS on the packaging for those! Although unfortunately my face looked weird, gurning sideways at the camera as I leapt over imaginary puddles in my long socks, miniskirt and blazer, clutching an umbrella. Still, my loyal mum stocked up. The lady at the till in Boots must've wondered why this petite lady needed so many socks.

Little jobs like these were lovely – it was undeniably thrilling that my pelvic area was such a hit (maybe I'd be recognised in the street and fans would want a picture with my hips?). They were also physical proof that I was working and enjoying some small successes. Dad loved my modelling photos; he was very proud – for years he had one of my composite cards in the side window of his wagon in the spot that was reserved in other wagons for Linda Lusardi.

Hilariously, I modelled a couple of times on *This Morning*, which was incredibly exciting but beyond nerve-wracking. With hindsight I now know why – when you're a model you're not there to talk, or have an opinion; you're not even mic'ed up, so even if someone asked you a question your answer wouldn't be heard. There's something unsettling about being muted. I was like the Little Mermaid after she's tricked into giving her voice to Ursula. Silently nodding, smiling, beatific.

When I started working as a television presenter I loved the freedom to chat, exclaim, laugh. I think that's why I talked so much, blurting out whatever came into my mind – my gag was gone, my voice and therefore my opinion, sense of humour and personality reinstated.

My modelling stints on *This Morning* happened during the golden years of Richard and Judy. We'd be herded around backstage by the model wrangler, whose job it was to get us organised and into our outfits. It was always quite a stressful gig; live television obviously put a bit of pressure on all the production team and this clearly seeped down to the women who had to get us sorted. They seemed constantly frazzled and ordered us about.

We'd then be cued on individually to stand there like a lemon while the fashion expert and the hosts chatted about the clothes.

Years later whenever I went on *This Morning* as a guest (WITH A MICROPHONE!!) plugging a TV show or charity campaign I'd tell Richard and Judy my tale of modelling on the show; they tried a few times to find the footage but luckily it never surfaced.

I used to joke on my Radio 1 show that Richard and Judy were my fantasy parents; in response when I went on their Channel 4 chatshow they surprised me by bringing on set a pony as a pretend present for me (thus only confirming their status as dream parents).

The floor manager had told me sternly beforehand that under no circumstances should I get on the pony because I didn't have a helmet on, which resulted in an Alan Partridge-esque stand-off on live telly with Richard shouting at me to 'GO ON!! GET ON THE PONY' while out of shot the poor floor manager stood shaking his head furiously at me, mouthing 'NO! DON'T!' Richard and Judy perfected that 'anything can happen' controlled chaos during their live shows and that's why I love them.

The modelling stints on *This Morning* weren't quite as crazy as that, though I was very unconfident. My body language didn't scream 'hot model', more 'cleaning lady who's accidentally come through the wrong door and stumbled onto the set and is trying to style it out'. I was an unsure, round-shouldered rabbit in the headlights.

One time on *This Morning* it was a 'Summer hats special' and to ensure all eyes were on the headgear we all had to bring along a black catsuit to wear. With the wide-brimmed summer bonnet atop my skinny body clad all in black I looked like a quivering floor lamp.

The irony wasn't lost on me that after an entire childhood being mocked for how I walked, to the extent that I didn't even like walking ahead of other kids en route to school, I was now expected to walk for a living in front of thousands. My crushing self-consciousness about how I moved meant I never cracked the knack of the proper model walk; despite the best efforts of model friends to teach me, the hip-swinging, determined stomp of the catwalk models was always out of my grasp. I walked instead like a wooden puppet whose strings were being held by someone in the throes of a sneezing fit.

I was good at standing still though (Go me!) and on one job I was even required to sway slowly and it was a triumph.

There was a casting at MMA for a pop video and I was chosen for the gig along with three other girls from the agency. We were pretty excited about this because the band was OMD, who I knew had had quite a few big hits in the eighties. Of course, now I've interviewed them and played their music loads on my *Sounds of the 80s* Radio 2 show, but back then I just knew they'd once been a pretty big deal – they were definitely from the cooler end of eighties pop, while I was busying myself with Wham! and Bros.

On the day of the shoot we arrived at the studio in a warehouse in Manchester and were told we were to be nymph-like creatures, hair pinned up, wrapped in long lengths of cream fabric that looked a lot like dust sheets. With youth on your side, it seems, you can even rock the 'protective covering on a statue during renovation' look.

We were to stand with the sides of our faces pressed against the wall as if trying to ear-wag on the neighbours' arguments through a thin wall. Lead singer Andy McCluskey was a bit grumpy that day and didn't seem to enjoy the shoot – it's worth saying here that whenever I've met him since he's been very nice, so maybe he was having a bad day. Also, video shoots are by their nature pretty repetitive: Andy's job was to sing along to the song again and again as we hugged the walls next to him.

It was nippy wrapped in just a sheet but once under the

lights, like newborn chicks under heat lamps, we felt warm again.

At the end of modelling shoots and indeed now, when I do photoshoots to promote a new show, it's always a joy to slip back into the comfort of my own jeans and jumper after being scantily clad, especially if everyone else on set – photographer, photographer's assistant, client, make-up artist, PR person – is fully clothed.

There's a certain vulnerability that's created by having on less clothing than everyone else and in my modelling days that was magnified by also not having any choice in what I wore. When you're a model no one cares if you're not keen on a skirt you're wearing or if you think the foundation that's been slapped on your face makes you look like Gollum's sister; you're there as a clothes horse, a blank canvas. On shoots, I'd feel equal to them again and able to have a voice, an opinion, only once I'd got fully dressed.

Obviously these days I do have a say. Hurrah. I only wear what I actually like and my definition these days of a 'scantily clad' shoot means I've maybe unbuttoned my cardigan a bit.

37. Three Thin People

S pring 1994. I was nineteen and was offered the chance to work in Milan.

I can't remember a lot about the place – I was there for a month but it was such a whirlwind that just a few memories rise like bubbles to the surface.

We were flown over by a sister agency of MMA and I shared an apartment with a few other girls. I was pretty naive and remember being shocked that we had to head out alone and find our way around the city to get to our castings. Luckily, thanks to Yvonne and my Paris trip I had some experience of navigating a new place armed with just a street map and a few quid in my pocket, although this time I was lacking even a GCSE-level grasp of the language. I did pick up a few phrases – hello, how are you, goodbye and f-off bastard.

The latter was basically the main one we needed while trooping around Milan, map in one hand and portfolio in the other. To say the men we encountered there were perverts is a little like saying a Premiership footballer is on a decent wage.

It may have changed now, but back then it was as if my visit coincided with the annual month-long sex pest convention. Wherever we walked in our little gang of girls, grown men reacted as if they'd been in solitary confinement and not clapped eyes on the female form for decades. They'd look at us like a starving dog would look at a T-bone steak. In the street, on the tube, they would make this strange hissing noise, the same one you'd make to get the attention of a cat. I don't know how any woman was supposed to react to being literally cat-called like that – 'Oh, how perfectly charming! You're hissing at me and clicking your fingers – we simply must have dinner some time.' We found it ludicrous and insulting.

There was no support from the sisterhood when we were getting blatantly ogled or harassed. Women on public transport didn't offer empathetic glances, they just glared disdainfully at us. I like to think if a man was being openly predatory towards a clutch of young ladies on the London tube now I'd at least, as a 43-year-old mum, keep an eye on the girls and make it obvious I disapproved of the man's behaviour.

When we were in groups of two or more and getting unwanted attention we'd use our new Italian phrase and tell the pervert to F off, but on the whole we hurried on and kept our heads down.

I imagine we were easy to identify as models thanks to us being foreign, tall, slim and, oh yes, holding our portfolios. Maybe models had a reputation as good-time girls and so were thought of as easy targets for sleazy men.

We were certainly used as a commodity; a few nights a week we'd be picked up by one of the bookers and taken out first for dinner with other people from the agency and then on to a club. I remember at dinner, even though I smoked, being disgusted at how everyone would puff on fags as the food was served and between mouthfuls, the smoke from their cigarettes constantly curling up from the ashtray. The bookers talked loudly to each other in Italian while the English models chatted among themselves and sipped the wine, hoping to appear grown-up and sophisticated.

Of course, a free dinner and a night out was not to be sniffed at for a nineteen-year-old girl but I soon sensed a darker side to it and started to feel uneasy about these nights out to clubs; we weren't there for our own entertainment, we were there as decoration for the club whose clientele was men old enough to be our dads.

We were just young women shipped in to make the place look pretty. The model bookers obviously had some sort of deal with the clubs that guaranteed they'd be treated like kings in return for furnishing the VIP area with models. I never felt in danger in the clubs – nothing was expected of us except to have fun and look the part – but I remember, as my trip neared its end, how I started to hate going out and to resent being one of the many pretty pawns in their shallow little game.

That month I spent in Milan felt hard; here I was, a model in an exciting city, one of the fashion capitals of the world, and all I wanted was to be at home on the flowery couch above the Pineapple pub, Mum shouting at me for not wiping up the dishes.

It was my first time working away and I was terribly homesick. I missed Mum, I missed Ani and hanging out with the lads. Everything was so (unsurprisingly, of course) foreign and I longed for the very streets I had thought I wanted to escape: walking up Blackburn Road to Phil's house, popping over the road to the massive Asda near the Pineapple, driving to Ani's to go for a drink by the log fire at the Bob Smithy pub. I should have felt slightly at home at least with the weather in Milan – it was very Mancunian and poured down almost every day, grey skies sluicing the streets with rain, soaking me on the way to my castings.

The castings themselves were depressing; each morning the agent would ring with a list of clients and locations, which I'd scribble down. The mornings were all a little bit like an episode of *The Apprentice*, with me looking frantically at maps of the city and public transport routes, working out the most logical way to get to all the castings, sometimes as many as six in a day, sprinkled liberally all over the city.

I'd take the metro, then a tram, then a bus to a grey miserable street. After walking around a bit in the drizzle trying to locate the building number, I'd schlep up four flights of stairs into a room containing three thin people dressed in black, with angular haircuts, smoking at a table. The people wouldn't even look up from their espressos; one would just thrust out an open hand, into which I'd slot my book. They'd flick through, looking at maybe three or four of the shots before mumbling 'Grazie' as they handed it back. That would be it. I'd slink out of the room and start my journey to the next casting.

Lunchtimes were equally disappointing. I was in a country famous for its love of good-quality, locally sourced fresh food and here I was, queueing in McDonalds for a Filet-O-Fish. What can I say? When you're nineteen and homesick you seek out the familiar. But it didn't taste the same as at home, and their McDonalds even served salads, proving to me once and for all that Milan was just plain weird.

Once back at the apartment I couldn't even escape by sinking into the sofa and gawping at the telly, because – surprisingly, I know – all of the channels except one were in Italian. The exception was MTV, which I watched endlessly – a background blurb or, if you actually watched it, a rolling visual and audio assault of candy-coloured ads and shouty hosts mixed with all the biggest nineties non-stop hits, interspersed with repeats of *Beavis and Butt-Head.*

I was pleased to return home after that month, no extra money in my pocket but a few new pictures in my book, which was at least to be helpful for getting my next gig.

38. Too Big for Japan

In August of 1994 there was a big casting for a contract in Japan. I'd always wanted to go to Tokyo – it had a reputation as a top destination for models, with quality work and great money. I was super-keen and the casting seemed to go well; I came out onto the mini catwalk and sashayed about in my usual 'accidentally walked through the wrong door' style, channelling Mrs Overall.

I wasn't worried. I knew Japan was all about the photographic work and wasn't catwalk-centric. I also knew my portfolio was quite strong. The Japanese agent loved my look, liked my book, but there was one stumbling block. Or rather two. My breasts. In Japan big boobs just wouldn't work – they liked their fashion models slim as reeds (check!) with narrow hips (check!) and flat chests (fail!) – so I was denied the chance of a Tokyo trip. The only positive part of this rejection was that I've been able to state ever since that 'My boobs were too big for Japan,' as if my mere presence in the country with such enormous breasts would cause natural disasters on a scale never seen before, my knockers disrupting equatorial weather systems.

However, there was a silver lining in the shape of South Korea. MMA had recently connected with an agency in Seoul called Classy and told me there could be an opportunity to work there.

It was explained to me that using western models in South Korea was a complicated business and although the agency was above board, there were laws regarding how many western models could be used on a shoot as a percentage had to be Korean. As I was soon to discover, that rule wasn't actually adhered to at all, although I was told to keep my passport hidden under my pillow just in case.

I wasn't concerned. I just wanted to go on another trip. So in September 1994, three months before my twentieth birthday, I found myself at Charles De Gaulle Airport waiting for a connecting flight to Seoul.

I wrote a diary about this trip. Its brown corrugated cardboard cover has 'KOREA' doodled on the front. The entries show that I'm wowed by the cultural shift I experience before I even board the plane – I wax lyrical like only a nineteen-year-old can about the different ethnicities of the passengers of the Air Korea flight, including 'an Indian man sat cross-legged as if to charm a snake' – a real Adrian Mole moment.

I don't mention the smoking area of the plane in this diary but I remember it well and the memory is enough to bring on a bronchial burst of coughing.

The smoking area used to be at the back, so all the smokers would congregate in the rear aisles of the 747 and stand puffing on their cigs as if at a bus stop or outside a bar. The thought of smoking on a plane is so ludicrous now that I can't quite believe it used to be OK – lots of people holding objects in their hands that burned and released deadly fumes while cruising at 35,000 feet.

*　　*　　*

After the eleven-hour flight and having had scant sleep I was collected from the airport at 10 a.m. by Mr Back, the Classy agency driver. I was fully expecting to be taken to the accommodation to unpack, shower, change traveller's cheques, ring home and generally recover from such a tiring flight (I even wrote 'Face pack here I come!' in my diary.)

What actually happened was I got driven straight to Seoul, where on the street outside the agency I met Mr Kim, Classy's owner, a stern, stocky man in his fifties who smiled so little that it looked like his face might crack when he attempted it.

Mr Kim demanded to see my book, which, as advised, I'd stashed deep in my suitcase, so I had to dig it out, bras, toiletries, shoes all tumbling out onto the dusty pavement. He flicked through it in seconds, grimacing in the manner of an elderly lady who's just found a fresh cat poo in her teapot, and thrust it back into my hands with a grunt.

I was then taken to six castings by Mr Back – one of the good things about South Korea was we weren't expected to find our way around. Either Mr Back or 'Young Mr Kim' would drive us to our castings every day. Negotiating the roads and public transport of Seoul would've been impossible as the Korean language when written is similar to Japanese, only with more squared-off shapes and symbols.

The roads in Seoul felt safe, although that feeling was undermined by a huge electronic sign above the Seongsu Bridge showing an up-to-date tally of the number of road collision casualties so far that year.

Mr Back drove a white sporty Hyundai, which wasn't the most practical car for squeezing four tall girls in, but we were grateful. Not only was South Korea an assault on the senses – huge skyscrapers lit by flashing colourful billboards, a rainbow of neon and LED plastered up the side of buildings – but the area where we were to live, Itaewon, was very complicated to navigate. It was made up of several bustling streets behind which was a huge hill, which was the residential area. To negotiate these without a driver, especially in those first few days, would've been impossible. The steep sides of the hill were smothered in thousands of apartment blocks, like dust on a dropped strawberry. The narrow one-car-width roads that were tangled tightly around the hill were so confusing – every blind corner looked the same as the last.

The blocks of flats weren't high-rise, just two storeys and higgledy-piggledy, balanced haphazardly like a toddler's tower of building blocks, many with extensions added on as an afterthought. They all clung to the sides of the hill, washing lines strung around, zig-zagging across the tiny concrete squares outside each apartment door that were occasionally dotted with bedraggled, thirsty-looking potted trees, the floor seasoned with discarded cigarette butts. People lived piled up on top of one another. The shadows of visitors descending from the apartment upstairs were accompanied by loud post-dinner belches ringing out as they made their way past our lounge window. In South Korea it is taken as a compliment to your cooking skills if guests burp after consuming your food and judging from the gassy cacophony coming from the stairwell outside, our neighbour must've been the Korean equivalent of Delia Smith.

On my first day Mr Back and I didn't arrive at my new home until nearly 9 p.m. – I was almost delirious with tiredness but was chuffed that one of the castings had resulted in a job the following day. I made my way up the steep concrete steps outside, following my new flatmate Diane who'd been on the castings too, dragging my massive case behind me.

On the second floor, through a dark wooden door we found a lounge with a lino floor, open-plan kitchen area to the rear and two bedrooms and a bathroom leading off it.

My two flatmates were both from Hawaii: Caroline was twenty with long dark hair and a perfect smile, an all-American sweetheart who looked like she'd just toppled out of a passing cheerleading troupe. Diane had pale skin and light auburn hair and seemed to me to be more worldly wise. It soon became clear why – despite being only eighteen she was married. This of course was a source of fascination and wonder for me and the other girls; that and the fact that she was a Mormon.

I had my own room, a tiny box room with a single mattress on the floor and a little wicker shelf unit next to it. No bed as such, but I would've happily slept on a pallet I was so knackered.

The apartment was harshly lit and furnished with a big boxy telly and the sort of ripped leather sofa usually found in the waiting area of a minicab office.

The fridge was filthy and on one of my first days there I write in my diary about cleaning it out and removing all the rotting food and cockroach carcasses.

Cockroaches became quite a feature of my time in South Korea. They were everywhere. There'd be an occasional one so big I didn't know whether to squash it or pop a saddle on it and ride it to the shops.

I generally have Buddhist leanings when it comes to killing things, but I had no qualms about bumping off roaches. I'm afraid they're in the same category as wasps on the squishlist – 'entirely killable'.

I became quite brave at squashing them. The bigger ones seemed to scream when I dealt them a deathly blow, especially the ones in the bathroom, where they thrived, forever scuttling up the shower wall. They were shiny and brown like polished mahogany and the size of one half of a Kinder Egg, with long antennae poking out the front like a couple of dressage whips.

They often met their end on the side of my Herbal Essences shampoo bottle.

The roaches I couldn't get to were the smaller ones I'd see in the fridge. This fridge was ancient and there were hiding places for them in various cracks in the back of it and in the rubber seal.

I didn't wage war on these ones, I just made sure my milk carton top was on properly. I used to quickly open and close the fridge door three times before looking in there, giving them time to scuttle off to their hiding places. Out of sight, out of mind. I didn't keep much fresh food in the fridge. I mainly lived on eggs on toast and, randomly, tinned pineapple.

Life in South Korea was pretty full on. The photoshoots would be long days. The best jobs to get were the catalogue shoots because they were the best money, but they were also the hardest graft. I know, I know, calling having your picture taken 'graft' sounds ridiculous, but the big shoots were genuinely knackering, often starting at 10 a.m. and finishing at 3 a.m.

There'd often be around twenty-five outfits to get through, so twenty-five outfit changes, twenty-five changes of background if you were outdoors or, if you were indoors, twenty-five tweaks of the lighting while you held a weird pose. The outfit changes were stressful. The Korean stylists often had a couple of assistants and getting undressed was a bit like being attacked by angry seagulls, each woman pulling at a different bit of clothing.

The styling itself was pretty random. We were shooting winter designs but September in Seoul was still a humid 25 degrees, so we were constantly boiling, in strange long leather macs and tweed baker boy caps. The trousers were always way too short, designed with a Korean body size in mind, not long-legged western models. To hide this fact, the stylists on nearly every shoot simply tucked the bottom of the trews into socks or boots.

We'd then see teenage girls wearing trousers tucked into their boots as if off on an impromptu hike; they'd religiously copied the look from the fashion pages. We'd cringe – this wasn't a new trend to follow, it was just because the trousers didn't fit!

Not speaking the same language as ninety-five per cent of people on the shoot was often stressful too. On a shoot the only word a photographer would know was 'Posey!' – this is what they'd holler again and again from behind their camera, meaning 'Pose'.

Every shoot it was 'Posey!' CLICK. 'Posey!' CLICK. 'Posey!' CLICK.

This took a little getting used to and on my second day on my very first job I struggled. In the UK and Milan the poses were much more relaxed and required just subtle changes every few clicks, usually instructed by the photographer – a chin lowered here, a gaze moved to the left, a hand on the hip. Usually while pouting.

I'd been a nymph wrapped in a dust sheet, of course, but this was something else. Being photographed in South Korea was a mixture of poorly improvised sign language and a weird Christmas parlour game.

I soon learned a variety of poses, and the dafter the better. The trick with posing was to lose all self-consciousness; the more wacky my expression and flamboyant my moves the more they clicked – and occasionally cheered.

A favourite of mine was cowgirl sharpshooter-inspired, making my fingers into pistols because then I could do so much stuff with them: hold 'pistols' by my face – CLICK! – 'shoot' at the camera – CLICK! – blow the invisible smoke from the end of my pistols – CLICK! – put the pistols in my invisible holster while winking to camera – CLICK! CLICK! CLICK!

I have to confess that when working with fellow Brits, for

our own amusement and if the photographer was particularly grumpy we'd joyfully flick the Vs at the camera as one of the poses while doing a big cheesy grin or a faux shocked face, mouth rounded in a big O.

Somewhere in some South Korean catalogues from the mid-nineties are pictures of a couple of young girls performing the British hand signal for Piss Off.

My first few days flew by, busy with either being on shoots or being driven around, and after a shaky start I started to settle into life in South Korea. I could find my way to the little local convenience store and perfected my chopstick technique by eating my breakfast cereal with them. I was still a little nervous at the agency. According to some other Classy models we saw on castings, Mr Kim was in the Korean mafia and had been in jail a lot. There was no basis for these rumours, but take a clutch of gossipy young girls with a penchant for melodrama plus Mr Kim's sour expression, then add to that the way his staff pandered to him, and it was easy to believe he was some sort of under-world big shot.

We heard from the agency that there was a new girl arriving from Manchester called Clare. I was really excited; I liked Diane and Caroline but I didn't have many shared reference points with the two girls from Hawaii, one of whom was a Mormon.

Clare arrived, exhausted after her long flight, and fell into bed immediately. Caroline, Diana and I arrived home from shopping like the three bears finding Goldilocks, except this Goldilocks hadn't eaten our porridge and had cropped brown hair and skin the colour of roast beef thanks to an enthusiastic application of fake tan.

I love that in my diary I talk about this mystery girl called Clare arriving from Manchester (she came from about four miles up the road from me), not knowing that she would go on to reveal herself as the most magnificent woman, my very best friend and soulmate to this day, and godmother to my children.

Of course I had no way of knowing all this as I peeped into Caroline's room and saw Clare passed out face down on a mattress, clothes and high heels spewing from her open suitcase.

We laugh now that the very first conversation we ever had, once she'd woken up, went like this:

Me: 'Hiya, d'ya smoke and drink coffee?'

Clare: 'Yeah.'

Me: 'Right, well there's some fags in me room if you want one and my coffee's over there, we can share it.'

Clare: 'Fanks.'

I liked Clare right away; she was a breath of fresh air in the apartment. She liked to party and, having been surrounded until now by non-drinking, all-American nice girls, it felt great to hook up with someone a bit naughty.

The more I chatted to Clare the more I warmed to her; we spoke about our backgrounds and school. I was wide-eyed when she informed me coolly that she'd been suspended from school eight times, once for setting off a firework in the girls' changing rooms.

Straight away we joined forces to lead Diane from the path of teetotal, married Mormonism and onto the road to Funsville. In fact, Funsville fell at our feet that night in the form of a phone call from England.

The dad of a male model called Ben who used to live in our apartment needed to get hold of him as there'd been a death in the family. Classy had stopped his contract and fired him, so they weren't any use – could we help? We were told that Ben used to drink at the Kettle, a bar about a ten-minute walk up the hill from the apartment.

Clare, Caroline, Diane and I quickly declared it our solemn duty to trace Ben (the fact that our intrepid mission involved discovering a nearby bar had absolutely no bearing on our decision . . .).

We found the Soju Kettle surprisingly easily. It had a small square glass frontage with empty bottle crates stacked outside. The illuminated sign was adorned, randomly, with the MTV logo and a huge dartboard as well as the neon outline of a teapot, guiding us in like the north star.

As we walked through the door two things became immediately apparent.

The first was that the clientele in there were largely male and western; in fact, as we'd soon discover, they were all GIs – American troops, based a couple of miles away at the Yongsan Garrison, the headquarters of the US military in South Korea.

The second was that they were clearly not expecting four young models to come storming into the bar. Indeed, if this had been in the Wild West, the music would've stopped as everyone turned to look in silence at these new visitors, saloon doors still gently swinging behind them.

As it was, the cheesy nineties R 'n' B kept playing but everyone did pause to stare at this walking shampoo advert – four girls with hair of different hues and styles striking a pose in the doorway.

Then the spell was broken and the GIs sprang to life, curious about these alien life forms suddenly inhabiting their orbit.

This colliding of worlds promised to be a lot of fun: young soldiers far from home suddenly in the company of some not-unattractive young women, two of whom bringing with them the familiarity and sunny outlook of Hawaii and the other two slightly feistier and from the UK.

Drinks were bought, introductions were made, accents were

mutually admired and we were treated with lots of respect. The soldiers all had impeccable manners – all that military training had certainly knocked off any rough edges.

We were called 'Ma'am', LIKE WHAT PEOPLE SAY IN THE MOVIES, which we found completely brilliant, and whenever one of us popped a cigarette in our mouths, four or five Zippo lighters would appear from nowhere, eager to be the one to ignite our smokes.

A Korean barmaid brought over a stack of plastic cups and three kettles on a tray – old-fashioned small tin kettles, the sort you'd put on a stove-top.

Inside each was a bright red, orange or yellow liquid that tasted like melted ice lollies – fruity, sickly sweet and slightly cloying. The alcohol in these kettles was soju – a clear spirit, the Korean equivalent of sake.

We soon learned that soju was very strong – it had an almost hallucinatory effect on you and you'd feel fantastically drunk very quickly, as well as slightly woozy. Rumour had it that soju contained loads of trace chemicals including formaldehyde and it was these ingredients that made the drink so potent.

Like only the young can, we absolutely relished the drama of drinking something that was not only considered pretty hardcore but would pickle your organs as you got sozzled on the alcohol content. Soju hangovers were legendary for their brutality, something I was on this first night still blissfully unaware of.

At our Kettle debut we proceeded to get stuck in. It felt magnificent to let loose – we got sloshed, danced, smoked and generally threw ourselves head first into the revelry.

Diane was surprisingly easy to influence and with minimal twisting of arm quietly forgot the whole teetotal Mormon thing and downed a few drinks.

Finally, some time in the early hours, we all linked arms and wound our slightly wobbly way back to the apartment high on life (and formaldehyde).

We never did find Ben that night – to be fair we didn't conduct a fingertip search, but we did ask around, and had no luck. We did, however, find the place that quickly became the very centre of our life in Seoul – all the dramas, drunkenness, fun and forging of lifelong friendships would happen inside those four walls.

The next day we hung limply from the jaws of a vicious hangover as we were driven by Mr Back to our castings. We probably could've fuelled his Hyundai with the soju fumes we were emitting.

Despite being green around the gills, both Clare and I were chosen for the first job of the day and were driven four hours out of Seoul on a coach with all the team – clients, photographer, make-up artists, stylists, numerous assistants and all the clothes. It was boiling on the coach, autumn sunshine streaming through the windows, and everyone slept, apart from myself and Clare. We laughed a lot on this trip – and learned a lot.

We learned that Koreans worked hard and played hard. After a long shoot, no matter how late the wrap, the client would always expect to take out the whole team for food and soju. The downside was that everyone would be roused out of their beds a handful of hours later, and would be expected to be ready to commence work on minimal sleep. This was why the Koreans napped every chance they got. On the coach en route to the next location it was as if someone had pressed the 'stand-by' button on the whole crew – they all instantly nodded off as the doors swung shut.

Clare and I couldn't sleep; we were too excited to be on a

trip away and by discovering we had so much in common. It was on this trip that Clare and I really bonded. Our belly laughs and non-stop larking about were probably massively irritating for the rest of the crew but we were having a ball. They got their revenge though. After a long day we all went for dinner. Obviously being teenagers a long way from home we were craving our usual Korean dinner – a Wendy's burger – but our options here were kimbap (sushi rolls) and bulgogi – slippery strips of beef and onion in a glossy thick gravy. Clare and I tried our best to be polite and eat it.

Despite the stereotype of age supposedly bringing with it a 'stuck in their ways' mentality, I believe that as you get older you become more, not less, open-minded. Back then I wasn't remotely adventurous with food, but now I'll try anything and in fact currently have in my fridge two jars of kimchi – the Korean fermented cabbage side dish that was my nemesis as a nineteen-year-old in the country of its origin.

After dinner and soju we went to our room, still giggling and overexcited, only to be woken up four hours later at 6 a.m. to set off for the location.

The shoot was exhausting and, probably to everyone's relief, Clare and I finally cottoned on to the snoozing thing and slept on the coach whenever we could.

Mid-morning we arrived at a new location and one of the make-up artists came over and gently woke me. She was wielding what I thought was a toothbrush but turned out to be a small razor blade with a long handle, not unlike a shank – the impro-vised weapon found hidden down the sock of any self-respecting high-security prison inmate. In broken English she explained she needed to trim my eyebrows.

Usually, of course, tweezers are adequate for this task but in South Korea the make-up artists preferred a razor. I agreed warily, but watched my brows in a hand mirror like a hawk and gently wrestled her away when I thought she'd chipped away at them enough.

She then made her way over to Clare while her assistant coloured in my eyebrows with eye make-up to the extent that it looked like someone had used their thumb to smear Marmite over them.

Clare, who was still sleepy, woke briefly to agree to the eyebrow trim before snoozing back off again. The brows were razored and then covered with the same dark brown streaks as mine.

It was later that evening, back home at the apartment, that Clare discovered the true extent of the trim. Once she'd washed off the eye make-up all that remained was a tiny patch of eyebrow on each side, like quotation marks framing her nose.

She screamed, and we all ran to look and guffawed supportively. They did grow back eventually, but to this day she still blames me for not waking her up.

As the ancient Korean proverb says, 'Snooze, you lose (your eyebrows).'

The shoot itself went well and by the end Clare and I were firm friends. It was a hot day but we were modelling winter fashions and had to wrap up in the usual trousers tucked into boots, long coats and hats.

The photographer had a great idea to recreate a classic snowy scene but we were shooting in a massive disused quarry, surrounded by a red dusty landscape that looked more like Mars than the Alps. They'd planned ahead though, which is how Clare and I found ourselves sitting on a wooden sleigh in sweltering heat as sacks of salt were emptied around us to look like snow.

I knew Clare and I had something special when for one of the shots we were asked to walk away from the camera, chatting.

We got on so well that we didn't hear the photographer yelling at us to stop, he'd got his shot. We were so busy talking and laughing that by the time we turned round the entire crew were dots on the horizon.

My month in Seoul was a real eye-opener. Different models came and went – friendships were intense but fleeting, made in the back of a stuffy Hyundai, on shoots and over kettles. The jobs rolled by and we settled into the rhythm of work, rest and play.

I will be forever indebted to South Korea for landing Clare at my feet and for all the good times we had there – dancing with her to hip-hop at Kings Niteclub up the road from the Kettle, laughing on shoots till our stomachs ached and generally behaving badly. I loved the chilled times too, at the apartment wearing face masks, watching movies like *A Few Good Men*, half-heartedly exercising to a Cindy Crawford workout video, writing our names on our boxes of eggs with biro so the others wouldn't nick them; they came not in a dozen per pack, but ten, so much to our amusement S-A-R-A-H and C-L-A-R-E fit perfectly, a letter per egg.

It was fantastic to earn half-decent money and build up my book as well as seeing a completely different world.

In fact, South Korea was like another planet. Wealth and poverty stood shoulder to shoulder: skyscrapers jostled for space in the city while at ground level tiny shacks smaller than a telephone box sold everything from chewing gum to razors to flip-flops through an envelope-sized hatch, the vendor crammed inside with all their produce closing in around them as if the whole thing had been in the jaws of a car crusher.

All of it was eye-opening, from the indoor market where all us girls ordered made-to-measure traditional dresses in red satin to the food on shoots, which often tested us – one breakfast was small grey crabs floating in what looked, to the untrained eye, like dishwater.

I was unadventurous when it came to the food, and stuck to only a few rice dishes when out with clients. In my own time I preferred a Wendy's or a McDonalds and once Clare and I even tried a vending machine hot dog on a stick wrapped in a smooth, lukewarm deep-fried spongey casing, which was as scrumptious as it sounds.

My struggles with the food also compounded my homesickness: home is where the belly is, that's what the saying should be. I longed for Mum's cooking and I missed her.

I was desperate to get home but at the same time I hoped to get a contract with a New York agency. I kept mithering MMA about it the whole time I was in South Korea. I'm guessing then that my homesickness was only half about missing home and the other half was about being sick of Seoul. Dad didn't call often but that wasn't a surprise – shooting the breeze on the phone wasn't really his thing; he always spoke with such urgency and distraction it sounded like there was a bovine emergency happening mere feet away from him that he was too polite to mention. Chatting on the phone was as awkward to Dad as smiling was to Mr Kim. I'd be all like 'It's mad here, Dad. The food is crazy – the beef isn't as good as British beef' (always on message). I'd prattle on about the friends I'd made: 'There's Clare from – guess where? Whitefield! I know! Up the road!' and downplay any nightlife – 'Oh we went out for a meal but that's about it, nothing too wild' – to which he'd reply, 'Right . . . right . . . well, OK then, love, I'd better go.'

Throughout all my trips Mum was the one steady thing. Whatever side of the world I was on, she'd always call and she'd always be there when I called. Again, Mum. Just there. Quietly by my side even when we were 5,000 miles apart.

This book began as an accidental love letter to my dad. But what's become so clear to me now, as I've continued to remember and rediscover those formative years, the memories and moments bubbling to the surface, is that it's Mum who's always been there, not wanting any credit, no ulterior motive, just driven by a maternal urge to be there for her kid whenever she's needed or wanted. As natural and instinctive to her as breathing. From donkeys to car crashes and long-distance phone calls. Even when I think I've not needed her, I have and she's known it.

Dad was different. It was always the thrill of the chase with him; I needed to work harder for his affection or attention, not because he wanted me to or because he was distant, but because he also had other pressures – his wife, work, the farm. Dad showed me he loved me in subtle ways – a look, a smile, a hug. Mum was much more vocal and in turn needed to know that love and appreciation was returned. It's only in recent years, since I've had kids of my own, that she's felt that love fully returned – and then some.

I love them both, of course. Loads. It's just now I see clearly just how much they each did for me in their own different ways.

The time came for me to leave South Korea and 'cash out' – when the agency would tot up all my earnings and take away the cost of the flights and roach-infested accommodation, leaving me with a decent chunk of money to take home, which I stashed away in a money belt. I waved goodbye to Clare and Korea and headed home, away from the Kettle and bulgogi and back to Bolton and Mum and to contemplate my next adventure.

39. Two-dollar Fried Egg

It was lovely to be home, back in my bed above the Pineapple, the familiar rumble of voices downstairs from the punters punctuated by the odd raucous moment like celebrating a flukey shot on the pool table. It was great to be back with Ani, out with the lads, but as my diary's final entry said, I'd been bitten by the travel bug: I wrote 'New York? Yes please!'

In January 1995 I had a casting at MMA with Wilhelmina's, a reputable agency in Manhattan. They liked my book and wanted me to go over for a three-month contract. I was beside myself. So excited. I'd never been to America, never mind New York.

I packed a woolly hat and my long black coat as I knew the winters were brutal, but it wasn't until we landed at JFK and I stepped outside and the chill slapped my cheek that I realised just how cold it would be. I would probably need to wear all of the contents of my suitcase at once. No matter – I was in New York, and as the yellow taxi hurtled along the highway towards Manhattan the long-flight fug dispersed and I tried to drink it all in.

It was like I'd landed in every movie I'd ever seen – the cars, the big lorries with their boxy long-nosed cabs, the highway itself – this was before I'd even swept over the Brooklyn Bridge and seen Manhattan stood proudly in the distance, that breathtaking skyline that still makes my eyes shine and my fingers tingle.

My time in New York was absolutely one of the biggest adventures of my life. I lived in a two-bedroomed eighth-floor apartment in midtown with six other girls, so it was a pretty chaotic flat, as you can imagine. The rooms each had two sets of bunkbeds, so we all lived and slept literally on top of each other. Girls from France, Holland and the UK thrown together in this amazing city.

The apartment was a complete state – the average age was twenty and the average attitude was 'mañana', so no one could be bothered to wash up. Piles of dirty plates and cereal bowls with solidified matter on them like something from an archaeological dig lay alongside coffee cups and saucers that doubled as ashtrays, with fag butts glued to them with spilt liquid. The work surfaces weren't visible underneath the stacks of crockery and jumbles of empty takeaway, juice and milk cartons that were piled chest-high. As you walked into the apartment the sour smell from the tiny kitchen sprang at your nostrils from its hiding place.

Once past the wall of stink, though, it was a nice big open-plan area with large curtainless windows and two doors leading off to the bedrooms.

These were just for bedtime and the lounge was definitely for lounging: leggy girls in jogging bottoms and face packs, happy to be home from shoots and castings, make-up free at last and slouching about, ringing home, watching Fox, eating takeaway noodles. The apartment was like being at the world's longest slumber party.

There were so many brilliant things about living in New York. From the little things – ringing for takeaway breakfast, a two-dollar fried egg roll and coffee arriving within ten minutes from the Korean-run cafe round the corner – to the bigger stuff like belonging. I just felt like I fitted in. There were times after work when I'd be making my way home from the store with a paper grocery bag in my arms, past all the commuters, sidestepping schoolkids, mums with buggies and the occasional crazy, and I'd feel like a New Yorker. Born and bred. I often fantasised that somehow my spirit had been jumbled up with that of a New York girl and somewhere in Manhattan there was a girl who'd never feel she fully fitted-in until she randomly visited Bolton one time, and strolled past Greggs thinking 'I'm home at last!'

It's easy to feel like you fit in in New York because the second you arrive you can find your way around like a native thanks to the grid system layout of Manhattan's streets. Every morning once I'd scribbled down all the addresses of the castings and worked out my route I'd set off on foot, preferring it to the tube, often walking ninety blocks a day.

Having learned my lesson in Milan that carrying a model portfolio can get you unwanted attention, I used a rucksack to carry my big black book, wrapped up warm in long black military-style coat (it WAS the nineties) and black woolly hat and set off, melting into the crowds going about their business as I went about mine, striding happily under the cold blue skies of New York.

There were test shoots with exciting new young photographers – daring outfits, blaring music, red lips, wind machines on full blast as I swayed and pouted and shouted – unpaid but a benefit for both, great, fun, sexy shots for the photographer and me.

My fellow models were brilliant fun too; there was Melissa

from London with a long straight nose and flashing, playful eyes, poker-straight dark-blond hair falling past her shoulders in a smooth sheet. And April, who was an Amazonian Marilyn Monroe with a Canvey Island accent. Very tall, platinum-blonde wavy bob, hourglass, striking. She couldn't pronounce her Rs and this coupled with her Essex twang meant lots of the Americans couldn't understand her pronunciation of her own name, resulting in her shouting 'January, February, March, APRIL!' until they did.

We'd go out to party only very rarely as we were too young to drink legally, but we had a ball having face packs and noodles back at the flat. I was still going out with Ani so was quite happy to chill at night and, once I'd made my phone calls home, would eat carbs and then crawl into my bunk. Ani and I fell back into the now familiar routine of a long-distance relationship, chatting for ten minutes at a time. Once he came over for a long weekend and I showed him the sights, navigating the city's tourist spots like a local.

The agency was really good, sending us on some great castings, and I got enough work to just about break even and cover the flights and accommodation costs while gaining some lovely pictures for my book.

I still had a few weeks left of my trip when my New York adventure was cut short by a phone call.

I was at a shoot and the agency had tracked me down to tell me I needed to call my mum urgently. My blood ran cold. This was before mobile phones and the very fact that Mum had tried so hard to reach me could only mean terrible news.

My heart was racing as I called home, hands shaking as I dialled the number from a landline in a quiet corner of the studio. I quickly ran through the possibilities – Grandad had died when I was fifteen, so it obviously wasn't him. I was praying it wasn't Dad and that Mum herself was all right. I had always been very close to Nana and she was getting on, so I feared the worst and my chest was thumping as the phone lines crackled and connected.

Mum picked up.

Turns out fearing the worst was pointless as what was to come was beyond even that. In fact, beyond all comprehension. Even now. It wasn't Nana. It was in fact my cousin Tracy. She'd died in the night. Tracy was like a third sister to me – kind and loving, yet hilarious and quick-witted. Sweetest nature, gentlest soul. Stolen from us aged just twenty-seven by what turned out to be natural causes from an undetected heart condition called viral myocarditis, a virus that causes the heart to stop beating.

I don't remember much of the following few hours. The agency was amazing and bundled me onto a flight home, where I drank too much white wine and sobbed until a stewardess came to calm me. Mum met me at the airport and I fell into her arms. Tracy's story isn't mine to tell; it's a story that belongs to the two children, now grown up, she left behind. I just know that the whole family's heart broke when she went, and nothing was really ever the same again. We carried on but it felt like our world had shifted on its axis.

40. Scorch Marks

I threw myself into trying to get away again. I didn't want to be in Bolton. I wanted to escape my home town with its memories round every corner. There was so much sadness. I needed to disappear.

I now had a great modelling book and it wasn't long until a contract came through for a new trip. Maybe I was a coward; this was a time for family to stick together and mourn but I couldn't – it was time to return to Korea.

My second trip to Seoul, in the summer of 1995, was a disaster from the beginning. It quickly became apparent that I wasn't ready to be away from my family and the very thing I thought I needed to escape from was actually the thing I needed to surround myself with: the sorrow, the sadness. The mourning, although hard, is all part of a process.

I was instantly homesick and hated the work. After New York the jobs seemed low-grade. On my first trip the castings and the city itself were an adventure, but this time I resented being schlepped around in the back of a Hyundai.

I tried to think of it as an easy way to get away and make money but it was a struggle. Also Clare wasn't there. She was working over in Thailand, although I was hoping she'd come to visit me during my stay. We'd hung out at home and were confirmed official best friends.

I returned to the Soju Kettle with my new crew and had fun, but it all seemed empty. The work was going well but I was homesick. Every night before drinking at the Kettle I'd stop off at a street stall and cheer myself up by tucking into some bokkeumbap – the most delicious egg fried rice with spring onions and beef – before getting stuck into some soju. If my second trip to Seoul was to be summed up by a montage it would show me wolfing fried rice and then rampaging around the Kettle downing drinks, and comfort-eating boiled eggs in the flat. It would end on a close-up of me on photoshoots struggling to zip up skirts, bloated and miserable, to the tune of the Chemical Brothers' 'Out of Control'.

I was already pushing my luck with the agency, being petulant and tired on castings, but then one night I nearly burned down the apartment and snuffed out my own life in one fell swoop.

I'd been out indulging in a few Kettles and had returned home to my little box room. I fell onto my little mattress on the floor and decided to read by candlelight. Very Jane Austen, except she probably wasn't used to downing ten units of Korean spirit of a night.

I fell fast asleep and the large church candle quickly burned down. In fact, it burned all the way down, and the thing that saved my life was I'd been stupid/clever enough to place the candle on top of a large box of cook's matches. I know that, normally, balancing a candle on top of matches wouldn't be advisable; however, on this occasion it saved me. As the candle burned down it set fire to the massive box of matches and as each match ignited it made a crackling, sharp, hissing noise. The matchbox was full so it sounded like a mini firework display was going off. It was enough to rouse me.

By the time I came round, though, the fire had started to take hold of the little plastic shelving unit underneath the candle. As I came to I screamed, waking the whole flat, and we all rushed around throwing water on the fire. The flames doused, I flopped back onto my mattress and slept again.

The next morning I saw the full extent of the damage – huge black scorch marks stained the wall and floor and the shelf was warped and melted to half its original size.

When Mr Back came to collect us he saw the damage and went crazy. He was furious and said that I would have to pay for the repairs.

I was miserable. The only good thing was that Clare was on her way from Thailand to visit me.

Unfortunately, when she arrived I felt empowered – she has that effect on me – and my attitude towards the agency soured even more; I resented their controlling ways, how they scolded me like a child, how they blew hot and cold with their affections.

We went out and had the night out to end all nights out – well, to end a modelling contract anyway. The next morning I missed the pickup for the castings and that was the final straw for the agency.

The partying, the extra pounds, the attitude. They'd had enough. It was a little like when you don't have the heart or the stomach to finish with someone so you behave badly in the hope they'll dump you first.

I was hauled into the office later that day and they told me it was over. 'You got too fat Sara and you party too much . . . you gotta go home.' I was going home a month early.

I was relieved.

It also turned out to be one of the best things that could've happened to me.

As I strolled through Seoul Incheon International Airport I remember feeling a strange sensation – that for the rest of my life on this earth I would never set foot in that country again. So far that's true but I'd never say never now, my feelings have mellowed over the years. But back in 1995 I'd had enough of Korea – and it'd certainly had enough of me.

41. Nubile Gulls

I felt instantly better as the Korean Air jumbo touched down and although I didn't exactly kiss the tarmac at Manchester International, I silently breathed a long, slow sigh of relief to be home. Mum was there to collect me and as we drove towards home I drank in the familiarity of Bolton – the wet streets, putty-coloured skies and Greggs.

It felt great to be back above the Pineapple. Back with Mum.

I got myself back on track: no boozing, more sleep. It felt fantastic to be home in my own bed; even the sound of the pool cues thudding on the floor of the pub, like some tribal celebration, sounded welcoming.

I was so excited to see my dad, I had butterflies as I bumped Mum's little blue Austin Metro up the farm lane. He was up at the top cattle pens on the tractor, deaf to my shouted greetings because of the roar of the engine, then jumping in shock as I popped up in front of him waving my arms like a drowning man.

Dad put the kettle on for a brew and hugged me to his chest, the fabric of his shirt soft from being washed so often. He smelled faintly of diesel and hay. Everything was familiar and a comfort. I felt like I could relax, like loosening my tie or undoing a top button.

Happy to be home, but I still needed to work out what to do next.

Models have a shelf life for sure, but also a boredom threshold – it had served me well but there's only so long you can find holding your belly in and pouting a worthwhile use of time. I wasn't making big bucks – to cash in I'd need to travel, but for now I just wanted to gather my family and friends to me like a lady gathering her skirts before stepping over a mucky puddle.

I began to ponder the idea of further education – maybe I'd have to bite the bullet and try university. After all, a model's life was pretty much the same as a student's (apart from everyone being a size 8 and having fewer nicked traffic cones knocking about) – I was already used to sharing a chaotic, untidy home with my peers, drinking and smoking too much, sleeping too little, being late, hungover and chased by figures of authority. As a student I'd just be a tad more skint.

In the meantime, I would do what I did best – tread water. I was twenty years old; there was no mad rush. The world may have been my oyster but for now I was content with scraps from the chippy while I pondered my next move.

A fortnight after arriving home I got a call from MMA – a good casting had come in. They said I should make the effort. The total train fare to Manchester was about £3.50 but I was completely skint. Could I be bothered? I asked Mum her opinion and she said 'Sweetheart, you've got to go in for it, what if it's something big? You'd be crackers not to,' and so, for the umpteenth time, she handed over the cash and the confidence I needed.

I set off for Manchester. A bus and two trains later I arrived at the agency to find an absolutely packed back room – a sea of skinny, a wall of waifs – and an accompanying racket of dozens of models squawking excitedly, the occasional slightly hysterical shriek ringing out, like nubile gulls.

There was a real buzz. Forget scrapping for fifty-quid fashion shoots for teen mags. This was a casting for television.

I imagined that if the producers were scouting round the model agencies they weren't after hard-nosed political broadcasters. Less Paxman, more pouting. What kind of show would it be?

I let the other girls go out before me, hoping to suss out the situation from their feedback.

One at a time they stepped out onto the mini catwalk and returned a few minutes later a little confused – they weren't being judged on their looks or on their walk but on their TALK!

Well hello. Talking was what I was good at. I'd barely drawn breath since birth – at school I was quieter, less confident, my natural propensity to perform and entertain dampened down by the bullies, but at home it was a different story. I'd always had an appreciative crowd in my mum and nana as I ran through my repertoire of impressions and general showing off. I was even used to working difficult crowds – Dad was often tired and busy but I'd always make him crack a smile with my gabbing on, jazz-handing around all over the shop.

At work, though, I was never particularly pushy and so on this day I continued to hang back until there was only me left. It was quite a cunning tactical move, with hindsight. Isn't it always best in any competition to go last so the judges remember you, the dozens who went before all having merged into one (long-limbed) mass?

I walked out on the stage clutching a hairbrush to hold like a microphone. This now makes me feel proud and curls my toes in equal measure. There was a guy and a woman sitting at the end of the catwalk. They looked really cool, very London. The man held a video camera and the woman, who had olive skin, dark wavy hair and denim jacket, started to ask me some questions – silly stuff about relationships like a quiz from *Cosmo* magazine: 'What's the worst date you've been on?' and that kind of thing. I was in my element. Being asked my opinion at a modelling casting was unheard of but joyful. I rattled off various humorous and wildly exaggerated anecdotes, speaking into my hairbrush mic and leaning in conspiratorially to the camera. Playing it for laughs.

The floodgates had officially opened. I had an audience for my musings, one that was even chuckling at them. I was hooked. Maybe I was imagining it but it seemed the woman's eyes had lit up a little as I talked, laughed and gurned down the lens.

Afterwards I asked the woman her name – she was called Esta (which I thought was, again, very London and arse-achingly cool) – and before leaving I grilled Georgina in the office about the job. It was a company called Rapido TV and they were making something called *The Girlie Show* for Channel 4.

As I strode through St Ann's Square towards Piccadilly Station I felt strangely confident. Kinetic energy was fizzing and building inside me and I felt like something was about to burst free. I allowed myself to dream, and hoped that this would be the beginning of a new chapter, the first domino in a line of thousands that was about to be flicked by the finger of fate, which would knock into a thousand more, revealing a bright, bold pattern – the next few years of my life. Hopefully.

*   *   *

This story began as a homage to my darling dad Len, for always being the calm at the eye of the storm; as a thank-you note to my siblings for shaping and moulding me and putting up with me, the show-off with the wonky legs; and as a love letter to the farm where we all grew up, where the brickwork of the buildings holds all our childhood memories.

It's still all of those things but as the tale slowly unfurled I found myself writing and thinking about (and finally appreciating) the unlikely hero of the story – my mum. The bespectacled supermum, and now grandma. The 4'11" heroine. Opinionated, funny, loving and complicated, but always there. Because if my twenty-year-old hunch was true and I was to embark on a big, new adventure it would all be thanks to Mum.

What would I do without her? Honestly. Where would I be if it wasn't for my mum? I've asked myself that question a lot, especially since that day. She's been my safety net, ready to catch me as I've spun and tumbled through life. The Post-it note parenting has made an indelible mark on me, for which I'm now so grateful. It, and she, showed me that working hard for what you want is important; to be independent and to provide is crucial; and no one is perfect, because being a grown-up doesn't mean you have all the answers. My own parenting style has ripples of her running through it – loud but loving.

All the times she annoyed and chivvied me, like a collie dog nipping the ankles of the slowest sheep in the flock, I now know were for my own good – she was simply herding me in the right direction so that eventually I'd grow up to be a good, useful, kind person. I think she succeeded, mostly.

So Mum, this story is for you for all your hard work, your support, your encouragement and for always believing in me and always being there, whether I knew I needed you or not.

Acknowledgements

This book would not have happened without the persistent prodding, poking and persuasion from my agent, Melanie Rockcliffe – half woman, half force of nature – who's been by my side through thick and thin. She always said I could write a book, whether I should have is another matter altogether. If it goes tits up Mel, I'm hiding in your basement till it all blows over.

Huge thanks to everyone at Hodder who held my hand during the whole first book thing, especially Hannah Black, who has the patience and skill of a terrorist negotiator and the soothing, encouraging tone of a thousand Mary Berrys.

Despite the tough times I had at secondary school there were some great teachers and lovely friends too. So I would just like to send a high-five to the people not featured in the book but who are still part of my story, who attended Smithills School 1986-1990 and Canon Stade Sixth Form 1990-1992, plus those who in recent times have come back into my life via the magic of social media: the girl who tried and failed to get me into Def Leppard, Rebecca Charnock; Tim Tatlock and Matt Gill.

Big thanks to my first best friend and fellow Brosette Joanne Lloyd for giving me permission to use photos displaying our unique teen hairdos.

Huge thank you to my kickass crew of best friends, the 'Five go French' gang – Emily, Anna, Eleanor and Megan. I'm awestruck by their continued love and support and capacity to consume rosé wine on our annual jaunt to the south of France. Special mention to Megan who came up with the title for this book. We settled on *Till the Cows Come Home* over her other gem: *A Cox and Bull Story*. Genius.

Thank you to Clare for being my soul mate and 'bestest friend and bridesmaid' – from the moment we clapped eyes on each other a spark ignited that'll never go out.

Thank you to my brilliant, kind, funny husband Ben; even though this book pre-dates him, without his love I wouldn't be as happy, settled and confident as I am and things like this book wouldn't ever come to fruition. I'd like to take this opportunity to warn Ben that at least three of my perms are featured in this book.

Love and thanks to my three awesome children who every day make me proud, make me laugh and make me shout a bit. I love you Lola, Isaac and Renee.

A bit like at the Oscars, I've saved the biggest till last – this thank you is the equivalent of Best Picture: my family.

To my siblings for always being there for me. I love you. Our family is big and complicated, but I know wherever I am in the world I have at least four people who'd fight my corner: Robert, David, Dot and Yvonne. A special thank you to Rob for always answering his phone during the writing of this book, even though he knew I was probably asking him a random question about a dog's name from 1976. Without his kindness, impressive memory and slightly obsessive logging of old photographs this book would not have been possible.

Thank you to my mum Jackie and dad Len. For their unwavering support, for their patience and advice, for the best bear hugs (Dad) and the scrambled egg when I was poorly (Mum). For letting me be myself but teaching me to think of others too (I got that one eventually), and for always loving me. I love you.

This book was created by
Hodder & Stoughton

Founded in 1868 by two young men who saw that the rise in literacy would break cultural barriers, the Hodder story is one of visionary publishing and globe-trotting talent-spotting, campaigning journalism and popular understanding, men of influence and pioneering women.

For over 150 years, we have been publishing household names and undiscovered gems, and today we continue to give our readers books that sweep you away or leave you looking at the world with new eyes.

Follow us on our adventures in books . . .

@HodderBooks /HodderBooks @HodderBooks

HODDER &
STOUGHTON